THE
OXFORD GUIDE
TO
ENGLISH USAGE

12/25/95

JEFF -

MERRY CHRISTMAS
HONEY! ENJOY!
LOVE,

Kim.

THE
OXFORD GUIDE
TO
ENGLISH USAGE

Second Edition

Compiled by
E. S. C. WEINER
and
ANDREW DELAHUNTY

CLARENDON PRESS · OXFORD
1993

Oxford University Press, Walton Street, Oxford OX2 6DP

Oxford New York Toronto
Delhi Bombay Calcutta Madras Karachi
Kuala Lumpur Singapore Hong Kong Tokyo
Nairobi Dar es Salaam Cape Town
Melbourne Auckland Madrid
and associated companies in
Berlin Ibadan

Oxford is a trade mark of Oxford University Press

Published in the United States
by Oxford University Press Inc., New York

First published 1983 as The Oxford Miniguide to English Usage
Hardback edition first published 1984
This second edition first published 1993

British Library Cataloguing in Publication Data
Data available

Library of Congress Cataloging in Publication Data
Data available
ISBN 0–19–863137–5

1 3 5 7 9 10 8 6 4 2

Typeset by Pure Tech Corporation, Pondicherry, India
Printed in Great Britain by
Bookcraft Ltd.
Midsomer Norton, Avon

PREFACE

THE *Oxford Guide to English Usage*, extensively revised for this edition, is intended for anyone who needs simple and direct guidance about the formation and use of English words —about spelling, pronunciation, meanings, and grammar—and who cannot claim any specialist training in these subjects.

This book is designed to answer the questions about English usage that ordinary people are constantly asking; it covers the known areas of difficulty and controversy, leaving aside the parts of the English language that cause most native speakers no trouble. Typical examples of the subjects covered are: whether to write *forego* or *forgo*, *Jones'* or *Joneses'*, *enrolment* or *enrollment*; where to place the stress in words like *contribute*, *controversy*, *nomenclature*, *subsidence*; the correct use of *data*, *media*, and *strata*; the difference between *deprecate* and *depreciate*, *imply* and *infer*, *militate* and *mitigate*; whether to say *different from* or *different than*; and when *shall* should be used rather than *will*. Clear and simple recommendations are given, highlighting correct and acceptable standard British English. Only the minimum knowledge of grammatical terminology is assumed (a glossary of all the terms employed is included), and technical symbols are entirely dispensed with.

This book differs from all other small usage guides in using a large number of examples drawn from the works of well-known twentieth-century writers to illustrate good usage. There are three appendices, dealing with punctuation, the perils of modish vocabulary, and some overseas varieties of English. Distinctive features of American English are pointed out wherever possible in the main body of the book. The index covers all the subjects discussed as well as giving the location of each of the 4,600 words and phrases mentioned in the book.

This work is based largely on the archives, experience, and resources of the Oxford English Dictionary Department of the Oxford University Press, and has the authority of the Oxford family of dictionaries behind its recommendations. I should like to record my gratitude to my colleagues in the Dictionary Department for their help and support. I am grateful in particular to the former Chief Editor of the Oxford English Dictionaries, Dr Robert Burchfield, CBE, to the late Miss J. M. Hawkins, and to Dr R. E. Allen for their guidance, criticisms, and suggestions; Mr A. J. Augarde, Miss E. M. Knowles, and Mr J. A. Simpson for their numerous contributions; and Mrs P. Lawton and Miss K. C. E. Vines for typing and re-typing sections of the text. Outside the Department I am grateful to Mrs M. Y. Offord for her contributions, to Mrs A. Whear for compiling the first edition's Word Index, and to Mr H. E. Boyce for his assistance with proof-reading.

E. S. C. W.

October 1993

CONTENTS

INTRODUCTION

> It is one thing to use language; it is quite another to
> understand how it works.
>
> (Anthony Burgess, *Joysprick*)

ENGLISH usage is a subject as wide as the English language
itself. By far the greater part of usage, however, raises no
controversies and poses no problems for native speakers of
English, just because it *is* their natural idiom. But there are
certain limited areas—particular sounds, spellings, words, and
constructions—about which there arise uncertainty, difficulty, or disagreement. The proper aim of a usage guide is to
resolve these problems, rather than describe the whole of
current usage.

The *Oxford Guide to English Usage* has this aim. Within the
limits just indicated, it offers guidance in as clear, concise, and
systematic a manner as possible. In effecting its aims it makes
use of five special features, explained below.

1. *Layout.* In the *Guide* the subject of usage is divided into
four fields: *word formation, pronunciation, vocabulary*, and
grammar. Each field is covered by a separate section of the
book, and each of the four sections has its own alphabetical
arrangement of entries. Each entry is headed by its title in **bold
type**. All the words that share a particular kind of spelling,
sound, or construction can therefore be treated together. This
makes for both economy and comprehensiveness of treatment. Note that Section II is in two parts: A deals with the
pronunciation of particular letters, or groups of letters, while
B is an alphabetical list of words whose pronunciation gives
trouble.

2. *Explanation.* The explanations given in each entry are
intended to be simple and straightforward. Where the subject
is inevitably slightly complicated, they begin by setting out
familiar facts as a basis from which to untangle the complex-
ities. The explanations take into account the approaches

developed by modern linguistic analysis, but employ the traditional terms of grammar as much as possible. (A glossary of all grammatical terms used will be found on pp. 1 ff.) Technical symbols and abbreviations, and the phonetic alphabet, are not used at all.

3. *Exemplification.* Throughout Sections III and IV, and where appropriate elsewhere, example sentences are given to illustrate the point being discussed. The majority of these are real, rather than invented, examples. Many of them have been drawn from the works of some of the best twentieth-century writers (many equally good writers happen not to have been quoted). Even informal or substandard usage has been illustrated in this way; such examples frequently come from speeches put into the mouths of characters in novels, and hence no censure of the style of the author is implied. The aim is to illustrate the varieties of usage and to display the best, thereby making it more memorable than a mere collection of lapses and solecisms would be able to do.

4. *Recommendation.* Recommendations are clearly set out. The blob ● is used in the most clear-cut cases where a warning, restriction, or prohibition is stated. The square □ is used, particularly in section I, where a recommendation is given alongside acceptable alternatives. The emphasis of the recommendations is on the degree of acceptability in standard English of a particular use, rather than on a dogmatic distinction of right and wrong. Much that is sometimes condemned as 'bad English' is better regarded as appropriate in informal contexts but inappropriate in formal ones. The appropriateness of usage to context is indicated by the fairly rough categories 'formal' and 'informal', 'standard', 'regional', and 'non-standard', 'jocular', and so on. Some of the ways in which American usage differs from British are pointed out.

5. *Reference.* Ease of access to the entry sought by the user is a priority of the *Guide.* The division into four sections, explained above, means that (roughly speaking) only a quarter of the total range of pages need be looked through in order to find a particular entry. But this should rarely be necessary, since there is an index in which every subject covered by the

Guide can be found (and this includes all endings, prefixes, and spellings), as well as every word cited. Within each section there are many cross-references to other entries; these are indicated by **bold type** and followed by the page number if necessary.

In addition to the four main sections described at 1 above, the *Guide* has three *appendices*: I is an outline of the principles of punctuation; II lists some of the clichés and overworked diction most widely disliked at present; and III gives a brief description of the characteristics of the five major overseas varieties of English.

Concise as it is, the *Guide* may be found by individual users to cover some ground that is already familiar and some that they consider it unnecessary to know about. It is impossible for an entry (especially in the field of grammar) not to include more facts than are strictly part of the question which the entry is designed to answer. Language is a closely woven, seamless fabric, not a set of building blocks or pigeon-holes, capable of independent treatment; hence there are bound to be some redundancies and some overlap between different entries. Moreover, every user has a different degree of knowledge and interest. It is the compiler's hope, however, that all will be instructed and enriched by any incidental gains in understanding of the language that the use of this *Guide* may afford.

GRAMMATICAL TERMS
USED IN THIS BOOK

WHERE an example is partly in italics and partly in roman type, it is the words in roman that exemplify the term being defined.

absolute used independently of its customary grammatical relationship or construction, e.g. Weather permitting, *I will come.*

acronym a word formed from the initial letters of other words, e.g. *NATO.*

active applied to a verb whose subject is also the source of the action of the verb, e.g. *We* saw *him*; opposite of **passive**.

adjective a word that names an attribute, used to describe a noun or pronoun, e.g. small *child, it is* small.

adverb a word that modifies an adjective, verb, or another adverb, expressing a relation of place, time, circumstance, manner, cause, degree, etc., e.g. *gently, accordingly, now, here, why.*

agent noun a noun denoting the doer of an action, e.g. *builder.*

agent suffix a suffix added to a verb to form an agent noun, e.g. *-er.*

agree to have the same grammatical number, gender, case, or person as another word.

analogy the formation of a word, derivative, or construction in imitation of an existing word or pattern.

animate denoting a living being.

antecedent a noun or phrase to which a relative pronoun refers back.

antepenultimate last but two.

antonym a word of contrary meaning to another.

apposition the placing of a word, especially a noun, syntactically parallel to another, e.g. *William the Conqueror.*

article *a/an* (**indefinite** article) or *the* (**definite** article).

attributive designating a noun, adjective, or phrase expressing an attribute, characteristically preceding the word it qualifies, e.g. *old* in *the old dog*; opposite of **predicative**.

auxiliary verb a verb used in forming tenses, moods, and voices of other verbs.

case the form (**subjective, objective,** or **possessive**) of a noun or pronoun, expressing relation to some other word.

clause a distinct part of a sentence including a **subject** (sometimes by implication) and **predicate**.

collective noun a singular noun denoting many individuals; see p. 179.

collocation an expression consisting of two (or more) words frequently juxtaposed, especially adjective + noun, e.g. *derisory offer, heavy drinker*.

comparative the form of an adjective or adverb expressing a higher degree of a quality, e.g. *braver, worse*.

comparison the differentiation of the **comparative** and **superlative** degrees from the positive (basic) form of an adjective or adverb.

complement a word or words necessary to complete a grammatical construction: the complement of a clause, e.g. *John is* (a) thoughtful (man), *Solitude makes John* thoughtful; of an adjective, e.g. *John is glad* of your help; of a preposition, e.g. *I thought of* John.

compound preposition a preposition made up of more than one word, e.g. *with regard to*.

concord agreement between words in gender, number, or person, e.g. *the girl* who is *here, you who* are *alive*, Those *men* work.

conditional designating (1) a clause which expresses a condition, or (2) a mood of the verb used in the consequential clause of a conditional sentence, e.g. (1) *If he had come*, (2) *I should have seen him*.

consonant (1) a speech sound in which breath is at least partly obstructed, combining with a **vowel** to form a syllable; (2) a letter usually used to represent (1); e.g. *ewe* is written with vowel + consonant + vowel, but is pronounced as consonant (y) + vowel (oo).

coordination the linking of two or more parts of a compound sentence that are equal in importance, e.g. *He sang and she played the piano*.

correlative coordination coordination by means of pairs of corresponding words regularly used together, e.g. *either . . or.*

countable designating a noun that refers in the singular to one and in the plural to more than one, and can be qualified by *a, one, every,* etc. and *many, two, three,* etc.; opposite of **mass (noun).**

diminutive denoting a word referring to a small, liked, or despised member of the class denoted by the corresponding root word, e.g. *ringlet, Johnny, princeling.*

diphthong: see **digraph,** p. 131.

direct object the **object** that expresses the primary object of the action of the verb, e.g. *He sent* a present *to his son.*

disyllabic having two syllables.

double passive: see p. 185.

elide to omit by **elision.**

elision the omission of a vowel or syllable in pronouncing, e.g. *let's.*

ellipsis the omission from a sentence of words needed to complete a construction or sense.

elliptical involving **ellipsis.**

feminine the gender to which words referring to female beings usually belong.

finite designating (part of) a verb limited by person and number, e.g. *I* am, *He* comes.

formal designating the type of English used publicly for some serious purpose, either in writing or in public speeches.

future the tense of a verb referring to an event yet to happen: **simple future,** e.g. *I shall go*; **future in the past,** referring to an event that was yet to happen at a time prior to the time of speaking, e.g. *He said he* would go.

gerund the part of the verb which can be used like a noun, ending in *-ing,* e.g. *What is the use of my* scolding *him?*

govern (said of a verb or preposition) to have (a noun or pronoun, or a case) dependent on it.

group possessive: see p. 189.

hard designating a letter, chiefly *c* or *g,* that indicates a guttural sound, as in *cot* or *got.*

if-**clause** a clause introduced by *if*.

imperative the mood of a verb expressing command, e.g. Come *here!*

inanimate opposite of **animate.**

indirect object the person or thing affected by the action of the verb but not primarily acted upon, e.g. *I gave* him *the book.*

infinitive the basic form of a verb that does not indicate a particular tense or number or person; the *to*-**infinitive**, used with preceding *to*, e.g. *I want* to know; the **bare infinitive,** without preceding *to*, e.g. *Help me* pack.

inflection a part of a word, usually a suffix, that expresses grammatical relationship, such as number, person, tense, etc.; also used to refer to the process by which this part is added.

informal designating the type of English used in private conversation, personal letters, and popular public communication.

intransitive designating a verb that does not take a direct object, e.g. *I must* think.

intrusive *r*: see pp. 81 f.

linking *r*: see pp. 80 f.

living designating a **prefix** or **suffix** that can be freely used to form new compounds.

loanword a word adopted by one language from another.

main clause the principal clause of a sentence.

masculine the gender to which words referring to male beings usually belong.

mass noun (or **uncountable noun**) a noun that refers to something regarded as grammatically indivisible, treated only as singular, and never qualified by *those, many, two, three,* etc.; opposite of **countable** noun.

modal relating to the **mood** of a verb; used to express mood.

mood form of a verb serving to indicate whether it is to express fact, command, permission, wish, etc.

monosyllabic having one syllable.

nominal designating a phrase or clause that is used like a noun, e.g. What you need *is a drink.*

nonce-word a word coined for one occasion.

non-finite designating (a part of) a verb not limited by person and number, e.g. the infinitive, gerund, or participle.

non-restrictive: see p. 209.

noun a word used to denote a person, place, or thing.

noun phrase a phrase functioning within the sentence as a noun, e.g. The one over there *is mine.*

object a noun or its equivalent governed by an active transitive verb, e.g. *I will take* that one.

objective the case of a pronoun typically used when the pronoun is the object of a verb or governed by a preposition, e.g. *me, him.*

paradigm the complete pattern of inflection of a noun, verb, etc.

participle the part of a verb used like an adjective but retaining some verbal qualities (tense and government of an object) and also used to form compound verb forms: the **present participle** ends in *-ing,* the **past participle** of regular verbs in *-ed,* e.g. *While* doing *her work she had* kept *the baby* amused.

passive designating a form of the verb by which the verbal action is attributed to the person or thing to whom it is actually directed (i.e. the logical object is the grammatical subject), e.g. *He* was seen *by us;* opposite of **active.**

past a tense expressing past action or state, e.g. *I* arrived *yesterday.*

past perfect a tense expressing action already completed prior to the time being spoken or written about, e.g. *I* had arrived *by then.*

pejorative disparaging, depreciatory.

penultimate last but one.

perfect a tense denoting completed action or action viewed in relation to the present; e.g. *I* have finished *now;* **perfect infinitive,** e.g. *He seems* to have finished *now.*

periphrasis a roundabout way of expressing something.

person one of the three classes of personal pronouns or verb-forms, denoting the person speaking **(first person),** the person spoken to **(second person),** and the person or thing spoken about **(third person).**

phrasal verb an expression consisting of a verb and an adverb (and preposition), e.g. *break down, look forward to.*

phrase a group of words without a predicate, functioning like an adjective, adverb, or noun.

plural denoting more than one.

polysyllabic having more than one syllable.

possessive the case of a noun or a pronoun indicating possession, e.g. *John's*; **possessive pronoun,** e.g. *my, his.*

predicate the part of a clause consisting of what is said of the subject, including verb + complement or object.

predicative designating (especially) an adjective that forms part or the whole of the predicate, e.g. *The dog is* old.

prefix a verbal element placed at the beginning of a word to qualify its meaning, e.g. *ex-, non-.*

preposition a word governing a noun or pronoun, expressing the relation of the latter to other words, e.g. *seated* at *the table.*

prepositional phrase a phrase consisting of a preposition and its complement, e.g. *I am surprised* at your reaction.

present a tense expressing action now going on or habitually performed in past and future, e.g. *He* commutes *daily.*

pronoun a word used instead of a noun to designate (without naming) a person or thing already known or indefinite, e.g. *I, you, he,* etc., *anyone, something,* etc.

proper name a name used to designate an individual person, animal, town, ship, etc.

qualify (of an adjective or adverb) to attribute some quality to (a noun or adjective/verb).

reflexive implying the subject's action on himself, herself, or itself; **reflexive pronoun,** e.g. *myself, yourself,* etc.

relative: see p. 209.

restrictive: see p. 209.

semi-vowel a sound intermediate between vowel and consonant, e.g. the sound of *y* and *w.*

sentence adverb an adverb that qualifies or comments on the whole sentence, not one of the elements in it, e.g. Unfortunately, *he missed his train.*

simple future: see **future**.

singular denoting a single person or thing.

soft designating a letter, chiefly *c* or *g*, that indicates a sibilant sound, as in *city* or *germ*.

split infinitive: see p. 216.

stem the essential part of a word to which inflections and other suffixes are added, e.g. *un*limit*ed*.

stress the especially heavy vocal emphasis falling on one (the **stressed**) syllable of a word more than on the others.

subject the element in a clause (usually a noun or its equivalent) about which something is predicated (the latter is the **predicate**).

subjective the case of a pronoun typically used when the pronoun is the subject of a clause.

subjunctive the mood of a verb denoting what is imagined, wished, or possible, e.g. *I insist that it* be *finished*.

subordinate clause a clause dependent on the main clause and functioning like a noun, adjective, or adverb within the sentence, e.g. *He said* that you had gone.

substitute verb the verb *do* used in place of another verb, e.g. '*He likes chocolate.*' 'Does *he*?'

suffix a verbal element added at the end of a word to form a derivative, e.g. *-ation, -ing, -itis, -ize*.

superlative the form of an adjective or adverb expressing the highest or a very high degree of a quality, e.g. *bravest, worst*.

synonym a word that means exactly or nearly the same as another.

transitive designating a verb that takes a direct object e.g. *I* said *nothing*.

uncountable noun: see **mass noun**.

unreal condition (especially in a **conditional** sentence) a condition which will not be or has not been fulfilled.

unstressed designating a word, syllable, or vowel not having **stress**.

variant a form of a word etc. that differs in spelling or pronunciation from another (often the main or usual) form.

verb a part of speech that predicates.

vowel (1) an open speech sound made without audible friction and capable of forming a syllable with or without a consonant; (2) a letter usually used to represent (1), e.g. *a, e, i, o, u.*

*wh-***question word** a convenient term for the interrogative and relative words, most beginning with *wh*: *what, when, where, whether, which, who, whom, whose, why, how.*

ABBREVIATIONS

Amer.	American
COD	*The Concise Oxford Dictionary* (edn. 8, Oxford, 1990)
Hart's Rules	*Hart's Rules for Compositors and Readers* (edn. 39, Oxford, 1983)
MEU	H. W. Fowler, *A Dictionary of Modern English Usage* (edn. 2, revised by Sir Ernest Gowers, Oxford, 1965)
OED	*The Oxford English Dictionary* (edn. 2, Oxford, 1989)
OWD	*The Oxford Writers' Dictionary* (Oxford, 1990)
TLS	*The Times Literary Supplement*

I
WORD FORMATION

THIS section is concerned with the ways in which the forms of English words and word elements change or vary. It deals primarily with their written form, but in many cases the choice between two or more possible written forms is also a choice between the corresponding spoken forms. What follows is therefore more than merely a guide to spelling, although it is that too. A great part is taken up with guidance on the way in which words change when they are inflected (e.g. the possessive case and plural of nouns, the past tense and past participle of verbs) or when derivational prefixes and suffixes are added (e.g. the adjectival -*able* and -*ible* suffixes, the adverbial -*ly* suffix). Because this is intended as a basic outline, little space has been given to the description of the meanings and uses of the inflected and compounded forms of words. Instead, the emphasis is on the identification of the correct, or most widely acceptable, written form. Particular attention is given to the dropping, doubling, and alteration of letters when derivatives are formed. Space has also been given to problems of spelling that are not caused by derivation, especially the different ways of spelling the same sound in different words (e.g. *y* or *i* in *cider*, *cipher*, *gypsy*, *pygmy*, etc.). A comprehensive coverage of all words requiring hyphens or capitals would require more space than is available here. The entries for these two subjects attempt only to offer guidelines in certain difficult but identifiable cases. For a fuller treatment the reader is referred to the *Oxford Writers' Dictionary* and *Hart's Rules*. Wherever possible, notes are added to indicate where the conventions of American spelling differ from those recommended here.

In cases where there is widespread variation in the spelling of a particular word or form, the spelling recommended here is that preferred (as its 'house style') by the Oxford University Press.

abbreviations

It is usual to indicate an abbreviation by placing a point (full stop) after it, e.g.

> *H. G. Wells, five miles S.* (= south), *B.Litt., Kt., Sun.* (= Sunday), *Jan.* (= January), *p. 7* (= page 7).

However, no point is used:

1. With a sequence of capitals alone, e.g. *BBC, MA, QC, NNE, BC, AD, PLC* (and not, of course, with acronyms, e.g. *Aslef, Naafi*).

2. With the numerical abbreviations *1st, 2nd,* etc.

3. *C, F* (of temperature), chemical symbols, and measures of length, weight, time, etc., e.g. *cm, ft, cwt, lb, kg.*

4. *Dr, Revd, Mr, Mrs, Ms, Mme, Mlle, St, Hants, Northants, p* (= penny or pence).

5. In words that are colloquial abbreviations, e.g. *co-op, decaf, demo, recap, trad, vac.*

-ability **and** *-ibility*

Nouns ending in these suffixes undergo the same changes in the stem as adjectives in *-able* and *-ible* (see next entry).

-able **and** *-ible*

Words ending in *-able* generally owe their form to the Latin termination *-abilis* or the Old French *-able* (or both), and words in *-ible* to the Latin *-ibilis*. The suffix *-able* is also added to words of 'distinctly French or English origin' (*OED*, s.v. *-ble*), and as a living element to English roots.

A. Words ending in *-able*. The following alterations are made to the stem:

1. Silent final *-e* is dropped (see p. 21).

Exceptions: words whose stem ends in *-ce, -ee, -ge, -le,* and the following:

blameable	*rateable*
dyeable	*ropeable*
giveable (but *forgivable*)	*saleable*
hireable	*shareable*
holeable	*sizeable*
likeable	*tameable*
liveable	*unshakeable*
nameable	

● Amer. spelling tends to omit -*e*- in the words above.

2. Final -*y* becomes -*i*- (see p. 51).

Exception: *flyable*.

3. A final consonant may be doubled (see pp. 19 ff.).

Exceptions:

inferable	*referable*
preferable	*transferable*
(but *conferrable*)	

4. Most verbs of more than two syllables ending in -*ate* drop this ending when forming adjectives in -*able*, e.g. *alienable*, *assimilable*, *calculable*, *demonstrable*, *navigable*, *separable*, etc. Verbs of two syllables ending in -*ate* form adjectives in -*able* regularly, e.g. *creatable*, *debatable*, *dictatable*, *rotatable*, etc.

B. Words ending in -*ible*. These are fewer, since -*ible* is not a living suffix (i.e. it cannot be freely used to form new words). Below is a list of the commonest. Almost all form their negative in *in-*, *il-*, etc., so that the negative form can be inferred from the positive in the list below; the exceptions are indicated by (*un*).

accessible	*comprehensible*
adducible	*contemptible*
admissible	*convertible*
audible	*corrigible*
avertible	*corruptible*
collapsible	*credible*
combustible	*defensible*
compatible	*destructible*

digestible	perceptible
dirigible	perfectible
discernible	permissible
divisible	persuasible
edible	plausible
eligible	possible
exhaustible	reducible
expressible	reprehensible
extensible	repressible
fallible	reproducible
(un)feasible	resistible
flexible	responsible
forcible	reversible
fusible	risible
gullible	sensible
horrible	(un)susceptible
indelible	tangible
(un)intelligible	terrible
irascible	vendible
legible	vincible
negligible	visible
ostensible	

ae and oe

In words derived from Latin and Greek, these are now always written as separate letters, not as the ligatures æ, œ, e.g. *aeon, aesthetic, Caesar, gynaecology; amoeba, diarrhoea, homoeopathy, Oedipus.* The simple *e* is preferable in several words once commonly spelt with *ae, oe,* especially *medieval* (formerly with *ae*) and *ecology, ecumenical* (formerly with initial *oe*).

● In Amer. spelling, *e* replaces *ae, oe* in many words, e.g. *gynecology, diarrhea.*

American spelling

Differences between Amer. and British spelling are mentioned at the following places: **-able and -ible** (p. 13); **ae and oe** (p. 14); **-ce or -se** (p. 18); **doubling of final consonant** (p. 20); **dropping of silent -e** (p. 22); **hyphens** (p. 30); **l and ll** (pp. 33 f.);

-oul- (p. 36); *-our* or *-or* (p. 36); **past of verbs, formation of** (pp. 37 ff.); *-re* or *-er* (pp. 46 f.); *-yse* or *-yze* (p. 51).

See also **difficult and confusable spellings** (pp. 52) passim.

ante- and *anti-*

ante- (from Latin) = 'before'; *anti-* (from Greek) = 'against, opposite to'. Note especially *antechamber* and *antitype*.

-ant or *-ent*

-ant is the noun ending, *-ent* the adjective ending in the following:

dependant	*dependent*
descendant	*descendent*
pendant	*pendent*
propellant	*propellent*

independent is both adjective and noun; *dependence, independence* are the abstract nouns.

The following are correct spellings:

ascendant, -ncy	*relevant, -nce*
attendant, -nce	*repellent, -nce, -ncy*
contribuent	*superintendent, -ncy*
expellent	*tendency*
impellent	*transcendent, -nce*
intendant, -ncy	

a or *an*

A. Before *h*.

1. Where *h* is pronounced, use *a*, e.g. *a harvest, hero, hope*.
2. Where *h* is silent, use *an*, e.g. *an heir, honour, honorarium*.
3. Where *h* is pronounced in words in which the first syllable is unstressed, use *a*, e.g. *a historic occasion, a hotel*.

● The older usage was not to pronounce *h* and to write *an*, but this is now almost obsolete.

B. Before capital letter abbreviations.

Be guided by the pronunciation.

1. Where the abbreviation is pronounced as one or more letter-names, e.g.

a B road	*a UN resolution*
a PS	*a VIP*

but

an A road	*an MP*
an H-bomb	*an SOS*

2. Where the abbreviation is pronounced as a word (an acronym), e.g.

a RADA student	*a SABENA airline typist*

but

an AIDS conference	*an OPEC minister*

But where the abbreviation would in speech be expanded to the full word, use *a* or *an* as appropriate to the latter, e.g. *a MS* 'a manuscript'.

-ative or *-ive*

Correct are:

(*a*) *authoritative*   *qualitative*
      exploitative   *quantitative*
      interpretative

(*b*) *absorptive*   *preventive*
      assertive   *supportive*

The forms *interpretive* (which has a special computing meaning) and *preventative* also occur.

by- prefix

'Tending to form one word with the following noun, but a hyphen is still frequently found' (*OWD*).

One word: *bygone, byline, byname, bypass, bypath, byplay, byroad, bystander, byway, byword*; the others (e.g. *by-election, by-product*) are hyphened.

• *Bye* (noun) in sport, *bye-bye* (= good-bye) are the chief words with final *-e*.

c and *ck*

Words ending in *-c* interpose *k* before suffixes which otherwise would indicate a soft *c*, chiefly *-ed*, *-er*, *-ing*, *-y*, e.g.:

bivouacker, *-ing*	*picnicked*, *-er*, *-ing*
colicky	*plasticky*
frolicked, *-ing*	*plastic-macked*
mimicked, *-ing*	*tarmacked*, *-ing*
panicky	*trafficked*, *-ing*

Exceptions: *arced*, *-ing*, *zinced*, *zincify*, *zincing*.

Before *-ism*, *-ist*, *-ity*, and *-ize c* (chiefly occurring in the suffix *-ic*) remains and is pronounced soft, e.g. *Anglicism*, *physicist*, *domesticity*, *italicize*.

capital or small initials

There are four classes of word that especially give trouble.

A. Compass points. Use capitals:

1. When abbreviated, e.g. *NNE for north-north-east.*
2. When denoting a region, e.g. *unemployment in the North.*
3. When part of a geographical name with recognized status, e.g. *Northern Ireland, East Africa, Western Australia.*
4. In bridge.

Otherwise use small initials, e.g. *facing (the) south, the wind was south, southbound, a southeaster.*

B. Parties, denominations, and organizations.

'The general rule is: capitalization makes a word more specific and limited in its reference: contrast a Christian scientist (man of science) and a Christian Scientist (member of the Church of Christ Scientist).' (*Hart's Rules*, pp. 10–11.)

So, for example, *Conservative, Socialist, Democratic* (names of parties); *Roman Catholic, Orthodox, Congregational*; but *conservative, socialist, democratic* (as normal adjectives), *catholic sympathies, orthodox views, congregational singing.*

C. Words derived from proper names.

When connection with the proper name is indirect or allusive (the meaning associated with or suggested by the proper name), use a small initial letter, e.g.

(nouns) *boycott, jersey, mackintosh, quisling*;
(adjectives) *herculean* (*labours*), *machiavellian* (*schemes*), *platonic* (*love*), *quixotic* (*temperament*);
(verbs) *blarney, bowdlerize, pasteurize.*

When the connection of a derived adjective or verb with a proper name is felt to be alive, use a capital, e.g.

Christian, Platonic (*philosophy*), *Rembrandtesque, Roman, Shakespearian*;
Anglicize, Christianize, Russify.

● Adjectives of nationality usually retain the capital even when used in transferred senses, e.g. *Dutch courage, go Dutch, French chalk, Russian salad, Turkish delight.* The chief exceptions are *arabic* (*numeral*), *roman* (*numeral, type*).

D. Proprietary names.

The name of a product or process, if registered as a trade mark, is a proprietary name, and should be given a capital initial, e.g. *Araldite, Coca-Cola, Filofax, Marmite, Olivetti, Pyrex, Quaker Oats, Vaseline, Xerox.*

-cede or *-ceed*

Exceed, proceed, succeed; the other verbs similarly formed have -*cede*, e.g. *concede, intercede, precede, recede.* Note also *supersede.*

-ce or *-se*

Advice, device, licence, and *practice* are nouns; the related verbs are spelt with -*se*: *advise, devise, license, practise.* Similarly *prophecy* (noun), *prophesy* (verb).

● Amer. spelling favours *license, practise* for both noun and verb; but the nouns *defence, offence, pretence* are spelt with *c* in Britain, *s* in America.

co- prefix

Most words with this prefix have no hyphen (even if a vowel, including *o*, follows the prefix). Those that are usually spelt with a hyphen are:

1. A few words with *o* following, e.g. *co-op, co-opt* (but *cooperate, uncooperative, coordinate*).

2. Words in which the hyphen preserves correct syllabication, so aiding recognition, e.g. *co-latitude, co-religionist, co-respondent* (distinguished from *correspondent*).

3. Words, especially recent or nonce coinages, in which *co-* is a living prefix meaning 'fellow-', e.g. *co-author, co-signatory, co-star*.

doubling of final consonant

1. When certain suffixes beginning with a vowel are added to nouns, adjectives, adverbs, and verbs, the final consonant of the stem word is doubled before the suffix:

(*a*) if the preceding vowel is written with a single letter (or single letter preceded by *qu*) and

(*b*) if that vowel bears the main stress (hence all monosyllables are included).

So *bed, bedding* but *head, heading*; *occúr, occúrred* but *óffer, óffered*; *befít, befítted* but *bénefit, bénefited*.

Suffixes which cause this doubling include:

(*a*) The verb inflections *-ed, -ing*, e.g.

> begged, begging   revved, revving
> bussed, bussing   trekked, trekking
> equipped, equipping

(*b*) The adjective and adverb suffixes *-er, -est*, e.g. *sadder, saddest*.

(*c*) Various derivational suffixes, especially *-able, -age, -en, -er, -ery, -ish, -y*, e.g.

> clubbable   waggery
> tonnage   priggish
> sadden   shrubby
> trapper

2. Words of more than one syllable, not stressed on the last syllable, do not double the final consonant, unless it is *l*, when a suffix beginning with a vowel is added, e.g.

biased	*gossipy*	*turbaned*
blossoming	*lettered*	*wainscoted*
combated	*pilotage*	*wickedest*
faceted	*targeted*	*womanish*
focusing		

Exception: *worship* makes *worshipped, -ing.*

Note that some other words in which the final syllable has a full vowel (not obscure *e* or *i*), some of which are compounds, also double the final consonant, e.g.

format	*humbug*	*periwig*
handicap	*kidnap*	*sandbag*
hobnob	*leap-frog*	*tear-gas*
horsewhip	*nonplus*	*zigzag*

● Amer. sometimes *kidnaped, kidnaping, worshiped, worshiping.*

3. Consonants that are never doubled are *c, h, w, x, y.*

4. When endings beginning with a vowel are added, *l* is *always* doubled after a single vowel wherever the stress falls, e.g.

controllable	*jeweller*
flannelled	*panelling*

Note also *woollen, woolly.*

Exceptions: *parallel* makes *paralleled, -ing; devil* makes *devilish.*

● In Amer. spelling *l* obeys the same rules as the other consonants (except *c, h, w, x, y*), e.g. *traveler, marvelous,* but *compelling, pally.*

Note also Amer. *woolen* (but *woolly*).

5. A silent final consonant is not doubled. Endings are added as if the consonant were pronounced, e.g.

crocheted, -ing	*rendezvouses* (third
pince-nezed	person singular)
précised	*rendezvousing*

dropping of silent -*e*

A. When a suffix beginning with a vowel (including -*y*) is added to a word ending in silent -*e* (including *e* following another vowel), the -*e* is dropped.

So:

1. Before suffixes beginning with *e*- (i.e. -*ed*, -*er*, -*ery*, -*est*), e.g.

braver, bravery, bravest	*hoed*
dyed, dyer	*issued*
eeriest	*manoeuvred*
freer, freest	*queued*

2. Before -*able*, e.g.

adorable	*imaginable*
analysable	*manoeuvrable*
bribable	*usable*

Exceptions:

(*a*) Words ending in -*ce* and -*ge* retain the *e* to indicate the softness of the consonant, e.g. *bridgeable*, *noticeable*, *peaceable*.

(*b*) In a number of -*able* adjectives, *e* is retained in order to make the root word more easily recognizable. See list on p. 13.

(*c*) *ee* is retained, e.g. *agreeable*, *feeable*, *foreseeable*.

(*d*) The few adjectives formed on verbs ending in consonant + -*le*; e.g. *handleable*.

3. Before -*age*, e.g. *cleavage*, *dotage*, *hectarage*, *linage* (number of lines).

Exceptions: *acreage*, *mileage*.

4. Before -*ing*, e.g. *centring*, *fatiguing*, *housing*, *manoeuvring*. With change of *i* to *y*: *dying*, *lying*, etc. (see p. 32).

Exceptions:

(a) *ee*, *oe*, and *ye* remain, e.g.

agreeing	*eyeing*	*shoeing*
canoeing	*fleeing*	*tiptoeing*
dyeing	*hoeing*	

(*b*) *blueing*, *cueing* (*gluing*, *issuing*, *queuing*, etc. are regular).
The forms *bluing*, *queueing* also occur but the spellings
given above are the recommended ones.

(*c*) *ageing* (*raging*, *staging*, etc. are regular). The form *aging* is
also common.

(*d*) *routeing*, *singeing*, *swingeing* are distinguished from *rout-
ing* 'putting to flight', *singing*, and *swinging*.

5. Before -*ish*, e.g.

bluish	nicish	roguish
latish	purplish	whitish

Exceptions: *moreish* and *ogreish* (though the forms *morish* and
ogrish also occur).

6. Before -*y*, e.g.

bony	mousy
chancy	nosy

Exceptions: see -*y* or -*ey* **adjectives,** pp. 49 f. Both *stagy* and
stagey are acceptable.

B. When a suffix beginning with a consonant (e.g. -*ful*, -*ling*,
-*ly*, -*ment*, -*ness*, -*some*) is added to a word ending in silent -*e*,
the -*e* is retained, e.g.

abridgement	houseful
acknowledgement	judgement (*judgment*
amazement	often in legal works)
awesome	useful
definitely	whiteness

Exceptions: *argument*, *awful*, *duly*, *eerily*, *eeriness*, *fledgling*,
truly, *wholly*.

● In Amer. spelling *e* is dropped after *dg* and before a suffix
beginning with a consonant, e.g. *abridgment*, *judgment*.

C. Final silent -*e* is omitted in Amer. spelling in several words
in which it is found in British spelling, and so often is final
silent -*ue* in the endings -*gogue*, -*logue*, e.g.

ax	adz	program
analog	epilog	pedagog

-efy or -ify

The chief words with *-efy* (*-efied*, *-efication*, etc.) are:

liquefy	*rubefy*	*tumefy*
putrefy	*stupefy*	
rarefy	*torrefy*	

All the others have *-ify* etc. See also **-ified or -yfied,** p. 30.

-ei- or -ie-

The rule '*i* before *e* except after *c*' holds good for nearly all words in which the vowel-sound is *ee*, as *Aries, hygienic, yield*.

Exceptions where *ie* follows *c* are: *prima facie, specie, species, superficies*.

Note also *friend, adieu, review, view*.

The following words which are, or can be, pronounced with the *ee*-sound have *ei*:

caffeine	*either*	*protein*
casein	*heinous*	*receipt*
ceiling	*inveigle*	*receive*
codeine	*Madeira*	*seise*
conceit	*neither*	*seize*
conceive	*perceive*	*seizure*
counterfeit	*peripeteia*	*weir*
deceit	*plebeian*	*weird*
deceive		

Note also *forfeit, surfeit*.

Many proper names pronounced with the *ee*-sound have *ei*, e.g. *Keith, Leith, Neil, Reid, Sheila*.

en- or in-

The following pairs of words can give trouble:

encrust (verb)	*incrustation*
engrain (verb) to dye in the raw state	*ingrain* (adjective) dyed in the yarn
	ingrained deeply rooted
enquire ask	*inquire* undertake a formal investigation

enquiry question   *inquiry* official investigation
ensure make sure   *insure* take out insurance
                          (against risk: note
                          assurance of life)

Although *enquire, enquiry* and *inquire, inquiry* are used almost interchangeably by many people, they are usually used in the meanings indicated above and the distinction in usage between the two pairs of words is a useful one.

-er and -est

These suffixes of comparison may require the following changes in spelling:

1. Doubling of final consonant (see pp. 19 ff.).
2. Dropping of silent -*e* (see p. 21).
3. *Y* to *i* (see p. 51).

-erous or -rous

The ending -*erous* is normal in adjectives related to nouns ending in -*er*, e.g. *murderous, slanderous, thunderous.* The exceptions are:

ambidextrous   *meandrous*
cumbrous   *monstrous*
disastrous   *wondrous*
leprous

final vowels before suffixes

A. For treatment of final -*e* and -*y* before suffixes see **dropping of silent -*e*,** pp. 21 ff., and *y* **to** *i*, pp. 51 f.

B. For treatment of final -*o* before -*s* (suffix), see **plural formation,** p. 39 and -*s* **suffix,** p. 47.

C. In nearly all other cases, the final vowels -*a*, -*i*, -*o*, and -*u* are unaffected by the addition of suffixes and do not themselves affect the suffixes. So:

echoer   *vetoer*
skier

areas	*gnus*
cameras	*(he) rumbas*
corgis	*(she) skis*
emus	*taxis*
echoing	*skiing*
radioing	*taxiing*
scubaing	*vetoing*
baaed	*mustachioed*
bikinied (girls)	*radioed*
concertinaed	*(they) rumbaed*
echoed	*subpoenaed*
hennaed	*taxied*
mascaraed	*tiaraed*

The -*ed* spelling is preferable for this last group of words, but an -'*d* spelling is also acceptable in many cases, especially when the suffix is preceded by the letter *a*, e.g. *rumba'd*. This spelling is preferable in *idea'd* (having ideas) and *ski'd* (from *ski*, contrasting with *skied* from *sky*).

D. Final -*é* in words taken from French is retained before all suffixes; the *e* of -*ed* is dropped after it, e.g.

appliquéd	*chasséing*
appliquéing	*clichéd*
attachés	*communiqués*
cafés	*émigrés*
canapés	*soufflés*

for- and *fore-*

The prefix *for-* 'means away, out, completely, or implies prohibition or abstention' (*MEU*). *Fore-* is the same as the ordinary word so spelt, = 'beforehand, in front'.

Note especially:

forbear refrain	*forebear* ancestor
forgather	*foreclose*
forgo abstain from	*forego* (esp.) in *foregoing (list)*, *foregone (conclusion)*
forfeit	

f to *v*

Certain nouns that end in *f* or *f* followed by silent *e* change this *f* to *v* in some derivatives. Most are familiar, but with a few derivatives there is variation between *f* and *v* or uncertainty about which consonant is correct; only these are dealt with below.

> *beef*: plural *beeves* oxen, *beefs* kinds of beef.
> *calf* (young bovine animal): *calfish* calflike; *calves-foot jelly.*
> *calf* (of leg): (*enormously*) *calved* having (enormous) calves.
> *corf* (basket): plural *corves.*
> *dwarf*: plural *dwarfs.* ● *Dwarves*, originally mainly in J. R. R. Tolkien's writings, is now increasingly found.
> *elf*: *elfish* and *elvish* are both acceptable; *elfin* but *elven* (in fantasy writings).
> *handkerchief*: plural *handkerchiefs.*
> *hoof*: plural usually *hooves*, e.g. *The useless tool for horses' hooves* (Graham Greene); *Listening for Sebastian's retreating hooves* (Evelyn Waugh); the historic form *hoofs* is also commonly found; adjective *hoofed* or *hooved.*
> *knife*: verb *knife.*
> *leaf*: *leaved* having leaves (*broad-leaved*, etc.) but *leafed* as past of *leaf* (*through a book*, etc.).
> *life*: *lifelong* lasting a lifetime; *livelong* (*day*, etc., poetic: the *i* is short); the plural of *still life* is *still lifes.*
> *oaf*: plural *oafs.*
> *roof*: plural *roofs.* ● *Rooves* is commonly heard and sometimes written, e.g. *Several acres of bright red rooves* (George Orwell). Its written use should be avoided.
> *scarf* (garment): plural *scarves*; *scarfed* wearing a scarf.
> *scarf* (joint): plural and verb keep *f.*
> *sheaf*: plural *sheaves*; verb *sheaf* or *sheave*; *sheaved* made into a sheaf.
> *shelf*: plural *shelves*; *shelvy* having sandbanks.
> *staff*: plural *staffs* but archaic and musical *staves.*
> *turf*: plural *turfs* or *turves*; verb *turf*; *turfy.*
> *wharf*: plural *wharves* or *wharfs.*
> *wolf*: *wolfish* of a wolf.

-ful suffix

The adjectival suffix -ful may require the following changes in spelling:

1. Change of y to i (see p. 51).
2. Simplification of -ll (see l and ll, p. 33).

hyphens

A. Hyphens are used to connect words that are more closely linked to each other than to the surrounding syntax. Unfortunately their use is not consistent. Some pairs or groups of words are written as a single word (e.g. *motorway, railwayman*), others, despite their equally close bond, as separate words (e.g. *motor cycle, pay phone*); very similar pairs may be found with a hyphen (e.g. *motor-cyclist, pay-bed*). There are no hard and fast rules that will predict in every case whether a group of words should be written as one, with a hyphen, or separately. A recommended style for individual items, based on current usage, can be found by consulting the most recent edition of *COD*.

1. Groups consisting of attributive noun + noun are probably the most unpredictable. It is the nature of English syntax to produce limitless numbers of groups of this kind. Such a group generally remains written as separate words until it is recognized as a lexical item with a special meaning, when it may receive a hyphen. Eventually it may be written as one word, but this usually happens when the two nouns are monosyllabic and there is no clash between the final letter of the first and the first letter of the second.

   This generalization is, however, a very weak guide to what happens in practice. Compare, for example, *coal tar, coal-sack, coalfield; oil well, oil-painting, oilfield; blood pressure, blood-money, bloodstream*.

2. Nouns derived from phrasal verbs, consisting of verb + adverb, are slightly more predictable. They are never written as two words, frequently hyphened, and sometimes written as one, e.g. *fall-out, play-off, set-back, turn-out; feedback, layout, runoff, turnover*. Phrases consisting of

agent-noun in *-er* + adverb are usually hyphened, e.g. *picker-up, runner-up*; those consisting of gerund in *-ing* + adverb are usually left as two words, e.g. *Your coming back so soon surprised me*, unless they have become a unit with a special meaning, e.g. *Gave him a going-over*.

3. Various collocations which are not hyphened when they play their normal part in the sentence are given hyphens when they are transferred to attributive position before a noun, e.g.

   (*a*) adjective + noun: *a common-sense argument* (but *This is common sense*), *an open-air restaurant* (but *eating in the open air*).

   (*b*) preposition + noun: *an out-of-date aircraft* (but *This is out of date*), *an in-depth interview* (but *interviewing him in depth*).

   (*c*) participle + adverb: *The longed-for departure* and *Tugged-at leaves and whirling branches* (Iris Murdoch) (but *the departure greatly longed for*; *leaves tugged at by the wind*).

   (*d*) other syntactic groups used attributively, e.g. *A tremendous wrapping-up-and-throwing-away gesture* (J. B. Priestley); *An all-but-unbearable mixture* (Lynne Reid Banks).

4. Collocations of adverb + adjective (or participle) are usually written as two words when attributive as well as when predicative, e.g. *a less interesting topic, an amazingly good performance*, but may very occasionally take a hyphen to avoid misunderstanding, e.g. *Sir Edgar, who had heard one or two more-sophisticated rumours* (Angus Wilson) (this does not mean 'one or two additional sophisticated rumours').

See also **well,** p. 171.

5. When two words that form a close collocation but are not normally joined by a hyphen enter into combination with another word that requires a hyphen, it may be necessary to join them with a hyphen as well in order to avoid an awkward or even absurd result, e.g. *natural gas* needs no hyphen in *natural gas pipeline*, but *natural-gas-producer*

may be preferred to the ambiguous *natural gas-producer*; *crushed ice + -making* looks odd in *crushed ice-making machine*, and so *crushed-ice-making machine* may be preferred. Occasionally a real distinction in meaning may be indicated, e.g. *The non-German-speakers at the conference used interpreters* versus *The non-German speakers at the conference were all Austrians*. Many people, however, prefer to avoid the use of long series of hyphened words.

6. A group of words that has been turned into a syntactic unit, often behaving as a different part of speech from the words of which it is composed, normally has hyphens, e.g. *court-martial* (verb), *happy-go-lucky* (adjective), *good-for-nothing*, *stick-in-the-mud*, *ne'er-do-well* (nouns).

7. A hyphen is used to indicate a common second element in all but the last word of a list, e.g. *two-, three-, or fourfold*.

B. Hyphens are also used within the word to connect a prefix or suffix to the stem. With most prefixes and suffixes it is normal to write the whole compound as a single word; the use of the hyphen is exceptional, and the writing of prefix or suffix and stem as two words virtually unknown.

The hyphen is used in the following cases:

1. After a number of prefixes that are considered to be living formative elements, i.e. prefixes that can be freely used to form new compounds:

   ex- (= formerly), e.g. *ex-President*; *neo-* (denoting a revived movement), e.g. *neo-Nazism*; *non-*, e.g. *non-stick*; *pro-* (= in favour of), e.g. *pro-marketeer*; *self-*, e.g. *self-destructive*.

   Exceptions: *Neoplatonism* (*-ic*, etc.); *selfsame, unselfconscious*.

2. After a number of prefixes to aid recognition of the second element, e.g. *anti-g*, or to distinguish the compound from another word identically spelt, e.g. *un-ionized* (as against *unionized*); see also **co- prefix**, **re- prefix**.

3. Between a prefix ending with a vowel and a stem beginning with the same vowel, e.g. *de-escalate, pre-empt*; see also **co- prefix**, **re- prefix**.

4. Between a prefix and a stem beginning with a capital letter, e.g. *anti-Darwinian, hyper-Calvinism, Pre-Raphaelite.*

5. With some living suffixes forming specially coined compounds, e.g. *Mickey Mouse-like*; or still regarded to some extent as full words, such as *-wise* (= as regards ——), e.g. *Weather-wise we have had a good summer.*

6. With suffixes in irregularly formed compounds, e.g. *unget-at-able.*

7. With the suffix *-like* after a stem ending in *-l*, e.g. *eel-like*, and when attached to a word of two or more syllables, e.g. *cabbage-like*; with the suffix *-less* after a stem ending in double *-l*, e.g. *bell-less, will-lessness.*

Note. In Amer. spelling there is a greater tendency than in British spelling to write compounds as one word, rather than hyphened, e.g. *nonplaying, nonprofit, roundhouse, runback, sandlot.*

-ified or *-yfied*

-ified is usual, whatever the stem of the preceding element, e.g.

citified	*gentrified*
countrified	*sissified*
dandified	*yuppified*
Frenchified	

But *ladyfied.*

in- or *un-*

There is no comprehensive set of rules governing the choice between these two negative prefixes. The following guidelines are offered. Note that *in-* takes the form of *il-, im-,* or *ir-* before initial *l, m,* or *r*.

1. *in-* is from Latin and properly belongs to words derived from Latin, whereas *un-*, as a native prefix, has a natural ability to combine with any English word. Hence

(*a*) *un-* may be expected to spread to words originally having *in-*. This has happened when the *in-* word has developed a sense more specific than merely the negative of the stem word:

unapt	inept
unartistic	inartistic
unhuman	inhuman
unmaterial	immaterial
unmoral	immoral
unreligious	irreligious
unsanitary	insanitary
unsolvable	insoluble

(b) It is always possible, for the sake of a particular effect, for a writer to coin a nonce-word with un-:

A small bullied-looking woman with unabundant brown hair (Kingsley Amis)

Joyce's arithmetic is solid and unnonsensical (Anthony Burgess)

2. Adjectives ending in -ed and -ing rarely accept in- (while participles can of course be formed from verbs like inactivate, indispose, etc.).

Exception: inexperienced.

3. in- seems to be preferred before the prefixes ad-, co- (col-, com-, con-, cor-), de-, di(s)-, ex-, per-.

Important exceptions are:

unadventurous	undeniable
uncommunicative	undesirable
unconditional	undetectable
unconscionable	unexceptionable
unconscious	unexceptional
uncooperative	unpersuasive
undemonstrative	

4. un- is preferred before the prefixes em-, en-, im-, in-, inte(r)-.

5. Adjectives ending in -able usually take in- if the stem preceding the suffix -able is not, by itself, an English word:

educable, stem educ-, negative in-
palpable, stem palp-, negative im-

Exceptions: *unamenable, unamiable, unconscionable.*

They usually take *un-* if the stem has only one syllable and is an English word:

> unbridgeable   unreadable
> unlovable   unsaleable

Exceptions: *incurable, immovable, impassable* (that cannot be traversed: but *impassible* = unfeeling).

But no generalization covers those with a polysyllabic English stem:

> illimitable   undeniable
> invariable   unmistakable

Note: Rule 2 overrides rule 3 (e.g. *uncomplaining, undisputed, unperturbed*); rule 3 overrides rule 5 (*unconscionable*); rule 4 overrides rule 5 (*unimpressible*).

i to *y*

When the suffix *-ing* is added to words (chiefly verbs) that end in *-ie*, *e* is dropped (see **dropping of silent *-e*,** p. 21), and *i* becomes *y*, e.g.

> dying   tying
> lying   vying

Exceptions: *hie, sortie,* make *hieing, sortieing.* Both *stymieing* and *stymying* are acceptable.

-ize and *-ise*

-ize should be preferred to *-ise* as a verbal ending in words in which both are in use, according to Oxford University Press house style. *-ize* is also usual in North America. Both spellings are common in the UK.

1. The choice arises only where the ending is pronounced *eyes*, not where it is *ice, iss,* or *eez.*
So: *precise, promise, chemise, expertise.*

2. The choice applies only to the verbal suffix (of Greek origin), added to nouns and adjectives with the sense 'make

into, treat with, or act in the way of (that which is indicated by the stem word)'.

Hence are eliminated

(*a*) nouns in -*ise*:

compromise	*franchise*
demise	*merchandise*
disguise	*revise*
enterprise	*surmise*
exercise	*surprise*

(*b*) verbs corresponding to a noun which has -*is*- as a part of the stem (e.g. in the syllables -*vis*-, -*cis*-, -*mis*-), or identical with a noun in -*ise*. Some of the more common verbs in -*ise* are:

advertise	*enterprise*
advise	*excise*
apprise	*exercise*
arise	*improvise*
chastise	*incise*
circumcise	*merchandise*
comprise	*premise*
compromise	*prise* (*open*)
demise	*revise*
despise	*supervise*
devise	*surmise*
disguise	*surprise*
enfranchise	*televise*

3. In most cases, -*ize* verbs are formed on familiar English stems, e.g. *authorize, familiarize, symbolize*; or with a slight alteration to the stem, e.g. *agonize, dogmatize, sterilize*. A few words have no such immediate stem: *aggrandize* (cf. *aggrandizement*), *appetize* (cf. *appetite*), *baptize* (cf. *baptism*), *catechize* (cf. *catechism*), *recognize* (cf. *recognition*); and *capsize*.

l and *ll*

Whether to write a single or double *l* can be a problem in the following cases:

1. Where a suffix is added to single final *l*: see **doubling of final consonants,** pp. 19 f.

2. *l* is single when it is the last letter of the following verbs:

annul	*enrol*	*fulfil*
appal	*enthral*	*impel*
distil	*extol*	*instil*

These double the *l* before suffixes beginning with a vowel (see pp. 19 f.), but not before *-ment*:

annulment	*enthralment*	*distillation*
enrolment	*fulfilment*	*enthralling*

● In Amer. spelling *l* is usually double in all these words except *annul*(*ment*), *extol*.

3. Final *-ll* is usually simplified to *l* before suffixes or word elements that begin with a consonant, e.g.

almighty, almost, etc.	*instalment*
chilblain	*skilful*
dully	*thraldom*
fulfil	*wilful*
gratefully	

Exception: Before *-ness*, *-ll* remains in *dullness*, *fullness*.

● In Amer. spelling *ll* is usual in *skillful, thralldom, willful*.

-ly

The suffix *-ly* is added to words (mainly nouns and adjectives) to form adjectives and adverbs, e.g. *earth, earthly; part, partly; sad, sadly*. With certain words one of the following spelling changes may be required:

1. If the word ends in double *ll*, add only *-y*, e.g. *fully, shrilly*.

2. If the word ends in consonant + *le*, change *e* to *y*, e.g. *ably, singly, subtly, supply, terribly*.

3. If the word ends in consonant + *y*, change *y* to *i* and add *-ly*, e.g. *drily, happily*.

Exceptions: *shyly, slyly, spryly, wryly*.

4. If the word ends in unstressed *-ey*, change *ey* to *i* and add *-ly*, e.g. *matily*.

5. If the word has more than one syllable and ends in *-ic*, add *-ally*, even if there is no corresponding adjective in *-ical*, e.g. *basically*, *scientifically*.

Exceptions: *politicly* (from the adjective *politic*, distinguished from *politically*, from the adjective *political*), *publicly* (● not *publically*).

6. Final *-e* is exceptionally dropped before *-ly* in *duly*, *eerily*, *truly*, *wholly* (*palely*, *solely*, *vilely*, etc., are regular).

7. Final *-y* is exceptionally changed to *i* before *-ly* in *daily*, *gaily* (*greyly*, *coyly* are regular).

-ness

As a suffix added to adjectives, it may require the change of *y* to *i*: see p. 51.

-or **and** *-er*

These two suffixes, denoting 'one who or that which performs (the action of the verb)' are from Latin (through French) and Old English respectively, but their origin is not a sure guide to their distribution.

1. *-er* is the living suffix, forming most newly-coined agent nouns; but *-or* is frequently used with words of Latin origin to coin technical terms.

2. *-er* is usual after doubled consonants (except *-ss-*), after soft *c* and *g*, after *-i-*, after *ch* and *sh*, and after *-er*, *-graph*, *-ion*, and *-iz-*, e.g.

    chopper, producer, avenger, qualifier, launcher, furnisher, discoverer, photographer, executioner, organizer.

Principal exceptions: *counsellor, carburettor, conqueror.*

3. *-or* follows *-at-* to form a suffix *-ator*, often but not always in words related to verbs in *-ate*, e.g. *duplicator, incubator.*

Exception: *debater.*

Note: nouns in *-olater*, as *idolater*, do not contain the agent suffix.

4. No rule can predict whether a given word having *-s-*, *-ss-*, or *-t-* (apart from *-at-*) before the suffix requires *-or* or *-er*. So *supervisor, compressor, prospector,* but *adviser, presser, perfecter. -tor* usually follows *-c*, unstressed *i*, and *u*, e.g. *actor, compositor, executor*; *-ter* usually follows *f, gh, l, r,* and *s*, e.g. *drifter, fighter, defaulter, exporter, protester*; but there are numerous exceptions.

5. A functional distinction is made between *-or* and *-er* in the following:

accepter one who accepts	*acceptor* (in scientific use)
caster one who casts, casting machine	*castor* beaver; plant giving oil; sugar (sprinkler); wheel
censer vessel for incense	*censor* official
resister one who resists	*resistor* electrical device
sailer ship of specified power	*sailor* seaman

6. A number of words have *-er* in normal use but *-or* in Law:

abetter	*mortgager*
accepter	*settler*
granter	*vender*

-oul-

In the words *mould, moulder, moult,* and *smoulder*, Amer. spelling favours *o* alone instead of *ou*.

-our or -or

1. In agent nouns, only *-or* occurs as the ending (cf. **-or and -er**), e.g. *actor, counsellor*.
Exception: *saviour*.

2. In abstract nouns, *-our* is usual, e.g. *colour, favour, humour*. Only the following end in *-or*:

error	pallor	terror
horror	squalor	torpor
languor	stupor	tremor
liquor		

● In Amer. English *-or* is usual in nearly all words in which British English has *-our* (*glamour* is the main exception).

3. Nouns in *-our* change this to *-or* before the suffixes *-ation*, *-iferous*, *-ific*, *-ize*, and *-ous*, e.g.

coloration, humorous, odoriferous, rigorous, soporific, vaporize, vigorous.

Exception: *colourize*.

But *-our* keeps the *u* before *-able*, *-er*, *-ful*, *-ism*, *-ist*, *-ite*, and *-less*, e.g.

armourer, behaviourism, colourful, favourite, honourable, labourite, odourless, water-colourist.

Exceptions: *humorist*, *rigorist*.

past of verbs, formation of

A. Regular verbs add *-ed* for the past tense and past participle, and may make the following spelling changes:

1. Doubling of final consonant (see pp. 19 ff.).
2. Dropping of silent *-e* (see p. 21).
3. Change of *y* to *i* (see p. 51).

Note *laid*, *paid*, and *said* from *lay*, *pay*, and *say*.

B. A number of verbs vary in their past tense and past participle between a regular form and a form with *-t* (and in some cases a different vowel-sound in the stem):

burn	leap	spell
dream	learn	spill
kneel	smell	spoil
lean		

The *-t* form is usual in Received Pronunciation* and should be written by those who pronounce it. The regular form is usual in Amer. English.

* See p. 65.

Bereave is regular when the reference is to the loss of relatives by death; *bereft* is used when the reference is to loss of immaterial possessions.

Cleave is a rare word with two opposite meanings: (i) = stick; *A man . . shall cleave unto his wife* (Genesis 2: 24) (regular). (ii) = split. The past tense *clave* is archaic; *clove, cleft*, and regular *cleaved* are all permissible, but *cleaved* is usual in scientific and technical contexts. The past participle, takes one of two forms in various fixed expressions, *cloven-footed, cloven hoof, cleft palate, cleft stick*; *cleaved* is technical, but probably also best used outside the fixed expressions.

● Earn is regular. There is no form *earnt* in standard English.

C. A number of verbs vary in the past participle only between the regular form and one ending in -(*e*)*n*:

hew, mow, saw, sew, shear, show, sow, strew, swell.

In most of these the latter form is to be preferred; in British English it is obligatory when the participle is used attributively as an adjective. So *new-mown hay, a sawn-off* (Amer. *sawed-off*) *shotgun, shorn* (not *sheared*) *of one's strength, a swollen gland*; *swollen* or *swelled head* (= conceit) is a colloquial exception.

D. The past tense has -*a*-, the past participle -*u*-, in

begin	*shrink*	*stink*
drink	*sing*	*swim*
ring	*sink*	

● It is an error to use *begun, drunk*, etc. for the past tense, as if they followed *clung, flung, spun*, etc.

E. The past tense and past participle of the following verbs can cause difficulty:

abide (*by*) makes *abided*
alight makes *alighted*
bet: betted is increasingly common beside *bet*
bid (make a bid): *bid*
bid (command; say (goodnight, etc.)): *bid* is usual (*bade, bidden* are archaic)

broadcast unchanged in past tense and past participle

chide: *chided* is now usual (older *chid*)

forecast unchanged in past tense and past participle

hang: *hanged* is frequent for the capital punishment; otherwise only *hung*

highlight makes *highlighted.*

knit: *knitted* is usual, but *knit* is common in metaphorical use (*he knit his brows*)

light makes past *lit*, past participle *lit* in predicative use (*a fire was lit*) but *lighted* attributively (*a lighted match*)

quit makes *quit*, but *quitted* is also occasionally found

reeve (nautical) makes *rove*

rid unchanged in past tense and past participle

speed makes *sped*, but *speeded* in the senses 'cause to go at (a certain) speed' and 'travel at illegal or dangerous speed'

spit makes *spat* ● Amer. *spit*

spotlight makes *spotlighted*

stave: (to dent) *staved* or *stove*; (to ward off) *staved*

sweat makes *sweated* ● Amer. *sweat*

thrive: *thrived* is increasingly common beside *throve, thriven*

plural formation

Most nouns simply add -*s*, e.g. *cats, dogs, horses, cameras.*

A. The regular plural suffix -*s* is preceded by -*e*-:

1. After sibilant consonants, where ease of pronunciation requires a separating vowel, i.e. after

   ch: e.g. *benches, coaches, matches* (but not *lochs, stomachs* where the *ch* has a different sound)

   s: e.g. *buses, gases, pluses, yeses* (note that single *s* is not doubled)

   sh: e.g. *ashes, bushes*

   ss: e.g. *grasses, successes*

   x: e.g. *boxes, sphinxes*

   z: e.g. *buzzes, waltzes* (note *fezzes, quizzes* with doubling of *z*)

Proper names follow the same rule, e.g. *the Joneses, the Rogerses, the two Charleses.*

● *-es* should not be replaced by an apostrophe, as *the Jones'.*

2. After *-y* (not preceded by a vowel), which changes to *i*, e.g. *ladies, soliloquies, spies.*

Exceptions: proper names, e.g. *the Willoughbys, the three Marys*; also *lay-bys, standbys, zlotys* (Polish currency).

3. After *-o* in certain words:

bravoes (= ruffians;	*mementoes*
bravos = shouts	*mosquitoes*
of 'bravo!')	*mottoes*
buffaloes	*Negroes*
calicoes	*noes*
cargoes	*peccadilloes*
dingoes	*porticoes*
dominoes	*potatoes*
echoes	*salvoes*
embargoes	*stuccoes*
goes	*tomatoes*
grottoes	*tornadoes*
haloes	*torpedoes*
heroes	*vetoes*
innuendoes	*volcanoes*
mangoes	

The forms *grottos, innuendos, mangos, mementos, porticos, salvos* also occur.

Words not in the above list add only *-s*.
It is helpful to remember that *-e-* is never inserted:

(*a*) when the *o* is preceded by another vowel, e.g. *cuckoos, embryos, ratios.*
(*b*) when the word is an abbreviation, e.g. *hippos, kilos.*
(*c*) with proper names, e.g. *Lotharios, Figaros, the Munros.*

4. With words which change final *f* to *v* (see pp. 26 f.), e.g. *calves, scarves.*

B. Plural of compound nouns.

1. Compounds made up of a noun followed by an adjective, a prepositional phrase, or an adverb attach -s to the noun, e.g.

    (a) *courts martial*   *heirs presumptive*
         cousins-german   *poets laureate*

But *brigadier-generals, lieutenant-colonels, sergeant-majors.*

    (b) *men-of-war*   *tugs of war*
         sons-in-law

    (c) *hangers-on*   *passers-by*
         runners-up   *whippers-in*

Note: In informal usage -s is commonly transferred to the second element of compounds of type (a).

2. Compounds which contain no noun, or in which the noun element is now disguised, add -s at the end. So also do nouns formed from phrasal verbs and compounds ending in -ful, e.g.

    (a) *ne'er-do-wells*   *will-o'-the-wisps*
         forget-me-nots

    (b) *pullovers*   *set-ups*
         run-throughs

    (c) *handfuls*   *spoonfuls*

3. Compounds containing *man* or *woman* make both elements plural, as usually do those made up of two words linked by *and*, e.g.

    (a) *gentlemen ushers*   *women doctors*
         menservants
    (b) *pros and cons*   *ups and downs*

C. The plural of the following nouns with a singular in -s is unchanged:

biceps	*means*	*species*
congeries	*mews*	*superficies*
forceps	*series*	*thrips*
innings		

The following are mass nouns, not plurals:

bona fides (= 'good faith'), *kudos*

● The singulars *bona-fide* (as a noun; there is an adjective *bona-fide*), *congery*, *kudo*, sometimes seen, are erroneous.

D. Plural of nouns of foreign origin. The terminations that may form their plurals according to a foreign pattern are given in alphabetical order below; to each is added a list of the words that normally follow this pattern. It is recommended that the regular plural (in -*s*) should be used for all the other words with these terminations, even though some are found with either type of plural.

1. -*a* (Latin and Greek) becomes -*ae*:

alga	*lamina*	*nebula*
alumna	*larva*	*papilla*

Note: *formula* has -*ae* in mathematical and scientific use.

2. -*eau*, -*eu* (French) add -*x*:

beau	*château*	*plateau*
bureau	*milieu*	*tableau*

The anglicized plurals *beaus*, *bureaus*, *milieus*, *plateaus* also occur and are acceptable variants.

3. -*ex*, -*ix* (Latin) become -*ices*:

appendix	*cortex*	*matrix*
codex	*helix*	*radix*

Note: *index*, *vortex* have -*ices* in mathematical and scientific use (otherwise regular).

4. -*is* (Greek and Latin) becomes -*es* (pronounced *eez*):

amanuensis	*hypothesis*
analysis	*metamorphosis*
antithesis	*oasis*
axis	*parenthesis*
basis	*synopsis*
crisis	*thesis*
ellipsis	

5. *-o* (Italian) becomes *-i*:

> *concerto grosso* (*concerti grossi*)
> *graffito*   *ripieno*
> *maestro*   *virtuoso*

The anglicized plurals *maestros, ripienos, virtuosos* also occur and are acceptable variants.

Note: *solo* and *soprano* sometimes have *-i* in technical contexts (otherwise regular).

6. *-on* (Greek) becomes *-a*:

> *criterion*   *parhelion*   *phenomenon*

Note: The plural of *automaton* is in *-a* when used collectively (otherwise regular).

7. *-s* (French) is unchanged in the plural (note: it is silent in the singular, but pronounced *-z* in the plural):

> *chamois*   *corps*   *fracas*
> *chassis*   *faux pas*   *patois*

Also (not a noun in French): *rendezvous*.

8. *-um* (Latin) becomes *-a*:

> *addendum*   *effluvium*
> *bacterium*   *emporium*
> *candelabrum*   *epithalamium*
> *compendium*   *erratum*
> *corrigendum*   *maximum*
> *cranium*   *minimum*
> *crematorium*   *quantum*
> *curriculum*   *scholium*
> *datum*   *spectrum*
> *desideratum*   *speculum*
> *dictum*   *stratum*

The forms *compendiums, emporiums, epithalamiums* also occur and are acceptable variants.

Note: *medium* in scientific use, and in the sense 'a means of communication' (as *mass medium*) has plural in *-a*; the collective plural of *memorandum* 'things to be noted' is in *-a*; *rostrum* and *vacuum* have *-a* in technical use; otherwise these words are regular. In the technical sense 'starting-point' *datum* has a regular plural.

9. *-us* (Latin) becomes *-i*:

alumnus	*fungus*	*nucleus*
bacillus	*gladiolus*	*radius*
bronchus	*locus*	*stimulus*
cactus	*narcissus*	*terminus*
calculus		

Note: *focus* has plural in *-i* in scientific use, but otherwise is regular; *genius* has plural *genii* when used to mean 'guardian spirit', but in its usual sense is regular; *corpus, genus, opus* become *corpora, genera, opera* (or, to avoid confusion, *opuses*).

● The following words of foreign origin are plural nouns; they should normally not be construed as singulars (see also as separate entries in Section III):

bacteria	*graffiti*	*phenomena*
candelabra	*insignia*	*regalia*
criteria	*media*	*strata*
data		

E. There is no need to use an apostrophe before *-s*:

1. After figures: *the 1890s.*
2. After abbreviations: *KOs, MPs, SOSs.*

But it is needed in: *dot the i's and cross the t's, fair do's, do's and don'ts.*

possessive case

To form the possessive:

1. Normally, add *-'s* in the singular and *-s'* (i.e. apostrophe following the plural suffix *-s*) in the plural, e.g.

Bill's book	*the Johnsons' dog*
his master's voice	*a girls' school*

Nouns that do not form plural in *-s* add *-'s* to the plural form, e.g.

children's books	*women's liberation*

2. Nouns ending in *s* add *'s* for the singular possessive, e.g.

boss's	*Hicks's*
Burns's	*St James's Square*
Charles's	*Tess's*
Father Christmas's	*Thomas's*

To form the plural possessive, they add an apostrophe to the *s* of the plural in the normal way, e.g.

bosses'	*the octopuses' tentacles*
the Joneses' dog	*the Thomases' dog*

French names ending in silent *s* or *x* add -*'s*, which is pronounced as *z*, e.g.

Dumas's (= Dumah's)   *Crémieux's*

Names ending in -*es* pronounced *iz* are treated like plurals and take only an apostrophe (following the pronunciation, which is *iz*, not *iziz*), e.g.

Bridges'	*Moses'*
Hodges'	*Riches'*

Polysyllables not accented on the last or second last syllable can take the apostrophe alone, but the form with -*'s* is equally acceptable, e.g.

Barnabas'	or	*Barnabas's*
Nicholas'	or	*Nicholas's*

It is the custom in classical works to use the apostrophe only, irrespective of pronunciation, for ancient classical names ending in -*s*, e.g.

Ceres'	*Mars'*
Demosthenes'	*Venus'*
Herodotus'	*Xerxes'*

Jesus' 'is an accepted liturgical archaism' (*Hart's Rules*, p. 31). But in non-liturgical use, *Jesus's* is acceptable (used, e.g., in the *Revised English Bible* (1989), *John* 2: 3).

With the possessive preceding the word *sake*, be guided by the pronunciation, e.g.

for goodness' sake	but	*for God's sake*
		for Charles's sake

After -*x* and -*z*, use -'*s*, e.g. *Ajax's, Berlioz's music, Leibniz's law, Lenz's law.*

3. Expressions such as:

a fortnight's holiday	*two weeks' holiday*
a pound's worth	*two pounds' worth*
your money's worth	

contain possessives and should have apostrophes correctly placed.

4. In *I'm going to the butcher's, grocer's,* etc. there is a possessive with ellipsis of the word 'shop'. The same construction is used in *I'm going to Brown's, Green's,* etc., so that properly an apostrophe is called for. Where a business calls itself *Brown, Green,* or the like (e.g. *Marks and Spencer, J. Sainsbury*) the apostrophe would be expected before -*s*. But many businesses use the title *Browns, Greens,* etc., without an apostrophe (e.g. *Debenhams, Barclays Bank*). No apostrophe is necessary in *a Debenhams store* or in (*go to* or *take to*) *the cleaners.*

5. The apostrophe must not be used:

(*a*) with the plural non-possessive -*s*: notices such as *TEA'S* are often seen, but are wrong.

(*b*) with the possessive of pronouns: *hers, its, ours, theirs, yours*; the possessive of *who* is *whose.*

● *it's* = *it is*; *who's* = *who is.*

● There are no words *her's, our's, their's, your's.*

-*re* or -*er*

The principal words in which the ending -*re* (with the unstressed *er* sound—there are others with the sound *ruh*, e.g. *macabre*, or *ray*, e.g. *padre*) is found are:

accoutre	*centre*
*acre	**euchre*
amphitheatre	*fibre*
*cadre	*goitre*
calibre	*litre*

louvre	*ochre*
*lucre	**ogre*
lustre	*philtre*
manoeuvre	*reconnoitre*
*massacre	*sabre*
meagre	*sceptre*
*mediocre	*sepulchre*
metre (note *meter*	*sombre*
the measuring	*spectre*
device)	*theatre*
mitre	*titre*
nitre	**wiseacre*

- All but those marked * are spelt with -er in Amer. English.

re- prefix

This prefix is followed by a hyphen:

1. Before another *e*, e.g. *re-echo, re-entry.*

2. So as to distinguish the compound so formed from the more familiar identically spelt word written solid, e.g.

> *re-cover* (put new cover on): *recover*
> *re-form* (form again): *reform*
> *re-sign* (sign again): *resign*

silent final consonants

Words borrowed from French having silent final consonants give difficulty when inflections are added to them:

A. In the plural: see p. 43.

B. In the possessive: see p. 45.

C. With verbal inflections: see p. 20.

-s suffix

A. As the inflection of the plural of nouns: see **plural formation**.

B. As the inflection of the third person singular present indicative of verbs, it requires the same changes in the stem as the plural ending, namely the insertion of -e-:

1. After sibilants (*ch, s, sh, x, z*), e.g. *catches, tosses, pushes, fixes, buzzes*; note that single *s* and *z* are subject to doubling of final consonant (see pp. 19 ff.), though the forms in which they occur are rare, e.g. *nonplusses, quizzes, whizzes*.
2. After *y*, which is subject to the change of *y* to *i* (see p. 51), e.g. *cries, flies, carries, copies*.
3. After *o*: *echo, go, torpedo, veto*, like the corresponding nouns, insert *-e-* before *-s*; *crescendo, radio, solo, zero* should follow their nouns in having *-s*, but in practice there is variation.

-xion or *-ction*

Complexion, crucifixion, effluxion, fluxion all have *-x-*; *connection, deflection, inflection, reflection* all have *-ct-*; both *genuflection* and *genuflexion* occur, though the former is more usual.

-y, *-ey*, or *-ie* nouns

The diminutive or pet form of nouns can be spelt *-y*, *-ey*, or *-ie*. The majority of nouns which end in the sound of *-y* are so spelt (whether diminutives or of other origin), e.g.

aunty	*granny*	*nappy*
baby	*missy*	*potty*

The following are the main diminutives spelt with *-ey* (*-ey* nouns of other kinds are excluded from the list):

goosey	*matey*
housey-housey	*nursey*
Limey	*Sawney*
lovey-dovey	*slavey*

The following list contains the diminutives in *-ie*, together with a number of similar nouns that are not in fact diminutives but do end in *-ie*. Note that most Scottish diminutives are spelt with *-ie*, e.g. *corbie, kiltie*.

beanie	*bookie*
birdie	*brownie*

budgie
caddie (golf; *tea caddy*)
chappie
charlie
clippie
cookie
coolie
dearie
doggie (noun; *doggy* adjective)
genie (spirit; plural *genii*)
Geordie
gillie
girlie
goalie
junkie

Kewpie (doll)
laddie
lassie
mealie (maize; *mealy* adjective)
Mountie
movie
nightie
oldie
pinkie (little finger)
pixie
quickie
rookie
sheltie
softie
Tin Lizzie
walkie-talkie
zombie

Note: *bogie* (wheeled undercarriage), *bogey* (score in golf, ghost).

-y or -ey adjectives

When -*y* is added to a word to form an adjective, the following changes in spelling occur:

1. Doubling of final consonant (see pp. 19 ff.).

2. Dropping of silent -*e* (see p. 21).

Exceptions:

(*a*) After *u*:

bluey   gluey
cliquey   tissuey

(*b*) In words that are not well established in the written language, where the retention of -*e* helps to clarify the sense:

cagey   dicey   pacey
cakey   dikey   pricey
chocolatey   matey   smiley
cottagey   orangey   villagey

Note also *holey* (distinguished from *holy*); *phoney*.

3. Insertion of *-e-* when *-y* is also the final letter of the stem:

clayey	*sprayey*
skyey	*wheyey*

Also in *gooey*.

4. Adjectives ending in unstressed *-ey* (2 (*a*) and (*b*) and 3 above) change this *-ey* to *-i-* before the comparative and superlative suffixes *-er* and *-est* and the adverbial suffix *-ly*, e.g.

cagey: cagily	*matey: matily*
cliquey: cliquier	*pacey: pacier*
dicey: dicier	*phoney: phonily*
gooey: gooier	*pricey: pricier*

Before *-ness* there is variation, e.g.

cagey: cageyness,	*phoney: phoneyness,*
caginess	*phoniness*
clayey: clayeyness	*wheyey: wheyiness*
matey: mateyness,	
matiness	

y or *i*

There is often uncertainty about whether *y* or *i* should be written in the following words:

Write *i* in:	Write *y* in:
cider	*dyke*
cipher	*gypsy*
Libya	*lyke-wake*
lich-gate	*lynch law*
linchpin	*pygmy*
sibyl (classical)	*style* (manner)
siphon	*stylus*
siren	*stymie*
stile (in fence)	*Sybil* (frequently as
timpani (drums)	Christian name)
tiro	*syllabub*

witch hazel	*sylvan* *syrup* *tyke* *tympanum* (ear-drum) *tyre* (of wheel) *wych-elm*

-yse or *-yze*

This verbal ending (e.g. in *analyse, catalyse, paralyse*) is not a suffix but part of the Greek stem *-lyse*. It should not be written with *z* (though *z* is normally used in such words in America).

y to *i*

Words that end in *-y* change this to *-i-* before certain suffixes. The conditions are:

A. When the *-y* is not preceded by a vowel (except *-u-* in *-guy, -quy*).

-y does not change to *-i-* when preceded by a vowel (other than *u* in *-guy, -quy*). So *enjoyable, conveyed, parleyed, gayer, gayest, donkeys, buys, employer, joyful, coyly, enjoyment, greyness*.

Exceptions: *daily, gaily,* and adjectives ending in unstressed *-ey* (see p. 50).

B. When the suffix is:

1. *-able*, e.g. *deniable, justifiable, variable.*

Exception: *flyable.*

2. *-ed* (the past tense and past participle), e.g. *carried, denied, tried.*

3. *-er* (agent-noun suffix), e.g. *carrier, crier, supplier.*

Exceptions: *fryer, shyer* (one who, a horse which, shies), *skyer* (in cricket). Note that *prier, trier* (one who tries) are regular, and that variation is possible with *flyer* (*flier* also occurs) and *drier* (person or thing that dries; *dryer* also occurs).

4. *-er, -est* (comparative and superlative); e.g. *drier, driest*; *happier, happiest.*

5. *-es* (noun plural and third person singular present indicative), e.g. *ladies, soliloquies, spies; carries, denies, tries.*
Exceptions: see p. 40.
6. *-ful* (adjectives), e.g. *beautiful, fanciful.* (*Bellyful* is a noun, not an adjective.)
7. *-less* (adjectives), e.g. *merciless, remediless.*
Exceptions: some rare compounds, e.g. *countryless, hobbyless, partyless.*
8. *-ly* (adverbs), e.g. *drily, happily, plaguily.*
Exceptions: *shyly, slyly, spryly, wryly.*
9. *-ment* (nouns), e.g. *embodiment, merriment.*
10. *-ness* (nouns), e.g. *happiness, cliquiness.*
Exceptions: *dryness, flyness, shyness, slyness, spryness, wryness; busyness* (distinguished from *business*).

Difficult and confusable spellings (not covered in previous entries)

The list below contains words (i) which occasion difficulty in spelling; (ii) of which various spellings exist; or (iii) which need to be distinguished from other words spelt similarly. In each case the recommended form is given, and in some cases, for the sake of clarity, is followed by the mark □ and the rejected variant. Misspellings which are not acceptable in standard English, and spellings which are essentially American, are preceded by the mark ●. Where the rejected variant is widely separated in alphabetical position from the recommended form, the former has been given an entry preceded by the mark □ and followed by 'use' and the recommended form. The wording added to some entries constitutes a guide to the sense, not an exhaustive definition or description.

accommodation
adaptation ● not *adaption*
adaptor
adviser
□ *aerie*: use *eyrie*
affront
agriculturist

ait □ not *eyot*
align, alignment ● not *aline, alinement*
allege
alleluia □ not *alleluya*
almanac (*almanack* only in some titles)

aluminium ● Amer.
  aluminum
ambiance (term in art)
ambience surroundings
amok □ not *amuck*
ampere
ancillary ● not *ancilliary*
annex (verb)
annexe (noun)
any one (of a number)
anyone anybody
any time
any way any manner
anyway at all events
apophthegm ● Amer.
  apothegm
apostasy
archaeology
artefact □ not *artifact*
assimilable ● not *assimilatable*
aubrietia □ not *aubretia*
aught anything □ not *ought*
autarchy despotism
autarky self-sufficiency
auxiliary
aye yes □ not *ay*
aye always
babu □ not *baboo*
bachelor
bail out obtain release,
    relieve financially □ not
    bale out
bale out parachute from
    aircraft □ not *bail out*
balk (verb)
balmy like balm
barbecue ● not *barbeque*
barmy (informal) mad
baulk timber
bayoneted, -ing

behove ● Amer. *behoove*
bivouac (noun and verb)
bivouacked, bivouacking
blond (of man or his hair)
blonde (of woman or her
  hair)
born: be born (of child)
borne: have borne have
  carried or given birth to;
  be borne be carried; *be
  borne by* be carried by or
  given birth to by (a
  mother)
brand-new
brier □ not *briar*
bur clinging seed □ not
  burr
burr rough edge, drill,
  rock, accent, etc. □ not
  bur
cabbala, cabbalistic □ not
  kabbala, kabbalistic
caftan □ not *kaftan*
calendar almanac
calender press
caliph
calligraphy
calliper leg support;
  (plural) compasses □ not
  caliper
callous (adjective)
callus (noun)
camellia shrub
canvas (noun) cloth
canvas (verb) cover with
  canvas (past *canvassed*)
canvass (verb) (past
  canvassed)
carcass □ not *carcase*
caviar □ not *caviare*

chameleon
chancellor
chaperon □ not *chaperone*
Charollais
cheque (bank)
chequer (noun) pattern
(verb) variegate;
● Amer. *checker*
chilli pepper
chivvy, chivvied
choosy
chord combination of
notes, line joining points
on curve
chukka boot
chukker (polo)
clarinettist ● Amer.
clarinetist
coco palm
cocoa chocolate
coconut
colander strainer
commit(ment)
committee
comparative
complement make
complete, that which
makes complete
compliment praise
computer
conjuror
connection
conqueror
conscientious
consensus
contractual ● not
contractural
cord string, flex, spinal or
vocal *cord*, rib of cloth
cornelian □ not *carnelian*

corslet armour, underwear
□ not *corselet*
cosy ● Amer. *cozy*
council assembly
councillor member of
council
counsel advice, barrister
counsellor adviser
court martial (noun)
court-martial (verb)
crape black fabric
crêpe crape fabric other
than black; rubber;
pancake
crevasse large fissure in ice
crevice small fissure
crosier □ not *crozier*
crumby covered in crumbs
crummy (informal) dirty,
inferior
curb restrain, restraint
curtsy □ not *curtsey*
□ *czar*: use *tsar*
dare say ● not *daresay*
database
debonair
depositary (person)
depository (place)
descendant
desiccated
□ *despatch*: use *dispatch*
desperate
deterrable
devest (only Law: general
use *divest*)
didicoi (tinker)
dilatation (medical)
dilator
dinghy boat
dingy grimy

disc ● Amer. *disk*
discreet judicious
discrete separate
disk (in computing) ● Amer.
  in all senses of *disc*
dispatch □ not *despatch*
dissect
dissociate □ not *disassociate*
disyllable
divest
doily □ not *doyley*
douse quench □ not *dowse*
dowse use divining rod
draft (noun) military party,
  money order, rough
  sketch (verb), sketch
  ● Amer. in all senses
  of *draught*
draftsman one who drafts
  documents
draught act of drawing, act
  of drinking, vessel's
  depth, current of air
  ● Amer. *draft*
draughtsman one who
  makes drawings, plans,
  etc.; piece in game of
  draughts
duffle □ not *duffel*
ecology
ecstasy
ecumenical
educationist □ not
  educationalist
effrontery
□ *eikon*: use *icon*
eirenicon □ not *irenicon*
elegiac ● not *elegaic*
embarrassment
embed □ not *imbed*

employee (masculine and
  feminine; no accent)
enclose
enclosure (but *Inclosure Acts*)
encroach
encyclopedia □ not
  encyclopaedia
envelop (verb)
envelope (noun)
erector
erupt break out
espresso □ not *expresso*
ethereal □ not *etherial*
everlasting
every one (of a number)
everyone everybody
exalt raise, praise
exceed
expatriate ● not *expatriot*
exult rejoice
□ *eyot*: use *ait*
eyrie □ not *aerie*
faecal
faeces
fascia □ not *facia*
fee'd (*a fee'd lawyer*) □ not
  feed
feldspar □ not *felspar*
feldspathic
felloe (of wheel) □ not *felly*
ferrule cap on stick
ferule cane
fetid □ not *foetid*
florescence flowering
flotation □ not *floatation*
flu □ not *'flu*
fluorescence light radiation
foetal, foetus □ Amer. and
  commonly in medicine,
  fetal, fetus

fogy □ not *fogey*
forbade (past tense of
  forbid) □ not *forbad*
forestall
for ever for always
forever continually
forty
fount (typeface) ● Amer.
  font
fungous (adjective)
fungus (noun)
furore ● Amer. *furor*
fusilier
fusillade
gaol (official use) □ Amer.
  jail (both forms used in
  Brit. English)
gaoler (as for *gaol*)
gauge measure
gazump ● not *gazoomph*,
  etc.
gibe jeer □ not *jibe*
gild make gold
□ *gild* association: use *guild*
glycerine
gormandize eat greedily
gormless
gourmand glutton
gram □ not *gramme*
gramophone
grandad
granddaughter
grayling (fish, butterfly)
grey ● Amer. *gray*
griffin fabulous creature □
  not *gryphon*
griffon vulture, dog
grill for cooking
grille grating □ not *grill*
grisly terrible

grizzly grey-haired; bear
groin (anatomy;
  architecture)
grommet □ not *grummet*
groyne breakwater
guerrilla
guild association
gybe (nautical) ● Amer. *jibe*
haema-, haemo- (prefix
  meaning 'blood')
haemorrhage
haemorrhoids
hairdos
hallelujah
harass
hark
harum-scarum
haulm stem
hearken
hiccup □ not *hiccough*
Hindu
homoeopathy
homogeneous having parts
  all the same
homogenize make
  homogeneous
homogenous having
  common descent
honorific
□ *hooping cough*: use
  whooping cough
horsy □ not *horsey*
horticulturist
hummus chick-pea spread
humous of humus
humus rich soil
hurrah, hurray ● not
  hoorah, hooray (except in
  Hooray Henry)
hussy ● not *huzzy*

hypocrisy
hypocrite
icon
idiosyncrasy
idyll
ignoramus plural
   ignoramuses
□ *imbed*: use *embed*
impinging
impostor
inadvisable
□ *inclose, inclosure*: use *en-*
incommunicado
inoculate
input, inputting
in so far
insomuch
inure
investor
irenic
□ *irenicon*: use *eirenicon*
irrupt enter violently
its of it
it's it is
jail (see *gaol*)
jailor (see *gaol*)
jalopy
jam pack tightly; conserve
jamb door-post
□ *jibe*: use *gibe, gybe*
   ● Amer. also = accord
   with
joust combat ● not *just*
□ *kabbala*: use *cabbala*
□ *kaftan*: use *caftan*
kebab
kerb pavement ● Amer.
   curb
ketchup
□ *khalif*: use *caliph*

kilogram
kilometre
koala
Koran □ not *Qur'an*
kowtow
labyrinth
lachrymal of tears
lachrymose tearful
lackey
lacquer
lacrimal (in science)
lacrimate, -ation, -atory (in
   science)
largesse □ not *largess*
ledger account book
leger line (in music)
liaison
licence (noun)
license (verb)
licensee
lickerish greedy
□ *licorice*: use *liquorice*
lightening making light
lightning (accompanying
   thunder)
limeade
linage number of lines
lineage ancestry
lineament feature
liniment embrocation
liqueur flavoured
   alcoholic liquor
liquor
liquorice □ not *licorice*
□ *litchi*: use *lychee*
literate
literature
littérateur
littoral
lodestone □ not *loadstone*

loath(some) (adjectives)
loathe (verb)
lodestar
longevity
longitude ● not *longtitude*
lour frown □ not *lower*
lychee □ not *litchi*
Mac (prefix) spelling
  depends on the custom
  of the one bearing the
  name, and this must be
  followed; in alphabetical
  arrangement, treat as
  Mac however spelt, *Mac,
  Mc, M^c or M'*.
mac (informal) mackintosh
mackintosh □ not *macintosh*
maharaja
maharanee
□ *Mahomet*: use
  Muhammad
mamma
mandolin
manikin dwarf, anatomical
  model
manila hemp, paper
manilla African bracelet
mannequin (live) model
manoeuvrable ● Amer.
  maneuverable
mantle(piece)
mantel cloak
marijuana □ not *marihuana*
marquis
marshal (noun and verb)
marten weasel
martial of war (*martial law*)
martin bird
marvellous ● Amer.
  marvelous

matins □ not *mattins*
matt lustreless □ not *mat*
medieval ● not *mediaeval*
menagerie
mendacity lying
mendicity the state of being
  a beggar
millenary of a thousand;
  thousandth anniversary
millennium thousand years
millipede □ not *millepede*
milli- (prefix meaning
  one-thousandth)
milometer ● not *mileometer*
miniature
minuscule ● not *miniscule*
mischievous ● not
  mischievious
miscible (in science)
missis (slang) □ not *missus*
misspell
mistle thrush □ not *missel
  thrush*
mistletoe
mixable
mizen (nautical)
mnemonic
moneyed
moneys □ not *monies*
mongoose (plural
  mongooses)
moustache ● Amer.
  mustache
mouth (verb) ● not *mouthe*
mucous (adjective)
mucus (noun)
Muhammad
murky
Muslim ● not *Moslem*
mynah (bird)

naive, naivety □ not *naïve,*
  naïvety, naïveté
naught nothing
negligée □ not *negligee,*
  négligé
negligible
nerve-racking ● not
  -wracking
net not subject to
  deduction □ not *nett*
nonet
nonplussed
nonsuch unrivalled person
  or thing □ not *nonesuch*
no one nobody
nought the figure zero
numskull □ not *numbskull*
nursling □ not *nurseling*
O (interjection) used to
  form a vocative (*O
  Caesar*) and when not
  separated by punctuation
  from what follows (*O for
  the wings of a dove*)
occurrence
octet
● *of*: not to be written
  instead of *have* in such
  constructions as '*Did you
  go?*' '*I would have, if it
  hadn't rained.*'
omelette □ not *omelet*
on to ● not *onto*
orangeade
Orangeism
orang-utan □ not
  orang-outang
outcast person cast out
outcaste (India) person
  with no caste

outputting
ouzel □ not *ousel*
oyez! □ not *oyes!*
paediatric
palaeo- (prefix = ancient)
palate roof of mouth
palette artist's board
pallet mattress, part of
  machine, platform for
  loads
pallor
panda animal
pander pimp; to gratify
panellist ● Amer. *panelist*
paraffin
parakeet
parallel, paralleled,
  paralleling
partisan □ not *partizan*
pasha
pastel (crayon)
pastille
pavior
pawpaw (fruit) □ not *papaw*
pedal (noun) foot lever
  (verb) operate pedal
peddle follow occupation of
  pedlar; trifle
pederast
pedigreed
pedlar vendor of small wares
  ● Amer. *peddler*
peewit □ not *pewit*
Pekingese dog, inhabitant
  of Peking □ not
  Pekinese
peninsula (noun)
peninsular (adjective)
pennant (nautical) piece of
  rigging, flag

pennon (military) long
  narrow flag
peony
phone (informal) telephone
  □ not *'phone*
phoney □ not *phony*
pi pious
pidgin simplified language
pie jumbled type
piebald
pigeon bird; *not one's*
  pigeon not one's affair
piggyback □ not *pickaback*
pi jaw
pilau □ not *pilaff, pilaw*
pimento aromatic spice
pimiento sweet pepper
plane (informal) aeroplane
  □ not *'plane*
plebeian
plenitude ● not *plentitude*
plimsoll (shoe) □ not
  plimsole
plough ● Amer. *plow*
pommel knob, saddle-bow
poppadam □ not *poppadom*
pore (*over* e.g. a map)
postilion □ not *postillion*
powwow
practice (noun)
practise (verb)
precede come before
précised
predacious □ not *predaceous*
predominant(*ly*) ● not
  predominate(*ly*)
premise (verb) to say as
  introduction
premises (plural noun)
  foregoing matters, building

premiss (in logic)
  proposition
primeval □ not *primaeval*
principal chief
principle fundamental
  truth, moral basis
prise force open
privilege
Privy Council
Privy Counsellor
proceed go on, continue
program (in computing)
  ● Amer. in all senses
programme (general use)
proletariat
promoter
protrude
protuberance ● not
  protruberance
pukka
pummel pound with fists
pupillage □ not *pupilage*
putt (in golf)
pyjamas ● Amer. *pajamas*
quadraphony, quadraphonic
  □ not *quadro-* ● not
  quadri-
quartet
quatercentenary ● not
  quarter-
questionnaire
quintet
□ *Qur'an*: use *Koran*
rabbet groove in woodwork
  (also *rebate*)
racket (for ball games) □
  not *racquet*
rackets game
racoon □ not *raccoon*
radical (chemistry)

radicle (botany)
raja □ not *rajah*
rarity
rattan plant, cane (also *ratan*)
raze □ not *rase*
razzmatazz □ not *razzamatazz*
recce (slang) reconnaissance
recompense
Renaissance ● not *Renascence*
renege □ not *renegue*
repairable (of material) able to be repaired
reparable (of loss) able to be made good
restaurateur
reverend (deserving reverence; title of clergy)
reverent (showing reverence)
review survey, reconsideration, report
revue musical entertainment
rhyme ● not *rime*
riband (sport, heraldry)
ribbon
rigor (medical) shivering-fit
rigour severity
Riley (slang: *the life of Riley*) □ also *Reilly*
rill stream
rille (on moon)
rime frost
rogues' gallery
role □ not *rôle*
roly-poly
Romania
rule the roost □ not *roast*

rumba □ not *rhumba*
saccharin (noun)
saccharine (adjective)
salutary beneficial
salutatory welcoming
sanatorium ● Amer. *sanitarium*
Sanhedrin □ not *Sanhedrim*
satire literary work
satiric(al) of satire
satyr woodland deity
satyric of Greek drama with satyrs
savannah □ not *savanna*
scallop □ not *scollop*
scallywag ● Amer. *scalawag*
sceptic ● Amer. *skeptic*
scrimmage tussle ● also term in Amer. football
scrummage (Rugby)
sear to scorch, wither(ed)
secrecy
seigneur feudal lord
seigneurial of a seigneur
seigniory lordship
selvage
separate
septet
sere catch of gunlock; term in ecology
sergeant (military, police)
serjeant (law)
sestet (in a sonnet)
□ *sett* (noun): use *set*
sextet (in music, etc.)
Shakespearian □ not *Shakespearean*
shanty hut, song
sharif Muslim leader □ not *sherif*

sheath (noun)
sheathe (verb)
sheikh
shemozzle rumpus
□ *sherif*: use *sharif*
sheriff county officer
Shia (branch of Islam)
show ● not *shew*
sibylline
Sinhalese □ not *Singhalese*
slew turn □ not *slue*
smart alec □ not *aleck*
smooth (adjective and verb)
 ● not *smoothe*
sobriquet □ not *soubriquet*
solemness
somersault □ not
 summersault
*some time (come and see
 me some time)*
sometime former, formerly
spinal cord □ not *spinal
 chord*
spirituel (masculine and
 feminine) having
 refinement of mind
sprightly ● not *spritely*
spurt □ not *spirt*
squirearchy □ not *squirarchy*
stanch (verb) stop a flow □
 not *staunch*
State (capital S for the
 political unit)
stationary (adjective) at
 rest
stationery (noun) paper, etc.
staunch loyal □ not *stanch*
step-parent
stoep (South Africa)
 veranda

storey division of building
 ● Amer. *story*
storeyed having storeys
storied celebrated in story
stoup for holy water, etc.
 □ not *stoop*
straight without curve
strait narrow
strait-jacket
strait-laced
sty for pigs; swelling on
 eyelid ● not *stye*
subsidiary
subtlety
subtly ● not *subtlely*
sulphur ● Amer. *sulfur*
sumac
summons (noun) a
 command to appear
 (plural *summonses*)
summons (verb) issue a
 summons (inflected
 summonsed)
supersede ● not *supercede*
swap □ not *swop*
swat hit sharply
swot study hard
sycamine, sycomore (Biblical
 trees)
sycamore (member of
 maple genus)
syllabication □ not
 syllabification
synthesist, synthesize ● not
 synthet-
teasel (plant)
teetotalism
teetotaller ● Amer.
 teetotaler
tee-hee (laugh)

tell (archaeology)
template □ not *templet*
tenet principle
tetchy
thank you ● not *thankyou*
thank-you (noun),
  thank-you letter
threshold
tic contraction of muscles
tick-tack semaphore □ not
  tic-tac
titbit ● Amer. *tidbit*
titillate excite
titivate smarten up □ not
  tittivate
today
tomorrow
tonight
tonsillar, tonsillitis
toupee
Trades Union Congress
trade union □ not *trades
  union*
traipse trudge □ not *trapes*
tranquil
tranquillity, tranquillize
transferable
transship(ment) □ not
  tranship(ment)
transonic □ not *transsonic*
transsexual □ not
  transexual
trolley
troop assembly of soldiers
trooper member of troop
troupe company of
  performers
trouper member of troupe
tsar □ not *czar*
T-shirt

Turco- (combining form of
  Turkish)
tympanum ear-drum
tyre ● Amer. *tire*
'un (informal for *one*)
unadvised
underlie, underlying
under way ● not *under
  weigh* or *underway*
unequivocal, -ally ● not
  unequivocable, -ably
valance curtain, drapery
valence (in chemistry)
Vandyke beard, brown
veld □ not *veldt*
vendor
veranda □ not *verandah*
vermilion
vice tool ● Amer. *vise*
villain evil-doer
villein serf
visor □ not *vizor*
vocal cord □ not *vocal chord*
wagon □ not *waggon*
waiver forgoing of legal
  right
warrior
wastable
waver be unsteady
weird
whiskey (Irish, Amer.)
whisky (Scotch)
Whit Monday, Sunday
Whitsunday (Scottish; not a
  Sunday)
whiz □ not *whizz*
whooping cough
who's who is
whose of whom
wisteria □ not *wistaria*

withhold
woebegone
woeful ● not *woful*
wrath anger

wreath (noun)
wreathe (verb)
wroth angry
yoghurt □ not *yogurt*

II
PRONUNCIATION

For one thing, you speak quite differently from Roy.
Now mind you, I'm not saying that one kind of voice is
better than another kind, although . . . the B.B.C. seems
to have very definite views on the subject.
                        (Marghanita Laski, *The Village*)

THIS section aims at resolving the uncertainty felt by many
speakers both about some of the general variations in the
pronunciation of English, and about a large number of individual words whose pronunciation is variable. Accordingly,
the section is in two parts: A, general points of pronunciation,
and B, a list of preferred pronunciations.

The aim of recommending one type of pronunciation rather
than another, or of giving a word a recommended spoken
form, naturally implies the existence of a standard. There are
of course many varieties of English, even within the limits of
the British Isles, but it is not the business of this section to
describe them. The treatment here is based upon Received
Pronunciation (RP), namely 'the pronunciation of that variety
of British English widely considered to be least regional, being
originally that used by educated speakers in southern England' (*OED*). This is not to suggest that other varieties are
inferior; rather, RP is here taken as a neutral national standard, just as it is in its use in broadcasting or in the teaching
of English as a foreign language.

A. *General points of pronunciation*

This first part of Section II is concerned with general variations and uncertainties in pronunciation. Even when RP
alone is taken as the model, it is impossible to lay down a set
of rules that will establish the correct pronunciation of every
word and hold it constant, since pronunciation is continually

changing. Some changes affect a particular sound in its every occurrence throughout the vocabulary, while others occur only in the environment of a few other sounds. Some changes occur gradually and imperceptibly; some are limited to a section of the community. At any time there is bound to be considerable variation in pronunciation. One of the purposes of the entries that follow is to draw attention to such variation and to indicate the degree of acceptability of each variant in standard English. Uncertainty about pronunciation also arises from the irregularity of English spelling. It is all too often impossible to guess how a particular letter or group of letters in an unfamiliar word should be pronounced. Broadly speaking, there are particular letters and letter sequences which repeatedly cause such uncertainty (e.g. *g* (hard and soft); final -*ed*; final -*ade*). To settle these uncertainties is the other main purpose of the entries that follow.

The entries are arranged in alphabetical order of heading; the headings are not, of course, complete words, but are either individual letters of the alphabet or sequences of letters making up parts (usually the beginnings or endings) of words. Some entries cover sounds that are spelt in various ways: the heading given is the typical spelling. There are also three entries of a different sort: they deal with (*a*) the main distinguishing features of American pronunciation, (*b*) the reduction of common words in rapid speech, and (*c*) patterns of stress.

a

1. There is variation in the pronunciation of *a* between the sound heard in *calm*, *father* and that heard in *cat*, *fan*, in

(*a*) the suffix -*graph* (in *photograph*, *telegraph*, etc.) and
(*b*) the prefix *trans*- (as in *transfer*, *translate*, etc.).

(*a*) In -*graph*, *a* as in *calm* seems to be the more generally acceptable form in RP. Note that when the suffix -*ic* is added (e.g. in *photographic*), only *a* as in *cat* can be used.
(*b*) In *trans*-, either kind of *a* is acceptable.

2. The word endings -*ada*, -*ade*, and -*ado* occasion difficulty, since in some words the pronunciation of the *a* is as in *calm*, in others as in *made*.

(a) In -*ada* words, *a* is as in *calm*, e.g. *armada, cicada.*

(b) In most -*ade* words, *a* is as in *made*, e.g. *accolade, barricade, cavalcade.*

Exceptions: *a* as in *calm* in

aubade	*façade*	*promenade*
ballade	*gambade*	*roulade*
charade	*pomade*	*saccade*

and in unassimilated loan-words from French, e.g. *dégringolade, oeillade.*

(c) In most -*ado* words, *a* is as in *calm*, e.g.

aficionado	*bravado*
amontillado	*desperado*
avocado	*Mikado*

Exceptions: *a* as in *made* in *bastinadó, tornado.*

3. *a* in the word-ending -*alia* is like *a* in *alien*, e.g. in *marginalia, pastoralia, penetralia.*

4. *a* before *ls* and *lt* in many words is pronounced either like *aw* in *bawl* or *o* in *doll*, e.g. in

alter	*halt*	*salt*
false	*palsy*	*waltz*

The same variation occurs with *au* in *assault, fault, somersault, vault.*

Note: in several words *a* before *ls* and *lt* can only be pronounced like *a* in *sally*, e.g.

Alsation	*altruism*	*peristalsis*
alter ego	*caltrop*	*peristaltic*
altitude	*contralto*	*salsify*
alto	*Malthusian*	*saltation*

5. The word endings -*ata*, -*atum*, and -*atus* occasion difficulty. In most words the *a* is pronounced as in *mate*, e.g. in

apparatus	*hiatus*
datum (plural *data*)	*meatus*
flatus	*ultimatum*

Exceptions: *cantata, cassata, chipolata, desideratum* (plural *desiderata*), *erratum* (plural *errata*), *serenata, sonata, toccata* with *a* as in *calm*; *stratum*, *stratus* with *a* as in *mate* or as in *calm*.

-age

The standard pronunciation of the following words of French origin ending in *-age* is with stress on the first syllable, *a* as in *calm*, and *g* as in *regime*.

arbitrage	*dressage*	*mirage*
barrage	*fuselage*	*persiflage*
camouflage	*garage*	*sabotage*
collage	*massage*	

Note that *montage* is stressed on the second syllable.

● The pronunciation of *-age* as in *cabbage* is non-standard in all of these words except for *arbitrage*. The placing of the stress on the final syllable in some of these words is a feature of Amer. pronunciation.

□ The substitution of the sound of *g* as in *large* for that in *regime* by some speakers in several of these words is acceptable and is commonly heard in *garage* in particular.

American pronunciation

Where the American pronunciation of individual forms and words significantly differs from the British, this is indicated as part of the individual entries in this Section. There remain certain constant features of 'General American'* pronunciation that, being generally distributed, are not worth noting for every word or form in which they occur. The principal features are these:

1. *r* is sounded wherever it is written, i.e. after vowels finally and before consonants, as well as before vowels, e.g. in *burn*, *car*, *form*.

2. The sound of *l* is 'dark' (as in British *bell*, *fill*) everywhere; the British sound of *l* as in *land*, *light* is not used.

---

* 'A form of U.S. speech without marked dialectal or regional characteristics' (*OED*).

3. (t)t between vowels sounds like d (and this d often sounds like a kind of r), e.g. in *latter*, *tomato*.

4. The vowel of *boat*, *dote*, *know*, *no*, etc. is a pure long vowel, not a diphthong as in British English.

5. Where British English has four vowels, (i) *a* as in *bat*, (ii) *ah* as in *dance*, *father*, (iii) *o* as in *hot*, *long*, and (iv) *aw* as in *law*, Amer. English has only three, differently distributed, viz.: (i) *a* as in *bat*, *dance*, (ii) *ah* as in *father*, *hot*, and (iii) *aw* as in *long*, *law*.

6. The sound of *you* (spelt *u*, *ew*, etc.) after *s*, *t*, *d*, *n*, is replaced by the sound of *oo*, e.g. in *resume*, *Tuesday*, *due*, *new*, etc.

7. The sound of *u* as in *up* (also spelt *o* in *come*, etc.) sounds like the obscure sound of *a* as in *aloft*, *china*.

8. *er* is pronounced as in *herd* in words where it is like *ar* in *hard* in British English, e.g. in *clerk*, *derby*.

9. The vowels in the first syllables of (*a*) *ferry*, *herald*, *merry*, etc., (*b*) *fairy*, *hairy*, *Mary*, etc., and (*c*) *carry*, *Harry*, *marry*, etc. (i.e. when *r* follows) are not distinguished from one another by most General American speakers.

10. In words of four syllables and over, in which the main stress falls on the first or second syllable, there is a strong secondary stress on the last syllable but one, the vowel of which is fully enunciated, not reduced as in British English, e.g. *cóntemplàtive*, *témporàry*, *térritòry*.

-arily

In a few adverbs that end in the sequence -arily there is a tendency to place the stress on the *a* rather than the first syllable of the word. The reason lies in the stress pattern of four- and five-syllable words.

Adjectives of four syllables ending in -ary which are stressed on the first syllable are generally pronounced with elision of one of the middle syllables, e.g. *military*, *necessary*, *temporary* pronounced milit'ry, necess'ry, temp'rary. This tri-syllabic pattern is much easier to pronounce.

The addition of the adverbial suffix -*ly* converts the word back into an unwieldy tetrasyllable that cannot be further elided: *milit(a)rily, necess(a)rily, temp(o)rarily*. Hence the use of these adverbs is sometimes avoided by saying *in a military fashion, in a solitary way*, etc.

A number of these adverbs are, however, in common use, e.g.

arbitrarily	*ordinarily*
momentarily	*temporarily*
necessarily	*voluntarily*

Because of the awkwardness of placing the stress on the first syllable, colloquial speech has adopted a pronunciation with stress on the third syllable, with the *a* sounding like *e* in *verily*. This is probably a borrowing from Amer. English, in which this pronunciation problem does not arise. In adjectives like *necessary* the ending -*ary* quite regularly receives a secondary stress (see **American pronunciation,** p. 68), which can then be converted into a main stress when -*ly* is added.

This pronunciation is much easier and more natural in rapid, colloquial speech, in which it would be pedantic to censure it.

The case of the word *primarily* is somewhat different. It contains only four syllables, which, with stress on the first, can be reduced by elision of the second syllable to the easily pronounced spoken form prim'rily.

● There is therefore no need to pronounce the word with stress on the second syllable. Pronunciations like pri-*merr*-ily or pri-*marr*-ily are not acceptable in careful speech.

-*ed*

1. In the following adjectives the ending -*ed* is pronounced as a separate syllable:

accursed	*naked*	*wicked*
cragged	*rugged*	*wretched*
deuced	*sacred*	

Note: *accursed* and *deuced* can also be pronounced as one syllable.

2. The following words represent two different spoken forms each with meanings that differ according to whether *-ed* is pronounced as a separate syllable or not. In most cases the former pronunciation indicates an adjective (as with the list under 1 above), the latter the past tense and past participle of a verb, but some are more complicated.

	(a) *-ed* as separate syllable	(b) *-ed* pronounced *'d*
aged	= very old (*he is very aged, an aged man*)	= having the age of (one, etc.) (*he is aged three, a boy aged three*); past of *to age* (*he has aged greatly*)
beloved	used before noun (*beloved brethren*); = beloved person (*my beloved is mine*)	used as predicate (*he was beloved by all*)
blessed	= fortunate, holy, sacred (*blessed are the meek, the blessed saints*); = blessed person (*Isles of the blessed*)	part of *to bless*; sometimes also in senses listed in left-hand column
crabbed	= cross-grained, hard to follow, etc.	past of *to crab*
crooked	= not straight, dishonest	= having a transverse handle (*crooked stick*); past of *to crook*
cursed	before noun = damnable	past of *to curse*

dogged		
	= tenacious	past of *to dog*
jagged		
	= indented	past of *to jag*
learned		
	= erudite	past of *to learn* (usually *learnt*)
ragged		
	= rough, torn, etc.	past of *to rag*

-edly, -edness

When the further suffixes *-ly* (forming adverbs) and *-ness* (forming nouns) are added to adjectives ending in the suffix *-ed*, an uncertainty arises about whether to pronounce this *-ed-* as a separate syllable or not. The adjectives to which these suffixes are added can be divided into three kinds.

1. Those in which *-ed* is already a separate syllable (*a*) because it is preceded by *d* or *t* or (*b*) because the adjective is one of those discussed in the entry for **-ed** above; e.g. *belated, decided, excited, level-headed, wicked.* When either *-ly* or *-ness* are added, *-ed-* remains a separate syllable, e.g. (i) *belatedly, decidedly, excitedly, wickedly*; (ii) *belatedness, level-headedness, wickedness.*

2. Those in which the syllable preceding *-ed* is unstressed, i.e. if *-(e)d* is removed the word ends in an unstressed syllable; e.g. *bad-tempered, embarrassed, hurried, self-centred.* When either *-ly* or *-ness* are added, *-ed-* remains non-syllabic (i.e. it sounds like 'd), e.g.

(i) *abandonedly* *hurriedly*
  bad-temperedly *ill-naturedly*
  biasedly *old-fashionedly*
  dignifiedly *self-centredly*
  embarrassedly *variedly*
  frenziedly *worriedly*
  good-humouredly

(ii) *bad-temperedness* *self-centredness* (= -center'dness)
  hurriedness *studiedness*

3. Those in which the syllable preceding -ed is stressed, i.e. if -(e)d is removed the word ends in a stressed syllable, or is a monosyllable, e.g. *assured, fixed.*

● (i) When -ly is added -ed becomes an extra syllable, e.g.

advisedly	*displeasedly*
allegedly	*fixedly*
amusedly	*inspiredly*
assuredly	*markedly*
avowedly	*professedly*
confessedly	*resignedly*
constrainedly	*surprisedly*
declaredly	*undisguisedly*
deservedly	*unfeignedly*
designedly	*unreservedly*

Exceptions:
There are a few definite exceptions to this rule, e.g. *subduedly, tiredly* (*ed* is not a separate syllable). There are also several words in which variation is found, e.g. *depravedly, depressedly, relievedly, shamefacedly, shockedly.*

● Note that some adverbs formed on adjectives in -ed sound awkward and ugly whether -ed- is pronounced as a separate syllable or not. Because of this, some authorities discourage the formation of words like *boredly, charmedly, discouragedly, experiencedly.*

(ii) When -ness is added, there is greater variation. In older usage -ed- seems usually to have been made an extra syllable. In *COD* only the following are so marked:

concernedness	*mixedness*
deservedness	*preparedness*
fixedness	*unashamedness*
markedness	

while *informedness* is given this pronunciation as an alternative.

Many other words are not specially marked, and it seems likely that it has become increasingly rare for -ed- to be separately sounded.

□ It is acceptable *not* to make -ed- a separate syllable in words of this type.

-ein(e)

The ending -*ein(e)* (originally two syllables) is now usually pronounced like -*ene* in *polythene* in

caffeine	*codeine*
casein	*protein*

Note: *casein* can also have the older pronunciation, with -*ein* disyllabic.

-eity

The traditional pronunciation of *e* in this termination is as in *me*, e.g. in

contemporaneity	*homogeneity*
corporeity	*simultaneity*
deity	*spontaneity*
heterogeneity	*velleity*

There is increasingly a tendency to substitute the sound of *e* in *café*, *suede*. The reasons for this are probably:

1. The difficulty of making the sounds of *e* (as in *me*) and *i* distinct when they come together. Cf. the words *rabies*, *species*, *protein*, etc. in which *e* and *i* were originally separate syllables but have now fused. Because of this difficulty, many users of the traditional pronunciation of *e* actually make the first two syllables of *deity* sound like *deer*, and so with the other words.

2. The influence of the reformed pronunciation of Latin in which *e* has the sound of *e* in *café*.

The same variation is found in the sequence -*ei*- in the words *deism*, *deist*, *reify*, *reification* (but not *theism*, *theist*).

-eur

This termination, occurring in words originally taken from French, in which it is the agent suffix, normally carries the stress and sounds like *er* in *deter*, *refer*, e.g. in:

agent provocateur	*connoisseur*
coiffeur	(con-a-*ser*)

entrepreneur	*saboteur*
littérateur	*sabreur*
masseur	*secateurs*
poseur	*seigneur*
raconteur	*tirailleur*
restaurateur	*voyeur*

Stress is on the first syllable usually in

> *amateur* (and *amateurish*: *am*-a-ter-ish)
> *chauffeur*

Stress can also be on the second syllable in *chauffeur*.

Feminine nouns can be formed from some of these by the substitution of *-se* for *-r*: the resulting termination is pronounced like *urze* in *furze*, e.g. *coiffeuse, masseuse, saboteuse*.

liqueur is pronounced li-*cure* (Amer. li-*cur*).

g

A. In certain less familiar words and words taken from foreign languages, especially Greek, there is often uncertainty as to whether *g* preceding *e, i*, and (especially) *y* is pronounced hard as in *get* or soft as in *gem*.

1. The prefix *gyn(o)-* meaning 'woman' now always has a hard *g*, as in *gynaecology, gynoecium*.

2. The element *-gyn-* with the same meaning, occurring inside the word, usually has a soft *g*, as in *androgynous, misogynist*.

3. The elements *gyr-* (from a root meaning 'ring') and *-gitis* (in names of diseases) always have a soft *g*, as in

gyrate	*gyro* (*-scope*,
gyration	*-compass*, etc.)
gyre (poetic, =	*laryngitis*
gyrate, gyration)	*meningitis*

4. The following, among many other more familiar words, have a hard *g*:

gibbous	*gill* (fish's organ)
gig (all senses)	*gingham*

● *g* should be hard in *analogous*.

5. The following have a soft *g*:

gibber	*gypsophila*
gibe	*gypsum*
gill (measure)	*gyrfalcon*
gillyflower	*longevity*
giro (payment system)	*panegyric*
gybe	

6. The following can vary, but usually have a hard *g*:

demagogic, -y,   *pedagogic, -y.*

7. The following can vary, but usually have a soft *g*:

gibberish,   *hegemony.*

B. See *-age,* p. 68.

-gm

g is silent in the sequence *gm* at the end of the word:

apophthegm	*paradigm*
diaphragm	*phlegm*

But *g* is pronounced when this sequence comes between vowels:

apophthegmatic	*paradigmatic*
enigma	*phlegmatic*

h

1. Initial *h* is silent in *heir, honest, honour, hour,* and their derivatives; also in *honorarium*. It is sounded in *habitué*.

2. Initial *h* used commonly to be silent if the first syllable was unstressed, as in *habitual, hereditary, historic, hotel*. This pronunciation is now old-fashioned. (See also *a* **or** *an*, p. 15.)

-ies

The ending *-ies* is usually pronounced as one syllable (like *ies* in *diesel*) in:

> caries   rabies
> congeries   scabies
> facies

● The reduction of this ending to a sound like the ending of the plural words *armies*, *babies*, etc., should be avoided in careful speech.

Exceptions: *series* and *species* can have either of the above pronunciations.

-ile

The ending *-ile* is normally pronounced like *isle*, e.g. in

> docile   fertile   sterile
> domicile   missile   virile

● The usual Amer. pronunciation in most words of this kind is with the sound of *il* in *daffodil* or *pencil*.

The pronunciation is like *eel* in:

> automobile   -mobile (suffix)
> imbecile

-ile forms two syllables in *campanile* (rhyming with *Ely*), *cantabile* (pronounced can-*tah*-bi-ly), and *sal volatile* (rhyming with *philately*).

ng

There is a distinction in Standard English between *ng* representing a single sound (which is represented by *n* alone before *c*, *k*, *q*, and *x*, as in *zinc*, *ink*, *tranquil*, and *lynx*) and *ng* representing a compound consisting of this sound followed by the sound of hard *g*.

1. The single sound is the only one to occur at the end of a word, e.g. in

> bring   song
> furlong   writing

2. The single sound also occurs in the middle of words, but usually in words that are a compound of a word ending in *-ng* (as in 1 above) + a suffix, e.g.

bringer	*kingly*	*stringy*
bringing	*longish*	*wrongful*
hanged	*singable*	

3. The compound sound, *ng + g*, is otherwise normal in the middle of words, e.g.

anger	*language*
hungry	*singly*

And exceptionally, according to rule 2, in *longer*, *-est*, *pro-longation*, *stronger*, *-est*, *younger*, *-est*.

● 4. It is non-standard:

(*a*) To use *-in* for *-ing* (suffix), i.e. to pronounce *bringing*, *writing* as bringin, writin.

(*b*) To use *n* for *ng* in *length*, *strength*. (The pronunciation lenkth, strenkth is acceptable.)

(*c*) To use *nk* for *ng* in *anything*, *everything*, *nothing*, *some-thing*.

(*d*) To use the compound sound *ng + g* in all cases of *ng*, i.e. in words covered by rules 1 and 2 as well as 3. This pronunciation is, however, normal in certain regional forms of English.

o

1. In many words the sound normally represented in English by *u* as in *butter*, *sun* is written instead with *o*, e.g. *above*, *come*, *front*. There are a few words in which there is variation in pronunciation between the above sound (as in *come*, etc.) and the more usual sound of *o* (as in *body*, *lot*, etc.). The earlier pronunciation of most of these was with the *u*-sound; the *o*-sound was introduced under the influence of the spelling.

(*a*) More usually with the *u*-sound:

accomplice	*constable*	*mongrel*
accomplish	*frontier*	*pommel* (verb)

(*b*) More usually with the *o*-sound:

combat	*dromedary*	*pomegranate*
comrade	*hovel*	*pommel* (noun)
conduit	*hover*	*sojourn*

2. Before *ff*, *ft*, *ss*, *st*, and *th*, in certain words, there was formerly a variety of RP in which *o* was pronounced like *aw* in *law* or *oa* in *broad*, so that *off*, *often*, *cross*, *lost*, and *cloth* sounded like *orf*, *orphan*, etc.

● This pronunciation is now non-standard.

3. Before double *ll*, *o* has the long sound (as in *pole*) in some words, and the short sound (as in *Polly*) in others.

(*a*) With the long sound:

boll	*roll*	*toll*
droll	*scroll*	*troll*
knoll	*stroll*	*wholly*
poll (vote, head)	*swollen*	

(*b*) With the short sound:

doll, *loll*, *moll*, *poll* (parrot), and most words in which another syllable follows, e.g. *collar*, *holly*, *pollen*, etc.

4. Before *lt*, *o* is pronounced long, as in *pole*, e.g. *bolt*, *colt*, *molten*, *revolt*.

● The substitution of short *o*, as in *doll*, in these words is non-standard.

5. Before *lv*, *o* is pronounced short, as in *doll*, e.g.

absolve	*evolve*	*revolve*
devolve	*involve*	*revolver*
dissolve	*resolve*	*solve*

● The substitution of long *o*, as in *pole*, in these words is non-standard.

ough

Difficult though this spelling is for foreign learners, most words in which it occurs are familiar to the ordinary English speaker. Pronunciation difficulties may arise, however, with the following words:

brougham	(a kind of carriage) *broo*-am or broom
chough	(bird) chuff
clough	(ravine) cluff

hough	(animal's joint), same as, and sounds like, *hock*
slough	(swamp) rhymes with *plough*
slough	(snake's skin) sluff
sough	(sound) rhymes with *plough* (also *tough*)

phth

This sequence should sound like *fth* (in *fifth, twelfth*), e.g. in *diphtheria, diphthong, monophthong, naphtha, ophthalmic.*

• It is non-standard to pronounce these as if written *diptheria*, etc.

Initially, as in the words *phthisical, phthisis*, the *ph* can be silent; it is also usually silent in *apophthegm*.

pn-, ps-, pt-

These sequences occur at the beginning of many words taken from Greek. In all of them it is normal not to pronounce the initial *p-*. The exception is *psi* representing the name of a Greek letter, used, e.g., as a symbol.

r

1. When *r* is the last letter of a word (always following a vowel, or another *r*) or precedes 'silent' final *e* (where it may follow a consonant, e.g. in *acre* which really = aker), it is normally silent in RP, e.g. in

aware	*four*	*pure*
err	*here*	*runner*
far	*kilometre*	

But when another word, beginning with a vowel sound, follows in the same sentence, it is normal to pronounce the final *r*, e.g. in

an acre *of land*	*to* err *is human*
*awa*re *of it*	*fa*r *away*
*clut*ter *up*	*fou*r *hours*

*he*re *it is*   *pu*re *air*
*a kilomet*re *of track*   *runne*r-*up*

This is called the 'linking *r*'.

• It is standard to use linking *r* and unnatural to try to avoid it.

2. A closely connected feature of the spoken language is what is called 'intrusive *r*'.

(*a*) The commonest occurrence of this is when a word ending with the obscure sound of *a*, as *china, comma, Jonah, loofah*, etc. is immediately followed by a word beginning with a vowel sound. An intrusive *r* is added to the end of the first word as if it were spelt with *-er* so as to ease the passage from one word to the next. Typical examples are:

the area-r *of the island*   *an umbrella*-r
the pasta-r *is cooked*   *organization*
sonata-r *in E flat*   *a villa*-r *in Italy*

Here the sound spelt *-a* at the end of *area, pasta*, etc., which sounds the same as *-er, -re* at the end of *runner, kilometre*, is treated as if it were spelt with an *r* following.

(*b*) In the same way, some speakers unconsciously equate (i) the spelling *a* or *ah* in *grandma, Shah* with the identical-sounding *ar* in *far*, (ii) the spelling *aw* in *law, draw* with the similar *our* in *four* or *ore* in *bore, tore*, and (iii) the spelling *eu* in *milieu, cordon bleu* with the similar *er(r)* in *err, prefer*. Thus, just as linking *r* is used with *far, four, bore, tore, err*, and *prefer*, such speakers introduce an intrusive *r* in, e.g.

is grandma-r *at home?*   a milieu-r *in*
The Shah-r *of Iran*   *which* . .
draw-r *a picture*   *a cordon bleu*-r
law-r *and order*   *in the kitchen*

(*c*) Intrusive *r* is often introduced before inflectional endings, e.g.

The boys are keen on scubering (i.e.
   scubaing)
oohing and ah-r-*ing*
draw-r-*ing room*

and even within the word *withdraw*-r-*al*.

Intrusive *r* has been noted since the end of the eighteenth century. In the mid-nineteenth century it was regarded as unpardonable in an educated person, but acknowledged to occur widely even among the cultivated. Its use after obscure *a* (as described under (*a*) above), where it greatly aids the flow of the sentence and is relatively unobtrusive, is acceptable in rapid, informal speech. The avoidance of intrusive *r* here by the insertion of a hiatus or a catch in the breath would sound affected and pedantic.

● The use of intrusive *r* after the sounds of *ah*, *aw*, and *eu* ((*b*) above) and before inflectional endings ((c) above) is very widely unacceptable and should be avoided if possible.

● In formal speech, the use of intrusive *r* in any context conveys an impression of unsuitable carelessness and should not be used at all.

3. There is a tendency in certain words to drop *r* if it is closely followed (or in a few cases, preceded) by another *r* at the beginning of an unstressed syllable, e.g. in

> *deteriorate* pronounced deteriate
> *February* pronounced Febuary
> *honorary* pronounced honary (prefer hon'rary)
> *itinerary* pronounced itinery
> *library* pronounced lib'ry
> *secretary* pronounced seketry or seketerry
> *temporary* pronounced tempary (prefer temp'rary)

● This pronunciation should be avoided, especially in formal speech.

reduced forms

In rapid speech, many of the shorter words whose function is essentially grammatical rather than lexical, being lightly stressed, tend to be reduced either by the obscuring of their vowels or the loss of a consonant or both. They may even be attached to one another or to more prominent words. Similarly, some words such as pronouns and auxiliary verbs are in rapid speech omitted altogether, while longer words of frequent occurrence are shortened by the elision of unstressed syllables. Typical examples are:

gonna, wanna = going to, want to
kinda, sorta = kind of, sort of
gimme, lemme = give me, let me
'snot = it's not
innit, wannit = isn't it, wasn't it
doncher, dunno = don't you, I don't know
what's he say, where d'you find it, we done it, what you want it for?
'spect or *I'xpect* = I expect
(*I*) *spose* = I suppose
cos, course, on'y, praps, probly = because, of course, only, perhaps, probably

● Most of these reduced forms (with the possible exception of *innit, wannit*) are natural in informal RP, but should be avoided in formal contexts.

s, sh, z, and *zh*

In certain kinds of word, where the spelling is *ci, si,* or *ti,* or where it is *s* before long *u,* there is variation between two or more of the four sounds which may be phonetically represented as:

s as in *sun*   *zh* representing the
sh as in *ship*   sound of *s* in *leisure*
z as in *zone*   or *g* in *regime*

1. There is variation between *s* and *sh* in words such as:

appreciate	*negotiate*
appreciation	*negotiation*
associate	*omniscient*
association	*sociology*
glacial	*uncial*

This variation does not occur in all words with a similar structure: only *s* is used in *glaciation, pronunciation* (= -see-*ay*-shon), and only *sh* in *partiality* (par-shee-*al*-ity). Only *sh* occurs in *initial, racial, sociable, spatial, special,* etc. It is possible that speakers avoid using *sh* in words that end in *-tion*, which also contains the *sh*-sound, so as to prevent the occurrence of this sound in adjacent syllables, e.g. in *appreciation* = appreshi-ashon.

2. There is variation between *s* and *sh* in *sensual, sexual, issue, tissue,* and between *z* and *zh* in *casual, casuist, visual.*

3. There is variation between *sh* and *zh* in *aversion, equation, immersion, version.*

☐ Either variant is acceptable in each of these kinds of word, although in all of them *sh* is the traditional pronunciation.

4. In the names of some countries and regions ending in *-sia,* and in the adjectives derived from them, there is variation between *sh* and *zh,* and in some cases *z(i)* and *s(i)* as well. So:

Asian	= *A*-shan or *A*-zhan
Asiatic	= A-shi-*at*-ic or A-zhi-*at*-ic or
	A-zi-*at*-ic or A-si-*at*-ic
Australasian	= Austral-*a*-zhan or -shan
Indonesian	= Indo-*nee*-shan or -zhan or
	-zi-an or -si-an
Persian	= *Per*-shan or *Per*-zhan

● The pronunciation with *sh* is traditional in RP and therefore the most widely acceptable. The pronunciation with *zh* is also generally acceptable.

5. There is variation between *zh* and *z(i)* in *artesian* (*well*), *Cartesian, Caucasian,* and *Friesian.*

☐ Either variant is acceptable.

stress

1. The position of the stress accent is the key to the pronunciation of many English polysyllabic words. If it is known on which syllable the stress falls, it is very often possible to deduce the pronunciation of the vowels. This is largely because the vowels of unstressed syllables in English are subject to reduction in length, obscuration of quality, and, quite often, complete elision. Compare the sound of the vowel in the stressed syllable in the words on the left with that of the vowel

in the same syllable, unstressed, in the related words on the right:

a:	humánity	húman
	monárchic	mónarch
	practicálity	práctically (-ic'ly)
	secretárial	sécretary (-t'ry)
e:	presént (verb)	présent (noun)
	protést	protestátion
	mystérious	mystery (= myst'ry)
i:	satírical	sátirist
	combíne	combinátion
	anxíety	ánxious (= anksh'ous)
o:	ecónomy	económic
	oppóse	ópposite
	histór ic	hístory (= hist'ry)
u:	luxúrious	lúxury
	indústrial	índustry

Because the position of the stress has such an important effect on the phonetic shape of the word, it is not surprising that many of the most hotly disputed questions of pronunciation centre on the placing of the stress. For example, in *controversy*, stress on the first syllable causes the four vowels to sound like those of *collar turning*, while stress on the second causes them to sound like those of *an opposite*: two quite different sequences of vowels.

2. It is impossible to formulate rules accounting for the position of the stress in every English word, whether by reference to the spelling or on the basis of grammatical function. If it were, most of the controversies about pronunciation could be cleared up overnight. Instead, three very general observations can be made.

(*a*) Within very broad limits, the stress can fall on any syllable. These limits are roughly defined by the statement that more than three unstressed syllables cannot easily be uttered in sequence. Hence, for example, five-syllable words with stress on the first or last syllable are rare. Very often in polysyllabic words at least one syllable besides the main stressed syllable bears a medium or secondary stress, e.g. *cáterpìllar, còntrovèrtibílity*.

(*b*) Although there is such fluidity in the occurrence of stress, some patterns of stress are clearly associated with some patterns of spelling or with grammatical function (or, especially, with variation of grammatical function in a single word). For example, almost all words ending in the suffixes *-ic* and *-ical* are stressed on the syllable immediately preceding the suffix. There is only a handful of exceptions: *Arabic, arithmetic* (noun), *arsenic, catholic, choleric, heretic, lunatic, politic(s), rhetoric.*

(*c*) If the recent and current changes and variations in stress in a large number of words are categorized, a small number of general tendencies can be discerned. Most of these can be ascribed to the influence exerted by the existing fixed stress patterns over other words (many of which may conform to other existing patterns of stress). It will be the purpose of the remaining part of this entry to describe some of these tendencies and to relate them to the existing canons of acceptability.

3. *Two-syllable words*

While there is no general rule that says which syllable the stress will fall on, there is a fixed pattern to which quite a large number of words conform, by which nouns and adjectives are stressed on the first syllable, and verbs on the second.

A large number of words beginning with a (Latin) prefix have stress on the first syllable if they are nouns or adjectives, but on the second if they are verbs, e.g.

accent	*import*	*transfer*
compound	*present*	*transport*
conflict	*suspect*	

The same distinction is made in some words ending in *-ment*, e.g.

ferment	*segment*
fragment	*torment*

And words ending in *-ate* with stress on the first syllable are usually nouns, while those with stress on the second are mainly verbs, e.g.

nouns: *climate*   verbs: *create*
       curate   *dictate*
       dictate   *frustrate*
       mandate   *vacate*

This pattern has recently exercised an influence over several other words not originally conforming to it. The words

ally   *defect*   *rampage*
combine   *intern*

were all originally stressed on the second syllable; as verbs, they still are, but as nouns, they are all usually stressed on the first. Exactly the same tendency has affected

dispute   *research*
recess   *romance*

but in these words, the pronunciation of the noun with stress on the first syllable is rejected in good usage. The following nouns and adjectives (not corresponding to identically spelt verbs) show the same transference of stress: *adept*, *adult*, *chagrin*, *supine*.

In the verbs *combat*, *contact*, *harass*, and *traverse*, originally stressed on the first syllable, a tendency towards stress on the second syllable is discernible, but the new stress has been fully accepted only in the word *traverse*.

4. *Three-syllable words*

Of the three possible stress patterns in three-syllable words, that with stress on the first syllable is the strongest and best established, exercising an influence over words conforming to the other two patterns.

(*a*) Words with stress on the final syllable are relatively rare. A number of them have been attracted to the dominant pattern; in some this pattern (stress on the first syllable) is acceptable in RP, e.g. *artisan*, *commandant*, *confidant*, *partisan*, *promenade*; in others it is not, e.g. *cigarette*, *magazine*.

(*b*) Many words originally having stress on the second syllable now normally or commonly have stress on the first, e.g.

abdomen	*decorous*	*recondite*
acumen	*obdurate*	*remonstrate*
albumen	*precedence*	*secretive*
aspirant	*precedent*	*sonorous*
communal	(noun)	*subsidence*
composite	*quandary*	*vagary*

Other words are also affected by this tendency, but the pronunciation with stress on the first syllable has not been accepted as standard, e.g. in

Byzantine	*contribute*
clandestine	*distribute*

Note: This tendency to move the stress back from the second to the first syllable of three-syllable words has been observed for at least a century. A case that typically illustrates it is the word *sonorous*. In 1884 W. W. Skeat, in his *Etymological Dictionary of the English Language* (edn. 2), wrote: 'Properly *sonórous*; it will probably, sooner or later, become *sónorous*.' The first dictionary to recognize the change was *Webster's New International* of 1909, which adds the newer pronunciation with the comment 'now often, esp. in British usage'. Fifty years after Skeat, G. B. Shaw wrote to *The Times* (2 Jan. 1934): 'An announcer who pronounced decadent and sonorous as dekkadent and sonnerus would provoke Providence to strike him dumb'—testifying both to the prevalence of the new pronunciation and to the opposition it aroused. In 1956 Compton Mackenzie, in an Oxford Union Debate, protested against the pronunciation of *quandary*, *sonorous*, and *decorous* with stress on the first syllable (B. Foster, *The Changing English Language*, 1968, p. 243). Foster (ibid.), however, records his surprise in about 1935 at hearing a schoolmaster use the older pronunciation of *sonorous*. The newer pronunciation was first mentioned in the *Concise Oxford Dictionary* in 1964; the two pronunciations are both heard, but the newer one probably now prevails.

(c) There is a tendency in a few words to move the stress from the first to the second syllable. It is generally resisted in standard usage, e.g. in

combatant	*exquisite*	*stigmata*
deficit	*patina*	

all of which have stress on the first syllable. But it has prevailed in *aggrandize, chastisement, conversant, doctrinal, environs, pariah, urinal.*

5. *Four-syllable words*

In a very large group of four-syllable words there is a clash between two opposing tendencies. One is the impulse to place the stress on the first syllable; the other is the influence of antepenultimate stress which is so prevalent in three-syllable words. Broadly speaking, it has been traditional in RP to favour stress on the first syllable, so that the shift to the second syllable has been strongly resisted in:

applicable	*formidable*
aristocrat	*illustrative*
capitalist	*intricacy*
controversy	*kilometre*
contumacy	*lamentable*
demonstrable	

With the words *controversy, formidable,* and *kilometre* in particular, a pronunciation with stress on the second syllable arouses strong disapproval on the part of many people.

In many words the two tendencies can be reconciled by the elision of one of the two middle unstressed syllables:

adversary	*participle*
comparable	*preferable*
migratory	*primarily*
momentary	*promissory*
necessary	*voluntary*

However, many words traditionally stressed on the first syllable have been, or arc bcing, adapted to the antepenultimate stress pattern, e.g.

centenary	*miscellany*
despicable	*nomenclature*
disputable	*pejorative*
explicable	*peremptory*
hegemony	*referable*
hospitable	*transferable*
metallurgy	

Because antepenultimate stress has been accepted in most of these words, it is difficult to reject it in the words in the first list simply on the ground of tradition. Analogy is the obvious argument in some cases, i.e. the analogy of *capital, demonstrate, illustrate, intricate, kilocycle* (or *centimetre*), and *remedy* for the words related to them in the list, but this cannot be used with the remaining words.

6. *Five-syllable words*

Five-syllable words originally stressed on the first syllable have been affected by the difficulty of uttering more than three unstressed syllables in sequence (see 2(*a*) above). The stress has been shifted to the second syllable in *laboratory, obligatory*, whereas in *veterinary* the fourth syllable is elided, and usually the second as well. For *arbitrarily, momentarily*, etc., see **-arily,** pp. 69 ff.

t

1. In rapid speech, *t* is often dropped from the sequence *cts*, so that *acts, ducts, pacts* sound like *axe, ducks, packs*.

• This should be avoided in careful speech.

2. The sounding of *t* in *often* is a spelling pronunciation: the traditional form in RP rhymes with *soften*.

th

1. Monosyllabic nouns ending in -*th* after a vowel sound (or vowel + *r*) form the plural by adding -*s* in the usual way, but the resulting sequence *ths* is pronounced in two different ways. In some words it is voiceless as in *myths*, in others voiced as in *mouths*.

(*a*) The following are like *myth*:

berth	girth	sleuth
birth	growth	sloth
breath	hearth	(animal)
death	heath	smith
faith	moth	wraith
fourth		

(*b*) The following are like *mouth*:

oath	*sheath*	*wreath*
path	*truth*	*youth*

bath, cloth, lath, swath vary, but are now commonly like *myth*.

2. Note that final *th* is like *th* in *bathe, father* in:

bequeath	*booth*
betroth	*mouth* (verb)

booth can also be pronounced to rhyme with *tooth*.

u

The sound of long *u*, as in *cube, cubic, cue, use* is also spelt *eu*, *ew*, and *ui*, as in *feud, few, pursuit*. It is properly a compound of two sounds, the semi-vowel *y* followed by the long vowel elsewhere written *oo*. Hence the word *you* (= y + oo) sounds like the name of the letter *U*, *ewe*, and *yew*.

When this compound sound follows certain consonants the *y* is lost, leaving only the *oo*-sound.

1. Where it follows *ch, j, r*, and the sound of *sh*, the *y* element was lost in the mid-eighteenth century.

So *brewed, chews, chute, Jules, rude*, sound like *brood, choose, shoot, joules, rood*.

The *y* element was also lost at about the same time or a little later where it follows an *l* preceded by another consonant; so *blew, clue, glue*, etc. sound as if they were spelt *bloo, cloo, gloo*, etc.

2. Where this compound sound follows an *l* not preceded by another consonant, loss of the *y*-element is now very common in a syllable that bears the main or secondary stress. *COD*, for instance, gives only the *oo* pronunciation in many words, e.g. *lubricate, lucid, Lucifer, lucrative, lucre, ludicrous*, etc., and either pronunciation for others, e.g. *lunar, lute, Lutheran*, etc. However, *lewd* and *lieu* are given only the *yoo* pronunciation.

Loss of the *y*-element is equally common in internal stressed syllables; in *COD* the words *allude, collusion, voluminous*, etc. are given both pronunciations. So also in a syllable which bears a secondary stress: *absolute, interlude*.

☐ In all syllables of these kinds, the *oo*-sound is probably the predominant type, but either is acceptable.

● In *unstressed* syllables, however, it is not usual for the *y*-element to be lost. The *yoo*-sound is the only one possible in, e.g.

curlew	*purlieu*	*value*
deluge	*soluble*	*volume*
prelude	*valuable*	

Contrast *solute* (= *sol*-yoot) with *salute* (= sa-*loot*).

3. After *s*, there is again variation between the compound sound and the *oo*-sound. The latter has now a very strong foothold. Very few people, if any, pronounce *Susan* and *Sue* with a *yoo*, and most people pronounce *super* (the word and the prefix) with *oo*. On the other hand, most people probably use *yoo* in *pseudo-* and in internal syllables, as in *assume*, *presume*, *pursue*. Common words such as *sewage*, *sewer*, *suet*, *suicide*, *sue*, and *suit* show wide variation: some people pronounce the first four (in which another vowel follows *ew* or *u*) with *oo*, but the last two with *yoo*, though most people now pronounced all these words with *oo*.

In an unstressed syllable, the *y*-sound is kept, as with *l* in 2 above:

capsule	*consular*	*insulate*
chasuble	*hirsute*	*peninsula*

☐ Apart from in *Susan* and *Sue*, and the words in which the vowel occurs in an unstressed syllable, either pronunciation is acceptable, although *yoo* is the traditional one.

4. After *d*, *n*, and *t*, the loss of the *y*-sound is non-standard, e.g. in *due*, *new*, *tune*.

Note: In Amer. English loss of the *y*-sound is normal after these consonants and *l* and *s*.

● The tendency to make *t* and *d* preceding this sound in stressed syllables sound like *ch* and *j*, e.g. *Tuesday*, *duel* as if *Choosday*, *jewel*, should be avoided in careful speech. In unstressed syllables (e.g. in *picture*, *procedure*) it is normal.

ul

After *b*, *f*, and *p*, the sequence *ul* sounds like *ool* in *wool* in some words, e.g. in *bull*, *full*, *pull*, and like *ull* in *hull* in others, e.g. in *bulk*, *fulminate*, *pulp*. In a few words there is uncertainty about the sound of *u*, or actual variation.

(*a*) Normally with *u* as in *hull*:

Bulgarian	*effulgent*	*pullulate*
catapult	*fulminate*	*pulmonary*
ebullient	*fulvous*	*pulverize*

(*b*) Normally with *u* as in *bull*:

bulwark	*fulsome*
fulmar	

(*c*) With variation: *fulcrum*.

urr

In Standard English the stressed vowel of *furry* and *occurring* is like that of *stirring*, not that of *hurry* and *occurrence*.

● The two sounds are identical in normal Amer. English.

wh

In some regions *wh* is distinguished from *w* by being preceded or accompanied by an *h*-sound.

□ This pronunciation is not standard in RP, but is acceptable to most RP-speakers.

B. *Preferred pronunciations*

The entries in this list are of three kinds. Some of the words in it have only one current pronunciation, which cannot, however, be deduced with certainty from the written form. These are mainly words that are encountered in writing and are not part of the average person's spoken vocabulary. Another class of words included here have a single, universally accepted pronunciation, which, in rapid or careless speech, undergoes a significant slurring or reduction. These reduced forms are noted, with a warning to use the fully enunciated form in careful speech so as to avoid giving an impression of sloppiness or casualness. Much the largest group are words for which two or more different pronunciations exist. Both (or all) are given, with notes giving a rough guide to the currency and acceptability of each.

The approach adopted here is fairly flexible, allowing for the inevitable subjectivity of judgements about pronunciation and the fact that there is variation and inconsistency even in the speech of an individual person.

Where the American pronunciation is significantly different from the British (disregarding the differences that are constant, such as the American pronunciation of *r* where it is silent in British speech), a note of it has been added, usually in brackets at the end of the entry. In a few cases the American pronunciation stands alone after the recommended one, implying that the use of the American form is incorrect in British speech. It will be found that in many cases the American pronunciation coincides with an older British one that is now being ousted. It is hoped that this will dispel the impression that all innovations are Americanisms, and give a clearer idea of the relationship between the two varieties of English pronunciation.

The symbol ● is used to warn against forms especially to be avoided; □ introduces most of the cases of peaceful coexistence of two variant pronunciations.

abdomen: stress on 1st syllable in general use; on 2nd in the speech of many members of the medical profession.

accomplice, accomplish: the older (and Amer.) pronunciation has 2nd syllable as in *comma*; but pronunciation as *come* is now predominant.

acoustic: 2nd syllable as *coo*, not *cow*.

acumen: stress on 1st syllable; the traditional pronunciation has stress on 2nd syllable.

adept (adjective): stress on 1st and 2nd syllable; (noun) on 1st syllable.

adult (adjective and noun): stress on 1st syllable.

adversary: stress on 1st syllable.

aficionado: a-fiss-eon-*ah*-do.

aggrandize: stress on 2nd syllable.

ague: 2 syllables.

albumen: stress on 1st syllable.

ally (noun): stress on 1st syllable; (verb) on 1st or 2nd syllable; **allied** preceding a noun is stressed on 1st syllable.

analogous: *g* as in *log*; not a-*na*-lo-jus.

Antarctic: ● do not drop the first *c*.

anti- (prefix): rhymes with *shanty*, not, as often Amer., *ant eye*.

antiquary: stress on 1st syllable.

apache (Indian): rhymes with *patchy*; (street ruffian) rhymes with *cash*.

apartheid: 3rd syllable like *hate*. ● Not *apart-ite* or *apart-hide*.

apophthegm: *a*-po-them.

apparatus: 3rd syllable like *rate*; not appar-*ah*-tus.

applicable: traditionally with stress on 1st syllable; now often on 2nd.

apposite: 3rd syllable like that of *opposite*.

arbitrarily: stress properly on 1st syllable, in informal speech on 3rd.

Arctic: ● do not drop the first *c*.

Argentine: 3rd syllable as in *turpentine*.

argot: rhymes with *cargo*.

aristocrat: stress on 1st syllable. ● Not (except Amer.) a-*rist*-ocrat.

artisan: stress originally on 3rd syllable; pronunciation with stress on 1st syllable is Amer., and now common in Britain.

aspirant: □ stress either on 1st syllable or on 2nd (the older pronunciation).

asthma: *ass*-ma is the familiar pronunciation; to sound the *th* is pedantic (Amer. *az*-ma).

ate: rhymes with *bet* or *bate* (also the Amer. pronunciation).

audacious: *au* as in *audience*, not as in *gaucho*.

auld lang syne: 3rd word like *sign*, not *zine*.

auxiliary: awg-*zil*-yer-ri.

azure: the older pronunciation was with -*zure* like -*sure* in *pleasure*; now usually *az*-yoor.

banal: 2nd syllable like that of *canal* or *morale* (Amer. rhymes with *anal*).

basalt: 1st *a* as in *gas*, 2nd as in *salt*; stress on either.

bathos: *a* as in *paper*.

bestial: 1st syllable like *best* not *beast*.

blackguard: *blagg*-ard.

bolero (dance): stress on 2nd syllable; (jacket) stress on 1st.

booth: rhymes with *smooth* (the traditional pronunciation) or *tooth*.

bouquet: first syllable as *book*, not as *beau*.

Bourbon (dynasty): 1st syllable as that of *bourgeois*; (US whisky) 1st syllable as *bur*.

breeches: rhymes with *pitches*.

brochure: stress on 1st syllable.

brusque: should be Anglicized: broosk or brusk.

bureau: stress on 1st syllable.

burgh (in Scotland): sounds like *borough*.

Byzantine: stress on 2nd syllable (Amer. *biz*-en-teen).

cadaver: traditionally with 2nd syllable as in *waver*; pronunciations as in *average* and *lava* are now commonly heard.

cadaverous: 2nd syllable like 1st of *average*.

cadre: rhymes with *harder*.

caliph: the traditional pronunciation, rhymes with *bailiff*, but 1st syllable as in *pal* is also heard.

camellia: rhymes with *Amelia*.

canine: □ 1st syllable may be as *can* or *cane* (the latter probably prevails).

canton (subdivision): 2nd syllable as 1st of *tonic*; (military, also in **cantonment**) 2nd syllable as that of *cartoon*.

capitalist: stress in 1st syllable.

Caribbean: stress on 3rd syllable is probably more usual, but stress on 2nd syllable is also acceptable.

carillon: rhymes with *trillion* (Amer. *carry*-lon).

caryatid: stress on 2nd *a*.

catacomb: 3rd syllable, in the older pronunciation, as *comb*; now frequently rhyming with *tomb*.

catechumen: stress on 3rd syllable (catty-*cue*-men).

centenary: sen-*tee*-nary (Amer. *sen*-te-nary).

cento: *c* as in *cent*, not *cello*.

centrifugal, centripetal: stress originally on 2nd syllable; but pronunciation with stress on 3rd syllable is now the usual one.

certification: stress on 1st and 4th syllables, not 2nd and 4th.

cervical: □ stress either on 1st syllable (with last two syllables as in *vertical*) or on 2nd (rhyming with *cycle*): both pronunciations have been common for at least a century and a half (Amer. only the first pronunciation).

chaff: rhymes with *staff*.

chagrin: stress on 1st syllable; 2nd as *grin* (Amer. stress on 2nd syllable).

chamois (antelope): *sham*-wah; (leather) shammy.

chastisement: traditionally with stress on 1st syllable; now often on 2nd.

chimera: *ch* = k, not sh.

chiropodist: strictly *ch* = k, but pronunciation as sh is common.

choleric: 1st two syllables like *collar*.

chutzpa: 1st syllable rhymes with p*uts*; this is of Yiddish origin and the initial sound should properly be pronounced like the *ch* in *loch*.

cigarette: stress on 3rd syllable (Amer. on 1st).

clandestine: stress on 2nd syllable.

clangour: rhymes with *anger*.

clientele: kleeon-*tell*.

clique: rhymes with *leak*, not *lick*.

coccyx: *cc* = ks.

colander: 1st syllable as *cull*.

combat (verb), **combatant, -ive:** stress on 1st syllable (Amer. on 2nd).

combine (noun): stress on 1st syllable.

commandant: stress originally on 3rd syllable; now often on 1st.

communal: stress on 1st syllable.

commune (noun): stress on 1st syllable.

comparable: stress on 1st syllable, not on 2nd.

compensatory: the older (and Amer.) pronunciation has stress on 2nd syllable, but stress on 3rd is now common.

compilation: 2nd syllable as *pill*.

composite: stress on 1st syllable; 3rd as that of *opposite* (Amer. stress on 2nd syllable).

conch: originally = *conk*; now often with *ch* as in *lunch*.

conduit: the older pronunciation has last three letters like those of *circuit*, but now usually *con*-dew-it.

confidant(e): the older pronunciation has stress on last syllable, which rhymes with *ant*; stress on 1st syllable is now common.

congener: stress on 1st syllable (the traditional pronunciation) or 2nd; *o* as in *con*; *g* as in *gin*.

congeries: □ con-*jeer*-eez or con-*jeer*-y-eez.

congratulatory: stress on 2nd syllable; pronunciation with stress on 4th syllable is also common.

conjugal: stress on 1st syllable.

consuetude: stress on 1st syllable; *sue* like *swi* in *swift*.

consummate (adjective): stress on 2nd syllable; (verb) on 1st syllable, 3rd syllable as *mate*.

contact (noun): stress on 1st syllable; (verb) stress on 1st or 2nd syllable.

contemplative: stress on 2nd syllable.

contrarily (on the contrary): stress on 1st syllable; (perversely) stress on 2nd syllable.

contribute: stress on 2nd syllable. ● The former pronunciation with stress on 1st syllable is frequently heard, but is not accepted as standard.

controversy: stress on 1st syllable. ● The pronunciation with stress on 2nd syllable seems to be increasingly common, but is strongly disapproved by many users of RP.

contumacy: stress on 1st syllable (Amer. on 2nd).

contumely: 3 syllables with stress on the 1st.

conversant: now usually stressed on 2nd syllable; formerly on 1st.

courier: *ou* as in *could*.

courteous: 1st syllable like *curt*.

courtesan: 1st syllable like *court*.

courtesy: 1st syllable like *curt*.

covert: 1st syllable like that of *cover*. ● The pronunciation *co*-vert is chiefly Amer.

cul-de-sac: 1st syllable may rhyme with *dull* or *full*.

culinary: *cul-* now usually as in *culprit*; formerly as in *peculiar*.

cyclical: 1st syllable like *cycle*, though *sick* is also commonly heard.

dais: originally one syllable; now only with two.

data: 1st syllable as *date*. ● Does not rhyme with *sonata*.

decade: stress on 1st syllable. ● The pronunciation with stress on 2nd syllable is quite common, but is not accepted as standard.

defect (noun): stress on 1st syllable is now usual.

deficit: stress on 1st syllable.

deify, deity: properly with *e* as in *me*; pronunciation with *e* as in *suede*, *fête* is increasingly common.

delirious: 2nd syllable as 1st of *lyrical*, not *Leary*.

demesne: 2nd syllable sounds like *main*.

demonstrable: the older pronunciation has stress on 1st syllable, but it is now usually on the 2nd.

deprivation: 1st two syllables like those of *deprecation*.

derisive, derisory: 2nd syllable like *rice*.

despicable: in formal speech, stress on 1st syllable; informally, especially for greater emphasis, on 2nd.

desuetude: as for **consuetude**.

desultory: stress on 1st syllable.

deteriorate: ● do not drop 4th syllable, i.e. not deteri-ate.

detour: *dee*-tour not *day*-tour (Amer. de-*tour*).

deus ex machina: *day*-us ex *mak*-ina, not ma-*shee*-na.

dilemma: 1st syllable like *dill* or, now commonly, like *die*.

dinghy: ding-gy is traditional, but pronunciation rhyming with *stringy* is also heard.

diphtheria, diphthong: *ph* = f not p.

disciplinary: the older (and Amer.) pronunciation has stress on 1st syllable, but it is now usually on the 3rd (with *i* as in *pin*).

disputable: stress on 2nd syllable.

dispute (noun): stress on 2nd syllable, not on 1st.

dissect: 1st syllable as *Diss*. ● Does not rhyme with *bisect*.

distribute: stress on 2nd syllable. • The pronunciation with stress on the 1st syllable is quite widespread but is considered incorrect by some people.

doctrinal: the older pronunciation has stress on 1st syllable, but it is now usually on the 2nd (with *i* as in *mine*).

dolorous, dolour: 1st syllable like *doll* (Amer. like *dole*).

dour: rhymes with *poor* not *power*.

dubiety: last 3 syllables like those of *anxiety*.

ducat: 1st syllable like *duck*.

dynast, dynastic, dynasty: 1st syllable like *din* (Amer. like *dine*).

ebullient: *u* as in *dull*, not as in *bull*.

economic: □ *e* as in *extra* or as in *equal*: both are current.

Edwardian: 2nd syllable as *ward*.

e'er (poetry, = *ever*): sounds like *air*.

efficacy: stress on 1st syllable, not 2nd.

ego: 1st syllable as that of *eager*.

egocentric, egoism, etc.: 1st syllable like *egg* (Amer. usually as ego).

either: *ei* as in *height* or *seize*: both are widely current (Amer. only the second pronunciation).

elixir: rhymes with *licks ear*.

enclave: *en-* as in *end, a* as in *slave*.

entirety: now usually entire-ety; formerly entire-ty.

envelope: *en-* as in *end*; the pronunciation as in *on* is widespread but disliked by many RP speakers.

environs: rhymes with *sirens*.

epoxy: stress on 2nd syllable.

equerry: stress properly on 2nd syllable, but commonly on 1st.

espionage: now usually with *-age* as in *camouflage*.

et cetera: etsetera. • Not eksetera.

explicable: stress originally on 1st syllable, but now usually on 2nd.

exquisite: stress originally on 1st syllable, but now usually on 2nd.

extraordinary: 1st *a* is silent.

fakir: sounds like *fake*-ear.

falcon: *a* as in *talk*, not as in *alcove*.

fascia: rhymes with *Alsatia*; in medicine, the 1st syllable is often like that of *fashion*.

fascism, fascist: 1st syllable like that of *fashion.*
February: ● do not drop the 1st *r*: feb-roor-y, not *feb*-yoor-y or *feb*-wa-ry or *feb*-yoo-erry (Amer. *feb*-roo-erry).
fetid, fetish: *e* as in *fetter.*
fifth: in careful speech, do not drop the 2nd *f.*
finance: □ stress on 1st syllable (only with *i* as in *fine*) or on 2nd (with *i* as in *fin* or *fine*).
flaccid: *cc* originally as in *accident*, but pronunciation rhyming with *acid* is now common.
forbade: 2nd syllable like *bad.*
formidable: in careful speech, stress on 1st syllable; informally, on 2nd.
forte (one's strong point): originally (and Amer.) like *fort*, but now usually like the musical term *forte.*
foyer: *foy*-ay or, less commonly, *fwah*-yay (Amer. *foy*-er).
fracas (singular): *frack*-ah, (plural) *frack*-ahz (Amer. *frake*-us).
fulminate: *u* as in *dull.*
fulsome: *u* formerly as in *dull*, now always as in *full.*
furore: 3 syllables (Amer. **furor** with 2).
Gaelic: 1st syllable as *gale.*
gala: 1st *a* as in *calm.* ● The former pronunciation with *a* as in *gale* is still used in the North and US.
gallant (brave, etc.): stress on 1st syllable; (polite and attentive to women) stress on 1st or 2nd syllable.
garage: stress on 1st syllable, *age* as in *camouflage* (or rhyming with *large*). ● Pronunciation so as to rhyme with *carriage* is common in some dialects but is disapproved of by many RP speakers.
garrulity: stress on 2nd syllable, which sounds like *rule.*
garrulous: stress on 1st syllable.
gaseous: 1st syllable like *gas.*
genuine: *ine* as in *engine.*
genus: *e* as in *genius*; **genera** (plural) has *e* as in *general.*
gibber, gibberish: now usually with *g* as in *gin*; *g* as in *give* was formerly frequent in the first word and normal in the second.
glacial: 1st *a* as in *glade.*
golf: *o* as in *got.* ● The pronunciation goff is old-fashioned.
gone: *o* as in *on.* ● The pronunciation gawn is non-standard.

government: ● In careful speech, do not drop the 1st *n* (or the whole 2nd syllable).

gratis: *a* originally as in *grate*; but grahtis and grattis are commonly heard.

greasy: □ *s* may be as in *cease* or *easy*.

grievous: ● does not rhyme with *previous*.

guacamole: gwark-er-*mole*-i.

gunwale: gunn'l.

half-past: ● In careful speech, avoid saying hah past or hoff posst.

hara-kiri: ● not harry-carry.

harass(ment): stress on 1st syllable. ● The pronunciation with stress on the second syllable is quite widespread but is considered incorrect by some people.

have: in rapid speech, the weakly stressed infinitive *have* is reduced to *'ve* and sounds like the weakly stressed form of the preposition *of*. When stress is restored to it, it should become *have*, not *of*, as in '*You couldn't 've done it*', '*I could* have' (not '*I could* of ').

hectare: 2nd syllable like *tare* or, less commonly, *tar*.

hegemony: stress on 2nd syllable, *g* as in *get* or (as also Amer.) as in *gem*.

Hegira: stress on 1st syllable, which is like *hedge*.

heinous: *ei* as in *rein*. ● The pronunciation rhyming with *Venus* is quite common but dislike by many RP speakers; the pronunciation rhyming with *genius* is erroneous

homo- (prefix = same): *o* now usually as in *hoe*.

homoeopath: 1st two syllables rhyme with *Romeo*.

homogeneous: last three syllables sound like *genius*.

honorarium: *h* silent, *a* as in *rare*.

hospitable: stress originally on 1st syllable, now usually on 2nd.

hotel: *h* to be pronounced.

housewifery: stress on 1st syllable, *i* as in *whiff*.

hovel, hover: *o* as in *hot*. ● The former pronunciation with *o* as in *love* is now only Amer.

idyll, idyllic: *i* as in *idiot*.

illustrative: stress on 1st syllable (Amer. on 2nd).

imbroglio: *g* is silent; rhymes with *folio*.

impious: stress on 1st syllable; on 2nd in **impiety**.

importune: stress on 3rd syllable or (with some speakers) on 2nd.

inchoate: stress on 1st syllable.

indict: *c* is silent; rhymes with *incite*.

indisputable: stress on 3rd syllable.

inexplicable: stress originally on 2nd syllable, but now usually on 3rd.

infamous: stress on 1st syllable.

inherent: 1st *e* as in *here* or *error*.

intaglio: *g* is silent, *a* as in *pal* or *pass*.

integral: stress on 1st syllable. ● The pronunciation with stress on the 2nd syllable is quite widespread but is considered incorrect by some people. The pronunciation *int*-re-gal, sometimes heard, is erroneous.

intern (verb): stress on 2nd syllable; (noun, Amer.) on 1st.

internecine: stress on 3rd syllable, last two syllables like *knee sign.*

interstice: stress on 2nd syllable.

intestinal: the traditional pronunciation has stress on 2nd syllable, 3rd syllable like *tin*; now commonly with stress on 3rd syllable, which is pronounced like *tine.*

intricacy: stress on 1st syllable.

invalid (sick person): stress on 1st syllable, 2nd *i* as in *lid* or *machine*; (verb) stress on 1st syllable, 2nd *i* as in *machine*; (not valid) stress on 2nd syllable.

inveigle: originally rhyming with *beagle*, but now commonly with second syllable as in *vague.*

inventory: like *infantry* with *v* instead of *f.*

irrefragable: stress on 2nd syllable.

irreparable: stress on 2nd syllable.

irrevocable: stress on 2nd syllable.

issue: *ss* as in *mission*; but pronunciation to rhyme with *miss you* is very common.

isthmus: in careful speech, do not drop the *th.*

January: *jan*-yoor-y (Amer. *jan*-yoo-erry).

jejune: stress on 2nd syllable.

jewellery: jewel-ry. ● Not jool-ery.

joule (unit): rhymes with *fool.*

jubilee: stress on 1st syllable. ● Not 3rd.

jugular: 1st syllable like *jug*: formerly as in *conjugal.*

junta: pronounce as written. • Hoonta, an attempt to reproduce the Spanish pronunciation, is the standard Amer. pronunciation.

karaoke: 1st two syllables properly like those of *caramel*, but (to avoid the awkward hiatus) often like *carry*.

kilometre: stress on 1st syllable, as with *kilocycle, kilolitre*. • The pronunciation with stress on the 2nd syllable is common but is considered incorrect by many people.

knoll: *o* as in *no*.

laboratory: stress on 2nd syllable. • The former pronunciation, with stress on 1st syllable, is now chiefly used by Amer. speakers (with *ory* as in *Tory*).

lamentable: stress on 1st syllable.

languor: as for **clangour**.

lasso: stress on 2nd syllable, *o* as in *do*.

lather: rhymes with *rather* or *gather*.

leeward (in general use): *lee*-ward; (nautical) like *lured*.

leisure: rhymes with *pleasure* (Amer. with *seizure*).

length: *ng* as in *long*. • Not *lenth*.

levee (reception, assembly): like *levy*; (Amer., embankment) may be stressed on 2nd syllable.

library: in careful speech avoid dropping the 2nd syllable (li-bry).

lichen: sounds like *liken*.

lieutenant: 1st syllable like *left* (Amer. like *loot*).

liquorice: licker-iss.

longevity: *ng* as in *lunge*.

longitude: *ng* as in *lunge* or as in *linger*. • Not (*latitude and*) *longtitude*, an error sometimes heard.

long-lived: originally rhyming with *arrived*, but now usually like past tense *lived*.

lour: rhymes with *hour*.

lugubrious: loo-*goo*-brious.

machete: *ch* as in *machine*, formerly as in *attach*; rhymes with *Betty*.

machination: *ch* as in *mechanical*, but pronunciation as in *machine* is increasingly common.

machismo, macho: *ch* as in *attach*, not as in *mechanical*.

magazine: stress on 3rd syllable (Amer. and Northern pronunciation has stress on 1st).

maieutic: 1st syllable like *may*.

mandatory: stress on 1st syllable.

margarine: *g* as in *Margery*.

marital: stress on 1st syllable.

massage: stress on 1st syllable (Amer. on 2nd).

matrix: *a* as in *mate*; **matrices** (plural) the same, with stress on 1st syllable.

medicine: two syllables (med-sin). ● The pronunciation with three syllables is normal in Scotland and the US, and increasingly so in the rest of the English-speaking world but is disapproved of by many users of RP.

mediocre: 1st syllable like *mead*.

metallurgy, -ist: stress on 2nd syllable. ● The older pronunciation with stress on 1st syllable, becoming rare in Britain, is chiefly Amer.

metamorphosis: stress on 3rd syllable.

metope: two syllables.

midwifery: stress on 1st syllable, *i* as in *whiff*.

mien: sounds like *mean*.

migraine: 1st syllable like *me* (Amer. like *my*).

migratory: stress on 1st syllable.

millenary: stress on 2nd syllable, which is like *Len*.

miscellany: stress on 2nd syllable (Amer. on 1st).

mischievous: stress on 1st syllable. ● Not rhyming with *previous*.

misericord: stress on 2nd syllable.

mnemonic: stress on 2nd syllable, 1st syllable like *nimble* not *Newman*.

mocha (coffee): originally (and Amer.) rhyming with *coca*, now usually like *mocker*.

momentary, -ily: stress on 1st syllable.

mullah: *u* as in *dull*.

municipal: stress on 2nd syllable.

nadir: *nay*-dear.

naive: nah-*Eve* or nigh-*Eve*.

naivety: has 3 syllables.

nascent: *a* as in *fascinate*.

necessarily: in formal speech, has stress on 1st syllable, with reduction or elision of *a*; informally, especially in emphatic use, stressed on 3rd syllable (e.g. *not necessarily!*).

neither: as for **either.**

nephew: the older pronunciation had *ph* like *v*, but now usually *neff*-you.

nicety: has three syllables.

niche: nitch has been the pronunciation for two or three centuries; neesh, now common, is remodelled on the French form.

nomenclature: stress on 2nd syllable. The pronunciation with stress on 1st and 3rd syllables is now chiefly Amer.

nonchalant: stress on 1st syllable, *ch* as in *machine*.

nuclear: *newk*-lee-er. ● Not as if spelt *nucular*.

nucleic: stress on 2nd syllable, which has *e* as in *equal*.

obdurate: stress on 1st syllable.

obeisance: 2nd syllable like *base*.

obligatory: stress on 2nd syllable.

obscenity: *e* as in *scent*.

occurrence: 2nd syllable like the 1st in *current*.

oche (darts): rhymes with *hockey*.

o'er (poetry, = over): traditionally like *ore*, now usually rhyming with *goer*.

of: see **have.**

often: the traditional pronunciation has a silent *t*, as in *soften*; the sounding of the *t* is a spelling pronunciation sometimes heard.

ominous: 1st syllable as that of *omelette*.

ophthalmic: *ph* = f not p.

opus: *o* as in *open*.

ormolu: *orm*-o-loo with weak 2nd *o* as in *Caroline*.

p (abbreviation for *penny, pence*): in formal context, say *penny* (after 1) or *pence*. ● 'Pee' is informal only.

pace (with all due respect to): like *pacey*.

paella: usually pie-*ell*-a rather than pah-*ell*-a, as the latter has an awkward vowel juncture.

panegyric: stress on 3rd syllable, *g* as in *gin, y* as in *lyric*.

paprika: stress on 1st syllable (Amer. on 2nd).

pariah: the older pronunciation has the stress on 1st syllable, rhyming with *carrier*; the pronunciation with stress on 2nd syllable, rhyming with *Isaiah*, is now common (and normal Amer.).

participle: stress on 1st syllable; 1st *i* may be dropped. • The pronunciation with stress on 2nd syllable is often heard though not yet accepted as standard.

particularly: in careful speech, avoid dropping the 4th syllable (particuly).

partisan: as **artisan**.

pasty (pie): *a* now usually as in *lass*; the older sound, as in *past*, is sometimes used in *Cornish pasty*.

patent: 1st syllable like *pate*. • Some who use this pronunciation for the general sense, have 1st syllable like *pat* in *Patent Office, letters patent*.

pathos: as for **bathos**.

patina: stress on 1st syllable.

patriarch: 1st *a* as in *paper*.

patriot(ic): *a* as in *pat* or *paper*.

patron, patroness: *a* as in *paper*.

patronage, patronize: *a* as in *pat*.

pejorative: stress on 2nd syllable. • The older pronunciation, with stress on 1st syllable, is now rare.

peremptory: stress on 2nd syllable (Amer. on 1st).

perhaps: in careful speech, two syllables with *h*, not *r*, sounded; informally praps.

pharmacopoeia: stress on *oe*; *-poeia* rhymes with *idea*.

philharmonic: 2nd *h* is traditionally silent.

phthisis: *ph* is silent.

pianist: stress on 1st *i*, *ia* as in *Ian*.

piano (instrument): *a* as in *man*; (musical direction) *a* as in *calm*.

piazza: *zz* = ts.

pistachio: *a* as in *calm*, *ch* as in *machine*.

plaid, plait: rhyme with *lad, flat*.

plastic: rhymes with *fantastic*. • The pronunciation with *a* as in *calm* sounds affected to many people.

plenty: • *plenny* is non-standard.

pogrom: originally with stress on the 2nd syllable (as in Russian); now usually on the 1st.

pomegranate: the older pronunciation was with 1st *e* silent, *o* as in *come* or *from*, and stress either on *o* or the 1st *a*; the pronunciation *pom*-gran-it is still used by some speakers, but *pommy*-gran-it is now usual.

porpoise: *oise* like *ose* in *purpose*.

posthumous: *h* is silent.

pot-pourri: stress on 2nd syllable (Amer. on 3rd), *pot-* like *Poe*.

precedence: originally with stress on 2nd syllable, now usually on 1st, which sounds like *press*.

precedent (adjective): stress on 2nd syllable; (noun) as for **precedence**.

precedented: as for **precedence**.

predilection: ● not as if spelt predeliction.

preferable: stress on 1st syllable.

premise (verb): stress on 2nd syllable, rhyming with *surmise*.

prestige: stress on 2nd syllable, *i* and *g* as in *regime*.

prestigious: rhymes with *religious*.

prima facie: *pry*-ma *fay*-shee.

primarily: stress on 1st syllable, with *a* reduced or elided. ● The pronunciation with stress on the 2nd syllable, used by some (but not all) Americans, is disapproved of by many users of RP.

Primates: (order of mammals) originally with 3 syllables, but now usually with 2.

primer (elementary school-book): *i* as in *prime*. ● The older pronunciation with *i* as in *prim* survives in Australia and New Zealand.

privacy: □ *i* as in *privet* or *private*; the former is probably commoner; the latter is the older and Amer. pronunciation.

probably: in careful speech, 3 syllables; informally often probbly.

proboscis: pro-*boss*-iss.

process (noun): *o* as in *probe*. ● An older pronunciation with *o* as in *profit* is now only Amer.

process (verb, to treat): like the noun; (to walk in procession) stress on 2nd syllable.

promissory: stress on 1st syllable.

pronunciation: 2nd syllable like *nun*. ● Not pro-*noun*-ciation.

prosody: 1st syllable like that of *prospect*.

protean: stress originally on 1st syllable, now commonly on 2nd.

protégé: 1st syllable like that of *protestant* (Amer. like that of *protest*).

proven: *o* as in *prove*, but pronunciaiton with *o* as in *woven* is widespread.

proviso: 2nd syllable as that of *revise*.

puissance (show-jumping): pronounced with approximation to French, *pui* = pwi, *a* nasalized; (in poetry) may be *pwiss*-ance or *pew*-iss-ance, depending on scansion.

pursuivant: *Percy*-vant.

pyramidal: stress on 2nd syllable.

quaff: rhymes with *scoff*.

quagmire: *a* originally as in *wag*, now usually as in *quad*.

qualm: rhymes with *calm*; the older pronunciation, rhyming with *shawm*, is now rare.

quandary: stress on 1st syllable; the older pronunciation, with stress on 2nd syllable, is rarely, if ever, heard.

quasi: the vowels are like those in *wayside*.

quatercentenary: *kwatt*-er–, not *quarter*-.

questionnaire: 1st two syllables like *question*.

rabid: 1st syllable like that of *rabbit*.

rabies: 2nd syllable like *bees*, not like the 2nd syllable of *babies*.

rampage (verb): stress on 2nd syllable; (noun) on 1st or 2nd syllable.

rapport: stress on 2nd syllable, which sounds like *pore* (Amer. like *port*).

ratiocinate: 1st two syllables like *ratty*, stress on 3rd.

rationale: *ale* as in *morale*.

really: rhymes with *ideally*, *clearly*, not with *freely*.

recess (noun and verb): stress on 2nd syllable.

recognize: ● do not drop the *g*.

recondite: stress on 1st or 2nd syllable. The former is the commoner, the latter, the older, pronunciation.

recuperate: 2nd syllable like the 1st of *Cupid*.

referable: stress on 2nd syllable.

remediable, -al: stress on 2nd syllable, *e* as in *medium*.

remonstrate: stress on 1st syllable; the older pronunciation, with stress on 2nd syllable, is rare.

Renaissance: stress on 2nd syllable, *ai* as in *plaice*.

renege: the traditional pronunciation rhymes with *league*. □ A pronunciation to rhyme with *plague*, for long dialectal, is now common. ● *g* is hard as in *get*, not as in *allege*.

reportage: *age* as in *camouflage*, but with stress.

research (noun): stress on 2nd syllable. ● The pronunciation with stress on the 1st syllable is Amer., and now quite widespread in Britain, but is considered incorrect by some people.

respite: stress on 1st syllable, 2nd like *spite* (Amer. like *spit*).

restaurant: pronunciation with final *t* silent and second *a* nasalized is preferred by many, but that with *ant* = ont is now more common.

revanchism: *anch* as in *ranch*.

ribald: 1st syllable like *rib*.

risible: rhymes with *visible*.

risqué: □ *riss*-kay or riss-*kay*.

romance: stress on 2nd syllable. ● Pronunciation with stress on 1st syllable, usually in sense 'love affair, love story', is considered incorrect by some people.

Romany: 1st syllable as that of *romp* or *rope*.

rotatory: stress on 1st syllable is traditional, but on 2nd is now usual.

rowan: *ow* often as in *low*, although in Scotland, from where the word comes, it is as in *cow*.

rowlock: rhymes with *Pollock*.

sacrilegious: now always rhymes with *religious*.

sahib: sounds like *Saab*.

salsify: *sal*-si-fee.

salve (noun, ointment; verb, soothe): properly rhymes with *halve*, but now usually with *valve* (Amer. with *have*).

salve (save ship): rhymes with *valve*.

satiety: as for **dubiety**.

Saudi: rhymes with *rowdy*, not *bawdy*.

scabies: as for **rabies**.

scabrous: *a* as in *skate* (Amer. as in *scab*).

scallop: rhymes with *wallop*. ● Pronunciation to rhyme with *gallop* is Amer. but sometimes heard in Britain.

scarify (make an incision): rhymes with *clarify*. ● Not to be confused with slang *scarify* (terrify) pronounced *scare*-ify.

scenario: *sc* as in *scene*, *ario* as in *impresario* (Amer. with *a* as in *Mary*).

schedule: *sch* as in *Schubert* (Amer. as in *school*).

schism: properly, *ch* is silent (siz'm); but skiz'm is often heard.

schist (rock): *sch* as in *Schubert*.
schizo-: skitso.
scilicet: 1st syllable like that of *silent* or *silly*.
scone: traditionally rhymes with *on*.
second (to support): stress on 1st syllable; (to transfer) on 2nd.
secretary: *sek*-re-try. ● Not *sek*-e-try or *sek*-e-terry or (Amer.) *sek*-re-terry.
secretive: stress on 1st syllable.
segue: *seg*-way.
seise, seisin: *ei* as in *seize*.
seismic: 1st syllable like *size*.
seraglio: *g* silent, *a* as in *ask*.
shaman: 1st syllable like *sham*, not *shame*; a pronunciation rhyming with *Brahman* is also sometimes heard.
sheikh: sounds like *shake* (Amer. like *chic*).
simultaneous: *i* as in *simple* (Amer. as in *Simon*).
sinecure: properly, *i* as in *sign*, but *i* as in *sin* is common.
Sinhalese: sin-(h)al-*ese*.
Sioux: soo.
sisal: 1st syllable like the 2nd of *precise*.
sixth: in careful speech, avoid the pronunciation sikth.
slalom: *a* as in *spa*.
slaver (dribble): *a* as in *have*.
sleight: sounds like *slight*.
sloth: rhymes with *both*.
slough (bog): rhymes with *bough*; (to cast a skin) with *tough*.
sobriquet: 1st syllable like that of *sober*.
sojourn: 1st *o* as in *sob* (Amer. as in *sober*).
solder: *o* as in *sob* (Amer. pronunciation is sodder or sawder).
solecism: *o* as in *sob*.
solenoid: stress on 1st syllable, *o* as in *sober* or as in *sob*.
sonorous: stress on 1st syllable, 1st *o* as in *sob*.
soporific: 1st *o* now usually as in *sob* (formerly also as in *sober*).
sough (rushing sound): rhymes with *plough*.
sovereignty: *sov*'renty. ● Not sov-*rain*-ity.
Soviet: *o* as in *sober*. The pronunciation with *o* as in *sob* is also very common.
species: *ci* as in *precious*. ● Not *spee*-seez.
spinet: □ may be stressed on either syllable.

spontaneity: as for **deify, deity.**

stalwart: 1st syllable like *stall.*

status: 1st syllable like *stay.* ● Not *statt*-us.

stigmata: stress on 1st syllable. ● Not with *ata* as in *sonata.*

strafe: rhymes with *staff.*

stratosphere: *a* as in *Stratford.*

stratum, strata: *a* of first syllable like 1st *a* of *sonata.*

strength: *ng* as in *strong.* ● Not *strenth.*

suave, suavity: *a* as 1st *a* in *lava.*

subsidence: stress originally on 2nd syllable with *i* as in *side*; pronunciation with stress on 1st syllable and *i* as in *sit* is increasingly common.

substantial: 1st *a* as in *ant*, not *aunt.*

substantive (in grammar): stress on 1st syllable; (having separate existence, permanent) on 2nd syllable.

suffragan: *g* as in *get.*

suit: now usually with an *oo* sound, though pronunciation with a *you* sound is still not uncommon.

supererogatory: stress on 4th syllable.

superficies: super-*fish*-(i-)eez.

supine (adjective): stress on 1st syllable (Amer, on 2nd).

suppose: ● in careful speech, avoid the elision of the *u*; informal *I s'pose so, s'posing it happens?*

surety: now usually three syllables (*sure*-et-y); originally two (*sure*-ty).

surveillance: ● do not drop the *l*; = sur-*vey*-lance, not sur-*vey*-ance.

suzerain: *u* as in *Susan.*

swath: traditionally with *a* as in *water*, but pronunciation to rhyme with *cloth* is now common.

syndrome: two syllables (formerly three).

Taoiseach: *tee*-sh'kh, the last sound pronounced like *ch* in *loch.*

taxidermist: □ stress on 1st syllable.

temporarily: stress on 1st syllable (with weakening or dropping of *o*): *temp*-ra-rily. ● Not tempo-*rar*-ily.

Tibetan: 2nd syllable like *bet*, not *beat.*

tirade: tie-*raid.*

tissue: as for **issue.**

tonne: sounds like *ton.* ● To avoid misunderstanding, *metric* can be prefixed; but in most spoken contexts the slight difference between the imperial and metric weights will not matter.

tortoise: as for **porpoise**.

tourniquet: 3rd syllable like the 2nd of *croquet* (Amer. turn-a-*kit*).

towards: the form with two syllables is now the most common; some speakers use the pronunciation tords in all contexts, others only in some.

trachea: stress on *e* (Amer. on 1st *a*, pronounced as in *trade*).

trait: 2nd *t* is silent (in Amer. pronunciation, it is sounded).

trajectory: stress properly on 1st syllable; now often (and Amer.) on 2nd.

transferable: stress on 2nd syllable.

transition: tran-*zish*-on. ● tran-*sizh*-on is now rare.

transparent: □ last two syllables either like those of *apparent* or like *parent*.

trauma, traumatic: *au* as in *cause* (Amer. as in *gaucho*).

traverse (noun): stress on 1st syllable; (verb) on 2nd syllable.

trefoil: stress on 1st syllable, *e* as in *even* or as in *ever*.

triumvir: 1st two syllables like those of *triumphant*.

troth: rhymes with *both* (Amer. with *cloth*).

trow: traditionally rhymes with *know*.

truculent: 1st *u* as in *truck*; formerly as in *true*.

turquoise: □ *tur*-kwoyz or *tur*-kwahz.

ululate: *yool*-yoo-late.

umbilical: stress on 2nd syllable.

unprecedented: 2nd syllable like *press*.

untoward: the older pronunciation rhymed with *lowered*, but the pronunciation with stress on the 3rd syllable is now usual.

Uranus: stress on 1st or 2nd syllable.

urinal: stress on 2nd syllable is usual, but the older pronunciation has stress on 1st.

usual: in careful speech, avoid complete loss of *u* (*yoo*-zh'l).

uvula: *yoo*-vyoo-la.

uxorious: 1st *u* as *Uxbridge*.

vacuum: traditionally three syllables, but now frequently two (*vak*-yoom).

vagary: the original pronunciation was with stress on 2nd syllable, but this has been almost entirely superseded by that with stress on 1st syllable.

vagina, vaginal: stress on 2nd syllable, *i* as in *china*.

valance: rhymes with *balance*.

valence, -cy (chemistry): *a* as in *ale*.

valet: those who employ them sound the *t*.

valeting: rhymes with **balloting**

Valkyrie: stress on 1st syllable.

vase: *a* as in *dance* (Amer. rhymes with *face* or *phase*).

veld: sounds like *felt*.

venison: the old pronunciation *ven*-z'n is now rare; *ven*-i-z'n or *ven*-i-s'n are usual.

veterinary: stress on 1st syllable, with reduction or elision of 2nd *e* and *a* (*vet*-rin-ry). ● Not *vet*-nary or (Amer.) *vet*-rin-ery.

vice (in *vice versa*): rhymes with *spicy*.

vicegerent: three syllables, 2nd *e* as in *errant*.

victualler, victuals: sound like *vitt*-ell-er, vittles.

viola (instrument): stress on 2nd syllable, *i* as in *Fiona*; (flower) stress on 1st syllable, *i* as in *vie*.

vitamin: *i* as in *hit* (Amer. as in *vital*).

viz. (= videlicet): when reading aloud, it is customary to substitute *namely*; 'viz' is chiefly jocular.

voluntarily: stress on 1st syllable.

waistcoat: the older pronunciation was *wess*-kot (with 2nd syllable like that of *mascot*); but the pronunciation as spelt has replaced it, except among older speakers.

walnut, walrus: ● do not drop the *l*.

werewolf: 1st syllable traditionally like *weir*, now often like *wear*.

whoop (cry of excitement, *whoop it up*): = woop; (cough, *whooping cough*) = hoop; both rhyme with *loop*.

wrath: rhymes with *cloth* (Amer. with *hath*).

wroth: as for **troth**.

yoghurt: *yogg*-urt (Amer. *yoh*-gurt).

zoology: in careful speech, best pronounced with 1st *o* as in *zone*; there are a number of other compounds of *zoo*- in technical use, in which this is the normal pronunciation. ● The pronunciation zoo-*ol*-ogy, although extremely common, is considered incorrect by some people.

III
VOCABULARY

> The perfect use of language is that in which every word
> carries the meaning that it is intended to, no less and no
> more.
>
> (C. Connolly, *Enemies of Promise*)

THIS section is concerned with problems of meaning, construction, derivation, and diction, associated with individual
words. The main aim is to recommend the meaning or construction most appropriate for serious writing or formal
speaking, but some attention is paid to informal and American usage.

aboriginal (noun) should be used in formal contexts as the
singular of *aborigines*. However, when referring to the
aboriginal inhabitants of Australia, *Aborigine* and *Aborigines* (with capitals) are now preferred.

account, to reckon, consider, is not followed by *as*, e.g. *Mere
morality . . was once accounted a shameful and cynical
thing* (G. B. Shaw).

affect, to have an influence on, e.g. *Hugh was immensely
affected by the way Randall had put it* (Iris Murdoch).
● Do not confuse with *effect* to accomplish, e.g. *He
picked at the German's lapel, hoping to effect a closer
relationship by touch* (Patrick White).
● There is a noun *effect* 'result, property', e.g. *to good
effect, personal effects, sound effects*; but there is no noun
affect except in the specialized language of Psychology.

affinity *between* or *with*, not *to* or *for*, since mutual relationship or attraction is meant, e.g. *Ann felt an affinity with
them, as if she too were an old dusty object* (Iris Murdoch);
Points of affinity between Stephen and Bloom (Anthony
Burgess).

afflict: see **inflict**.

aftermath can be used of any after-effects, e.g. *The aftermath of the wedding seemed to mean different things to different people* (*The Times*). It is pedantic to object to the sense 'unpleasant consequences' on the ground of derivation.

agenda (from a Latin plural) is usually a singular noun (with plural *agendas*), e.g. *It's a short agenda, by the way* (Edward Hyams). But it is occasionally found in its original use as a plural meaning 'things to be done' or 'items of business to be considered' (singular *agendum*).

aggravate (1) To make worse, e.g. *The war .. simply aggravates the permanent human situation* (C. S. Lewis). (2) To annoy, exasperate.

● Sense (2) is regarded by some people as incorrect, but is common informally. The participial adjective *aggravating* is often used in sense (2) by good writers, e.g. *He had pronounced and aggravating views on what the United States was doing for the world* (Graham Greene).

ain't (= are not, is not, have not, has not) is not used in Standard English except in representations of dialect speech, or humorously. *Aren't* (= are not) is also a recognized colloquialism for *am not* in the interrogative construction *aren't I*.

alibi, a claim that when an alleged act took place one was elsewhere.

● The sense 'an excuse' is informal and to some people unacceptable, e.g. *Low spirits make you seem complaining .. I have an alibi because I'm going to have a baby* (L. P. Hartley).

all of (= the whole of, the entirety of, every one of) is usual before pronouns, e.g. *And so say all of us*, or emphatically, often paralleling *none of* etc., before nouns, e.g. *Marshall Stone has all of the problems but none of the attributes of a star* (Frederic Raphael). Otherwise *all* + noun is normal, e.g. *All the King's men*.

● The general use of *all of* before nouns is Amer. only.

all right. This phrase is popularly thought of as a unit, e.g. *an all-right bloke*, but its unitary nature has not yet been recognized in spelling by the standard language, probably because the expression remains largely an informal one.

● *Alright*, though widely seen in the popular press, remains non-standard, even where the standard spelling is somewhat cumbersome, as in: *I just wanted to make sure it was all all right* (Iris Murdoch).

allude means 'refer indirectly'; an *allusion* is 'an indirect reference', e.g. *He would allude to her, and hear her discussed, but never mention her by name* (E. M. Forster).
● The words are not, except very informally, mere synonyms for *refer, reference.*

alternative (adjective and noun). The use of *alternative* with reference to more than two options, though sometimes criticized, is acceptable, e.g. *We have been driven to Proletarian Democracy by the failure of all the alternative systems* (G. B. Shaw).
● Do not confuse with *alternate* happening or following in turns, e.g. *Expressed that conflict of feeling by alternate waggings of his tail, and displays of his teeth* (Dickens). The use of *alternate* for *alternative* is, however, acceptable in Amer. English: *Liaison and Reserve watched alternate exits in buildings* (Norman Mailer).

altogether. ● Beware of using *altogether* (meaning 'in total') when *all together* (meaning 'all at once, all in one place') is meant, e.g. *They went up all together to the hotel and sat down to tea* (John Galsworthy). The reverse error, of using *all together* for the adverb *altogether*, should also be avoided; *altogether* is correct in *There's too much going on altogether at the moment* (Evelyn Waugh).

amend, to alter to something that sounds better, make improvements in; to make better, e.g. *If you consider my expression inadequate I am willing to amend it* (G. B. Shaw); *I have amended my life, have I not?* (James Joyce); noun *amendment.*
● Do not confuse with *emend* to remove errors from (something written), e.g. *An instance of how the dictionary may be emended or censored* (Frederic Raphael); noun *emendation.* An *emendation* will almost always be an *amendment*, but the converse is not true.

analogous means 'similar in certain respects'. It is not a mere synonym for *similar.*

anticipate (1) To be aware of (something) in advance and take suitable action, to deal with (a thing) or perform (an action) before someone else has had time to act so as to gain an advantage, to take action appropriate to (an event) before the due time, e.g. *His power to . . anticipate every change of volume and tempo* (C. Day Lewis); *I shall anticipate any such opposition by tendering my resignation now* (Angus Wilson); *She had anticipated execution by suicide* (Robert Graves); *Some unknown writer in the second century . . suddenly anticipated the whole technique of modern . . narrative* (C. S. Lewis).
(2) To take action before (another person) has had the opportunity to do so, e.g. *I'm sorry—do go on. I did not mean to anticipate you* (John le Carré).
(3) To expect, regard as probable (used only with an event as a direct object), e.g. *Serious writers . . anticipated that the detective story might supersede traditional fiction; Left-wing socialists really anticipated a Fascist dictatorship* (A. J. P. Taylor).
● Sense (3) is well established in informal use, but is regarded as incorrect by many people. Use *expect* in formal contexts. In any case, *anticipate* cannot be followed, as *expect* can, by infinitive constructions (*I expect to see him* or *him to come*) or a personal object (*I expect him today*) and cannot mean 'expect as one's due' (*I expect good behaviour from pupils*).
antithetical to means 'characterized by direct opposition to'; it is not a mere synonym for *opposed to*.
appraise, to estimate the value or quality of, e.g. *He was appraising the women present, as if he were a talent scout who only recognized one talent* (Nicholas Monsarrat).
● Do not confuse with *apprise*, to inform, *be apprised of*, be aware of, e.g. *Apprised, sir, of my daughter's sudden flight . ., I followed her at once* (Oscar Wilde).
approve (1) (Followed by direct object) authorize, e.g. *On 28 January the naval plan was approved by the war council* (A. J. P. Taylor).
(2) (Followed by *of*) consider good, e.g. *All the books approved of by young persons of cultivated taste* (C. P. Snow).

● *Approve* should not be used in sense (2) with a direct object, as (wrongly) in *Laziness, rudeness, and untidiness are not approved in this establishment* (correctly, *approved of*).

apt, followed by the *to*-infinitive, carries no implication that the state or action expressed by the infinitive is undesirable from the point of view of its grammatical subject (though it often is from that of the writer), e.g. *In weather like this he is apt to bowl at the batsman's head* (Robert Graves). It indicates that the subject of the sentence is habitually predisposed to doing what is expressed by the verb, e.g. *Time was apt to become confusing* (Muriel Spark). Compare **liable,** which, however, is not complementary to *apt to,* but overlaps with it; *apt to,* followed by a verb with undesirable overtones, = 'habitually or customarily liable to'.

Arab is now the usual term for 'native of Arabia' or an Arabic-speaking country, not *Arabian.*

aren't: see **ain't.**

Argentine, Argentinian can be both noun (= a native of Argentina) and adjective (= belonging to Argentina).

● Only the former is used in *Argentine Republic,* and it also has the advantage of brevity when used in other contexts. It rhymes with *turpentine.*

artiste, a professional singer, dancer, or similar public performer: used of persons of either sex.

as (1) = *that, which,* or *who* (relative) is now non-standard except after *same, such,* e.g. *Such comments as seem to be needed* (George Orwell); but not *I know somebody who knows this kid as went blind* (Alan Sillitoe, representing regional speech).

(2) = *that* (conjunction), introducing a noun clause, is now non-standard, e.g. in *I don't know as you'll like it.*

Asian (1) *Asian* is to be preferred when used of persons to *Asiatic,* which is now widely considered derogatory; the formation of *Asian* is in any case more closely parallel to that of *European, African,* etc. *Asiatic* is acceptable in other contexts, e.g. *Asiatic coastal regions; The Royal Asiatic Society; Asiatic cholera.*

(2) In Britain *Asian* is also the usual term for a person

who comes from (or whose parents come from) the Indian subcontinent.

as from is used in formal dating to mean 'from' or 'after' and followed by an actual date, e.g. *As from 10 p.m. on 15 October. As of*, originally Amer., has the same meaning and use.

● *As of now, yesterday*, and the like, are informal only.

aside from: Amer., = apart from, except for.

as if, as though (1) Followed by the past tense when the verb refers to an unreal possibility (i.e. when the statement introduced by *as if, as though* is untrue, or unlikely), e.g. *Every critic writes as if he were infallible* (Cyril Connolly); *It's not as though he lived like a Milord* (Evelyn Waugh). (2) Followed by the present tense when the statement is true, or might be true; this is especially common when the verbs *look* or *sound* precede, e.g. *I suppose you get on pretty well with your parents. You look as though you do* (Kingsley Amis); *He speaks as though even the rules which we freely invent are somehow suggested to us in virtue of their being right* (Mary Warnock).

attention. *Someone called it to my attention* (Alison Lurie) represents an illogical reversal of the idiom, not uncommon in speech; *someone called* (or *drew*) *my attention to it* or *someone brought it to my attention* would be better in formal contexts.

author (verb) is a rarely required synonym for *write*; *co-author*, however, is acceptable as a verb.

avenge: one avenges an injured person or oneself *on* (occasionally *against*) an offender, or a wrong *on* an offender; the noun is *vengeance* (*on*), and the idea is usually of justifiable retribution, as distinct from **revenge,** though the distinction is not absolute.

avert, to prevent or ward off (an undesirable occurrence), e.g. *Many disastrous sequels to depression might be averted if the victims received support* (William Styron).

● Do not confuse with *avoid*, as this writer has done: *On a couple of occasions he only narrowly averted being arrested.*

aware is normally a predicative adjective followed by an *of*-phrase or a *that*-clause, but can also be preceded by an adverb in the sense 'aware of, appreciative of (the subject indicated by the adverb)', a chiefly Amer. use, e.g. *The most intellectually ambitious and the most technically aware* (W. S. Graham).

• In popular usage *aware* is sometimes used without any qualifying word in the sense 'well-informed', e.g. *a very aware person*. This use should be avoided in formal contexts.

bacteria is the plural of *bacterium*, not a singular noun.

baluster, a short pillar with a curving outline, especially in a balustrade; *banister*, an upright supporting a stair handrail (usually in the plural).

beg the question, to assume the truth of the thing which is to be proved, e.g. *I scoffed at that pompous question-begging word 'Evolution'* (H. G. Wells).

• It does not mean (1) to avoid giving a straight answer; or (2) to invite the obvious question (that . .).

behalf: *on behalf of X* (= in X's interest, as X's representative) should not be confused with *on the part of X* (= proceeding from or done by X); *behalf* cannot replace *part* in *His death was largely due to panic on his part*.

benign (in Medicine) has *malignant* as its antonym.

beside (preposition) is used of spatial relationships, or in figurative adaptations of these, e.g. *Beside oneself with joy*; *Quite beside the question*; *We all seemed children beside him* (Evelyn Waugh); *besides* = in addition to, other than, e.g. *Eros includes other things besides sexual activity* (C. S. Lewis).

between. There are no grounds for objection to the use of *between* to express relations, actions, movements, etc. involving more than two parties; *among* should not be substituted in, e.g., *Cordial relations between Britain, Greece, and Turkey*.

See also **choose between**.

bi- (prefix). *Biannual* = appearing (etc.) twice a year, half-yearly; *biennial* = recurring (etc.) every two years, two-yearly. *Bimonthly*, *biweekly*, and *biyearly* are ambiguous in sense, meaning either 'twice a month (etc.)' or 'every two months (etc.)'; they are best avoided.

• Use *twice a month* or *semi-monthly*, *twice a week* or *semi-weekly*, and *twice a year* in the first sense, and *every two months, fortnightly* or *every two weeks,* and *every two years* in the second sense.

billion, etc. (1) Traditional British usage has a *billion* = a million million ($1,000,000,000,000 = 10^{12}$), a *trillion* = a million^3 (10^{18}), and a *quadrillion* = a million^4 (10^{24}); the logic is that the initial *bi-, tri-, quadri-,* etc. relate to the powers of a million.

(2) The US usage makes each 'step' from *million* to *quadrillion,* and beyond, a power of 1,000; i.e. *million* = 1000^2, *billion* = 1000^3, *trillion* = 1000^4, *quadrillion* = 1000^5.

(3) For the quantity 'thousand million' ($1000^3 = 10^9$), the older British term *milliard* is now rare. Many people who have frequent need to refer to the quantity, namely astronomers and economists, use the American *billion* for this. Most British national newspapers have officially adopted it too.

● In general contexts it is probably safer to use *thousand million* (X,000 m.). But where the sense is vague, e.g. *A billion miles away, Billions of stars,* the exact value is immaterial. Note that American *trillion* (10^{12}) = traditional British *billion.*

but = 'except', followed by a pronoun: see pp. 178 f.

candelabra is strictly speaking the plural of *candelabrum* and is best kept so in written English.

● *Candelabra* (singular), *candelabras* (plural) are often found in informal use.

censure, to criticize harshly and unfavourably, e.g. *Laura censured his immoral marriage* (E. M. Forster).

● Do not confuse with *censor* to suppress (the whole or parts of books, plays, etc.).

centre about, (a)round, meaning (figuratively) 'to revolve around, have as its main centre' is criticized by many authorities, though used by good writers, e.g. *A rather restless, cultureless life, centring round tinned food,* Picture Post, *the radio and the internal combustion engine* (George Orwell). It can be avoided by using *to be centred in* or *on,* e.g. *My universe was still centred in my mother's fragrant person* (Richard Church).

century. Strictly, since the first century ran from the year 1 to the year 100, the first year of a given century should be that ending in the digits 01, and the last year of the preceding century should be the year before, ending in two noughts.

• In popular usage, understandably, the reference of these terms has been moved back one year, so that the twenty-first century will commonly be regarded as running from 2000 to 2099. Beware of ambiguity in their written use.

character. The use of this word after an adjective as a substitute for an abstract-noun termination (*-ness*, *-ty*, or the like), or for the word *kind*, devalues it and should be avoided, e.g. *the uniqueness and antiquity of the fabric*, not *the unique and ancient character of the fabric*.

charisma (1) Properly, a theological word (plural *charismata*) designating any of the gifts of the Holy Spirit (see I Corinthians 12). (2) In general use (usually as a mass noun, with no plural), a term (drawn from the works of the German sociologist Max Weber) for the capacity to inspire followers with devotion and enthusiasm.

charismatic (1) Designating a Christian movement that lays stress on the *charismata*. (2) Generally, 'having the capacity to inspire with devotion and enthusiasm', e.g. *A forcefully charismatic hero compensating in physical presence for what he politically lacks* (Terry Eagleton).

choose between: this construction, and *choice between,* are normally followed by *and* in written English; informally *or* is sometimes used, e.g. *The poorest girl alive may not be able to choose between being Queen of England or Principal of Newnham; but she can choose between ragpicking and flowerselling* (G. B. Shaw).

chronic is used of a disease that is long-lasting, though its manifestations may be intermittent (the opposite is *acute* 'coming sharply to a crisis'); it is used in much the same way of other conditions, e.g. *The chronic unemployment of the nineteen-twenties* (A. J. P. Taylor); *The commodities of which there is a chronic shortage* (George Orwell).

• The sense 'objectionable, bad, severe' is very informal.

cohort is a collective noun with a number of different meanings:

(1) Originally, an ancient Roman military unit, equal to $1/10$ of a legion; (2) a band of warriors; (3) a group of

persons banded together in common cause; (4) a group of persons with a common statistical characteristic.

● The sense 'companion, ally', though quite common, especially in American English, is criticized by many people and should be avoided.

comparable is followed by *with* in sense (1) of **compare** and by *to* in sense (2). The latter is much the more usual use, e.g. *The little wooden crib-figures . . were by no means comparable to the mass-produced figures* (Muriel Spark).

compare. In formal use, the following distinctions of sense are made: (1) 'Make a comparison of x with y', followed by *with*, e.g. *You've got to compare method with method, and ideal with ideal* (John le Carré).

(2) 'Say to be similar to, liken to', followed by *to*, e.g. *To call a bishop a mitred fool and compare him to a mouse* (G. B. Shaw).

(3) Intransitively, = 'to be compared, stand comparison', followed by *with*, e.g. *The American hipsters' writings cannot begin to compare with the work of . . Celine and Genet* (Norman Mailer).

● *Compare with* is loosely used in sense (2); the senses overlap, e.g. *How can you compare the Brigadier with my father?* (John Osborne). Conversely, in the separate clause (*as*) *compared with* or *to x*, only sense (1) is possible, but *to* occurs as well as *with*, e.g. *Tarzan . . bewails his human ugliness as compared to the beauty of the apes* (Tom Stoppard); *Earth is tractable stuff compared with coal* (George Orwell).

comparison is usually followed by *with,* especially in *by* or *in comparison with*. It is followed by *to* when the sense is 'the action of likening (to)', e.g. *The comparison of philosophy to a yelping she-dog* (Jowett).

complaisant, disposed to please others or comply with others' wishes; noun *complaisance*, e.g. *The indulgent complaisance which Horace did not bother to disguise* (Frederic Raphael).

● Do not confuse with *complacent* self-satisfied (noun *complacency*).

compose can be used to mean 'constitute, make up' with the constituents as subject and the whole as object, e.g. *The* *tribes which composed the German nation.* It is more commonly used in the passive with the whole as subject and the constituents as object, e.g. *His face was .. composed of little layers of flesh like pallid fungus* (Iris Murdoch).

comprise. The proper constructions with *comprise* are the converse of those used with **compose**. (1) In the active, meaning 'consist of', with the whole as subject and the constituents as objects, e.g. *The faculty comprises the following six departments.*

● In sense (1), *comprise* differs from *consist* in not being followed by *of*. Unlike *include*, *comprise* indicates a comprehensive statement of constituents.

(2) In the passive, meaning 'to be embraced or comprehended *in*', with the constituents as subject and the whole as object, e.g. *Fifty American dollars comprised in a single note* (Graham Greene).

● *Comprise* is often used as a synonym of **compose,** e.g. *The twenty-odd children who now comprise the school* (Miss Read). This is regarded as incorrect by many people. It is especially objectionable in the passive, since *comprise* is not followed by *of*; write *The faculty is composed* (not *comprised*) *of six departments.*

condole, to express sympathy, is always followed by *with,* e.g. *Many .. had come .. to condole with them about their brother* (*Revised English Bible*).

● Do not confuse with *console* 'to comfort', followed by direct object, e.g. *This consoles us for the undeniable secondrateness of the people we .. know* (G. B. Shaw).

conduce, to lead or contribute (to a result), is always followed by *to*; similarly *conducive* (adjective); e.g. *The enterprise was popular, since it conduced to cut-price jobs* (J. I. M. Stewart).

conform may be followed by *to* or *with,* e.g. *The United Nations .. conformed to Anglo-American plans* (A. J. P. Taylor); *Having himself no particular opinions or tastes he relied upon whatever conformed with those of his companion* (John le Carré).

congeries, a collection of things massed together, is a singular noun, e.g. *A congeries of halls and inns on the site* (J. I. M. Stewart); it is unchanged in the plural.

● The form *congery*, formed in the misapprehension that *congeries* is plural only, is incorrect.

connote, denote. *Connote* means 'to imply in addition to the primary meaning, to imply as a consequence or condition', e.g. *Literature has needed to learn how to exploit all the connotations that lie latent in a word* (Anthony Burgess). *Denote* means 'to be the sign of, indicate, signify', e.g. *A proper name .. will convey no information beyond the bare fact that it denotes a person* (Stephen Ullman).

● The two terms are kept rigidly distinct in Logic, but in popular usage *connote* is frequently used to mean 'convey to the mind', or 'mean in actual use' and hence verges on the sense of *denote*. *Denote* cannot be used in the senses of *connote*, e.g. in *His silence does not connote hesitation* (Iris Murdoch).

consequent, following as a result, adverb *consequently*, e.g. *Two engaged in a common pursuit do not consequently share personal identity* (Muriel Spark). These are nearly always to be used rather than *consequential* 'following as an indirect result' and *consequentially*, which are rarer and more specialized.

consist: *consist of* = be composed of, made up of; *consist in* = have as its essential quality, e.g. *All enjoyment consists in undetected sinning* (G. B. Shaw).

continual, always happening, constantly or frequently recurring; *continuous*, unbroken, uninterrupted, connected throughout; similarly the adverbs; e.g. *He was continually sending Tiberius not very helpful military advice* (Robert Graves); *There was a continuous rattle from the one-armed bandits* (Graham Greene).

continuance, continuation. The former relates mainly to the intransitive senses of *continue* (to be still in existence), the latter to its transitive senses (to keep up, to resume), e.g. *The great question of our continuance after death* (J. S. Huxley); *As if contemplating a continuation of her assault* (William Trevor).

cousin (1) The children of brothers or sisters are *first cousins* to each other. (2) The children of first cousins are *second cousins* to each other. (3) The child of one's first cousin, or the first cousin of one's parent, is one's *first cousin once* *removed.* (4) The grandchild of one's first cousin, or the first cousin of one's grandparent, is one's *first cousin twice removed*; and so on. (5) *Cousin-german* = first cousin.

credible, able to be believed.

● Do not confuse with *credulous*, too ready to believe things, as e.g. in *Even if one is credible* (correctly *credulous*) *enough to believe in their ability.*

crescendo, used figuratively, means 'a progressive increase in force or effect'. Do not use it when *climax* is meant, e.g. in *The storm reached a crescendo* (correctly *a climax*) *at midnight.*

criteria is the plural of *criterion,* not a singular noun.

crucial, decisive, critical, e.g. *His medical studies were not merely an episode in the development of his persona but crucial to it* (Frederic Raphael).

● The weakened sense 'important' is informal only.

data (1) In scientific, philosophical, and general use, usually considered as a number of items and treated as plural, e.g. *Let us give the name of 'sense-data' to the things which are immediately known in sensation: such things as colours, sounds,* (etc.) (Bertrand Russell); *The optical data are incomplete* (*Nature*); the singular is *datum,* e.g. *Personality is not a datum from which we start* (C. S. Lewis).

(2) In computing and allied fields it is treated as a mass noun (i.e. a collective item), and used with words like *this, that,* and *much,* and with singular verbs; it is sometimes so treated in general use, e.g. *Useful data has been obtained* (Winston Churchill).

● Some people object to use (2), though it is more common than use (1).

● *Data* is not a singular countable noun and therefore cannot be preceded by *a, every, each, either, neither,* and cannot be given a plural form *datas.*

decidedly, decisively. *Decidedly,* definitely, undoubtedly, e.g. *The bungalow had a decidedly English appearance* (Muriel Spark). *Decisively* (1) conclusively, so as to decide the question, e.g. *The definition of 'capital' itself depends decisively on the level of technology employed* (E. F. Schumacher); (2) resolutely, unhesitatingly, e.g. *The* *young lady, whose taste has to be considered, decisively objected to him* (G. B. Shaw).

decimate, (originally) to kill or destroy one in every ten of; (now usually) to destroy or remove a large proportion of, e.g. *All my parents' friends, my friends' brothers were getting killed. Our circle was decimated* (Rosamond Lehmann).

● *Decimate* does not mean 'defeat utterly'.

decline (verb: to refuse an invitation) has no derived noun; we have to make do with *refusal* if *declining* cannot be used.

definitive, decisive, unconditional, final; (of an edition) authoritative; e.g. *The Gold Cup flat handicap, the official and definitive result of which he had read in the Evening Telegraph* (James Joyce).

● Do not use instead of *definite* (= having exact limits, distinct, precise). A *definite no* is a firm refusal, precisely expressed. A *definitive no* is a final, authoritative decision that something is not the case.

delusion, illusion. A general distinction can be drawn, though it is not absolute. *Delusion* would naturally occur in psychiatric contexts, and is used similarly outside them, to denote a false idea, impression, or belief held tenaciously, arising mainly from the internal workings of the mind; e.g. *delusions of grandeur*, and *He's been sent here for delusions. His most serious delusion is that he's a murderer* (Robert Graves).

Illusion denotes a false impression derived either from the external world, e.g. *optical illusion*, and *A partition making two tiny boxes, giving at least the illusion of privacy* (Doris Lessing), or from faulty thinking, e.g. *I still imagine I could live in Rome, but it may be an illusion* (Iris Murdoch). It is in this second sense that *illusion* is almost equivalent to *delusion*; cf. *I hope to strike some small blows for what I believe to be right, but I have no delusions that knock-outs are likely* (Frederic Raphael). It should be remembered that *delusion* carries the sense of *being deluded* (by oneself or another), whereas no verb is implied in *illusion*; on the other hand, one can be said to be *disillusioned*, whereas *delusion* forms no such derivative.

demean (1) *Demean oneself* = conduct oneself, behave (usually with adverbial expression), e.g. *He would see what he was to be in this life, how he was to demean himself, and how he should meet his death* (A. C. Parker). This is now rather rare. (2) *Demean* (*someone* or *something*) = lower in status, especially with *oneself*, e.g. *Nor must you think that you demean yourself by treading the boards* (W. Somerset Maugham).

denote: see **connote**.

depend, to be controlled or determined by (a condition or cause), is followed by *on* or *upon*.
 ● The use of *it depends* followed, without *on* or *upon*, by an interrogative clause, is informal only, e.g. *It depends what you have .. in mind in forming a library of gramophone records whether you think it worth acquiring* (*The Times*).

depreciate, deprecate. *Depreciate* (1) to make or become lower in value; (2) to belittle, disparage, e.g. *To defend our record we seem forced to depreciate the Africans* (*Listener*); *To become a little more forthcoming and less self-depreciating* (Richard Adams).
 Deprecate (1) (with a plan, proceeding, purpose, etc. as the object) to express a wish against or disapproval of, e.g. *I deprecate this extreme course, because it is good neither for my pocket nor for their own souls* (G. B. Shaw); *Polly .. patted her father's head in deprecation of such forcible metaphor* (Anthony Powell). (2) (with a person as the object) to express disapproval of, to reprove; to disparage, e.g. *Anyone who has reprinted his reviews is in no position to deprecate our reprinter* (Christopher Ricks).
 ● Sense (2) of *deprecate* tends to take on the sense of *depreciate* (2), especially in conjunction with *self*. This use is frequently found in good writers, e.g. *A humorous self-deprecation about one's own advancing senility* (Aldous Huxley); *The old, self-deprecating expression* (Susan Hill). It is, however, widely regarded as incorrect.

derisive = scoffing; *derisory* = (1) scoffing, (2) so small or unimportant as to be ridiculous (now the more usual sense), e.g. *A part .. once looked upon as discreditable and derisory* (Anthony Powell); *The £40 .. you'll pay for* *any of the current sets is derisory compared with the £16.50 charged . . 39 years ago* (*Independent*).

dialect (form of speech) forms *dialectal* as its adjective; *dialectic* (form of reasoning) can be adjective as well as noun, or can have *dialectical* as its adjective.

dice is the normal singular as well as the plural (*one dice, two dice*); the old singular, *die*, is found only in *the die is cast*, *straight* (or *true*) *as a die*, and in mathematical discussions, e.g. *Rolling a die will generate a stream of random numbers*.

dichotomy in non-technical use means 'differentiation into contrasting categories' and is frequently followed by *between*, e.g. *An absolute dichotomy between science and reason on the one hand and faith and poetry on the other*.

● It does not mean *dilemma* or *ambivalence*.

die (noun): see **dice**.

different can be followed by *from*, *to*, or *than*.

(1) *Different from* is the most usual expression in both written and spoken English; it is the most favoured by good writers, and is acceptable in all contexts, e.g. *It is also an 'important' book, in a sense different from the sense in which that word is generally used* (George Orwell).

(2) *Different to* is common informally. It sometimes sounds more natural than *different from*, and should then be used; e.g. when yoked with *similar* and followed by a phrase introduced by *to*: *His looks are neither especially similar nor markedly different to those of his twin brother*.

(3) *Different than* is an established idiom in American English, but is not uncommon in British use, e.g. *Both came from a different world than the housing estate outside London* (Doris Lessing). Both *different to* and *different than* are especially valuable as a means of avoiding the repetition and the relative construction required after *different from* in sentences like *I was a very different man in 1935 from what I was in 1916* (Joyce Cary). This could be recast as *I was a very different man in 1935 than I was in 1916* or *than in 1916*. Compare *The American theatre, which is suffering from a different malaise than ours*, which is greatly preferable to *suffering from a different malaise from that which ours is suffering from*.

Uses (2) and (3) are especially common when *different* is part of an adverbial clause (e.g. *in a different way*) or when the adverb *differently* is used, and have been employed by good writers since the seventeenth century, e.g. *Things were constructed very differently now than in former times* (Trollope); *Sebastian was a drunkard in quite a different sense to myself* (Evelyn Waugh); *Puts one in a different position to your own father* (John Osborne).

differential, a technical term in Mathematics, an abbreviation for *differential gear*, or a term for a maintained difference in wage between groups of workers.
  ● It is not a synonym for *difference*.

digraph = a group of two letters standing for a single sound, e.g. *ea* in *head*, *gh* in *cough*; *ligature* = a typographical symbol consisting of two letters joined together, e.g. fi, fl. The term *diphthong* is best restricted to the sense for which there is no synonym, namely 'a union of two vowels pronounced in one syllable', which is something primarily spoken and heard, not written; *i* in *find*, *ei* in *rein*, and *eau* in *bureau* all *represent* diphthongs. One cause of confusion is that Latin had two *diphthongs* (*ae* and *oe*) often printed as the *ligatures* æ and œ; in English words derived from Latin these are now *digraphs ae* and *oe* (sometimes modified into *e*: see p. 14) representing single vowel sounds.

dilemma (1) A choice between two (or sometimes more than two) undesirable or awkward alternatives, e.g. *The dilemma of cutting public services or increasing taxes* (*The Times*). (2) More loosely, a perplexing situation in which a choice has to be made, e.g. *The dilemma of the 1960s about whether nice girls should sleep with men* (Alan Watkins).
  ● It is not merely a synonym for *problem*.

diphthong: see **digraph**.

direct is used as an adverb in two of the main senses of the adjective: (1) straight, e.g. *Another door led direct to the house* (Evelyn Waugh); (2) without intermediaries, e.g. *I appeal now, over your head, . . direct to the august oracle* (G. B. Shaw).

directly is used in most of the main senses of the adjective, e.g. *Why don't you deal directly with the wholesalers?*

(G. B. Shaw); *The wind is blowing directly on shore*; *directly opposite, opposed.*

• It is not usually used to mean 'straight', since it has an extra sense, used in similar contexts, 'immediately, without delay', e.g. *Just a night in London—I'll be back directly* (Iris Murdoch).

discomfit, to thwart, disconcert; similarly *discomfiture*; e.g. *He discomfited his opponents by obliging them to disagree with a great logician* (Frederic Raphael).

• Do not confuse with *discomfort* (now rare as a verb, = make uneasy).

disinterest, lack of interest, indifference, e.g. *Buried the world under a heavy snowfall of disinterest* (Christopher Fry).

• The use of *disinterest* in this sense may be objected to on the same grounds as sense (2) of **disinterested**; but the word is rarely used in any other sense, and the possible alternative *uninterest* is very rare indeed.

disinterested (1) Impartial, unbiased, e.g. *Thanks to his scientific mind he understood—a proof of disinterested intelligence which had pleased her* (Virginia Woolf). The noun is *disinterestedness*. (2) Uninterested, indifferent, e.g. *It is not that we are disinterested in these subjects, but that we are better qualified to talk about our own interests* (*The Times*). The noun is **disinterest**.

• Sense (2) is common in informal use, but is widely regarded as incorrect and is avoided by careful writers, who prefer *uninterested*.

disposal is the noun from *dispose of* (get off one's hands, deal with); *disposition* is the noun from *dispose* (arrange, incline).

distinctive, serving to distinguish, characteristic, e.g. *It had smelled like this soap today, a light, entirely distinctive smell* (Susan Hill).

• Do not confuse with *distinct*, separate, individual, definite, e.g. *Trying to put into words an impression that was not distinct in my own mind* (W. Somerset Maugham).

drunk, drunken. In older and literary usage, the predicative and attributive forms respectively; now usually allocated to distinct senses, namely 'intoxicated' and 'fond of drinking', e.g. *They were lazy, irresponsible, and drunken;*

but on this occasion they were not drunk. **Drunken** also means 'caused by or exhibiting drunkenness', e.g. *a drunken brawl.*

due to (1) That ought to be given to, e.g. *He felt for Franz the respect due to the boss's nephew* (Vladimir Nabokov). (2) To be ascribed to, e.g. *Half the diseases of modern civilization are due to starvation of the affections in the young* (G. B. Shaw). *Due* is here an adjective with a complementary prepositional phrase, like *liable* (*to*), *subject* (*to*). As an adjective it needs to be attached to a noun as complement (see example above), or as part of a verbless adjective clause, e.g. *A few days' temporary absence of mind due to sunstroke was . . nothing to worry about* (Muriel Spark). (3) = *owing to.* A sentence conforming to type (2) above like *He suffered a few days' absence of mind due to sunstroke* can be equated with *He suffered a few days' absence of mind, owing to sunstroke.* In this way *due to* has borrowed from *owing to* the status of independent compound preposition, a use not uncommon even with good writers, e.g. *It . . didn't begin until twenty past due to a hitch* (William Trevor); *Due to an unlikely run of nineteens and zeros, I gained the equivalent of three hundred pounds* (Graham Greene).

● The use of *due to* as a compound preposition is widely regarded as unacceptable. It can often be avoided by the addition of the verb *to be* and *that*, e.g. It is *due to your provident care* that . . *improvements are being made* (*Revised English Bible*).

effect: see **affect**.

e.g., i.e.: *E.g.* (short for Latin *exempli gratia*) = for example, for instance; it introduces one or more typical examples of what precedes it: *Many countries of Asia, e.g. India, Indonesia, and Malaysia, were once ruled by European powers. I.e.* (short for Latin *id est*) = that is; it introduces an amplification or explanation of what precedes it: *It was natural that the largest nation (i.e. India) should take the lead*; *The United States presence, i.e. the maintenance of American military personnel, in south-east Asia.*

egoism, -ist(ic), egotism, -ist(ic). *Egoism* is the term used in Philosophy and Psychology, and denotes self-interest (often contrasted with *altruism*), e.g. *Egoistic instincts concerned with self-preservation or the good of the Ego* (Gilbert Murray). *Egotism* is the practice of talking or thinking excessively about oneself, self-centredness, e.g. *He is petty, selfish, vain, egotistical; he is spoilt; he is a tyrant* (Virginia Woolf).

● In practice the senses tend to overlap, e.g. *Human loves don't last, . . they are far too egoistic* (Iris Murdoch); *A complete egotist in all his dealings with women* (Joyce Cary).

egregious, remarkable in a bad sense; flagrant, gross, outrageous; used mainly with words like *ass, impostor, liar, blunder, folly, waste,* e.g. *Wark tenderly forgives her most egregious clerical errors* (Martin Amis). It does not mean simply 'offending, errant' as in *If sanctuary officers spot a particularly egregious diver they will direct him to the surface.*

either (adjective and pronoun). (1) One or other of the two, e.g. *Simple explanations are for simple minds. I've no use for either* (Joe Orton). (2) Each of the two, e.g. *Every few kilometres on either side of the road, there were Haitian and Dominican guard-posts* (Graham Greene).

● *Either* is frequently used in sense (2), in preference to *each*, with reference to a thing that comes naturally in a pair, e.g. *end, hand, side.* This use is sometimes ignorantly condemned but is both the older sense of *either* and commonly found in good writers of all periods.

elder (adjective) the earlier-born (of two related or indicated persons), e.g. *The first and elder wife . . returned . . to Jericho* (Muriel Spark); *He is my elder by ten years. Eldest* first-born or oldest surviving (member of family, son, daughter, etc.).

elusive (rather than *elusory*) is the usual adjective related to *elude*; *illusory* (rather than *illusive*) is the usual adjective related to *illusion*.

enjoin: one can enjoin an action, etc., *on* someone, or enjoin someone *to* do something; the latter is more usual; e.g. *To . . enjoin celibacy on its laity as well as on its clergy* and *That enables and enjoins the citizen to earn his own living* (G. B. Shaw). In legal writing, *to enjoin* (a person) *from* (doing something) is also found.

enormity (1) Great wickedness (of something), e.g. *Hugh was made entirely speechless . . by the enormity of the proposal* (Iris Murdoch); a serious crime or offence, e.g. *They had met to pass sentence on Wingfield for his enormities* (David Garnett). (2) Enormousness, e.g. *The war in its entire magnitude did not exist for the average civilian . . The enormity of it was quite beyond most of us* (G. B. Shaw).

• Sense (2) is commonly found, but is regarded by many people as incorrect.

enthuse, to show or fill with enthusiasm, is chiefly informal.

• **equally as** (+ adjective) should not be used for *equally*, e.g. in *How to apply it in a calm, unruffled manner was equally as important*, or for *as*, e.g. *The Government are equally as guilty as the Opposition.*

event: *in the event of* is followed by a noun or gerund, e.g. *In the event of the earl's death, the title will lapse.*

• *In the event that,* treated as a compound conjunction, is ungainly and avoided by good writers; it is even less acceptable with *that* omitted, e.g. *In the event the car overturns.*

ever. When placed after a *wh*-question word in order to intensify it, *ever* should be written separately, e.g. *Where ever have you been?, when ever is he coming?, who ever would have thought it?, why ever did you do it?, how ever shall I escape?* When used with a relative pronoun or adverb to give it indefinite or general force, *ever* is written as one word with it, e.g. *Wherever you go I'll follow; whenever he washes up he breaks something; there's a reward for whoever* (not *whomever*) *finds it; whatever else you do, don't get lost; however it's done, it's difficult.*

evidence, evince. *Evidence* (verb), to serve as evidence for the existence or truth of, e.g. *There was an innate refinement . . about Gerty which was unmistakably evidenced in her delicate hands* (James Joyce).

Evince, to show that one has a (hidden or unseen) quality, e.g. *Highly evolved sentiments and needs* (*sometimes said to be distinctively human, though birds and animals . . evince them*) (G. B. Shaw).

- *Evince* should not be confused with *evoke* to call up (a response, a feeling, etc.), e.g. *A timely and generous act which evoked a fresh outburst of emotion* (James Joyce).

exceedingly, extremely; *excessively*, beyond measure, immoderately, e.g. *The excessively rational terms employed by people with a secret panic* (Muriel Spark).

excepting (preposition) is only used after *not* and *always*.

exceptionable, to which exception may be taken; *unexceptionable* with which no fault may be found, e.g. *The opposite claim would seem to him unexceptionable even if he disagreed with it* (George Orwell).

- Do not confuse with *(un)exceptional*, that is (not) an exception; (not) unusual or outstanding, e.g. *It's a good enough book in its way, modest, unexpectional, competent, but small in its ambition* (Amanda Cross).

excess. *In excess of* 'to a greater amount or degree than' forms an adverbial phrase.

- Prefer *more than* where the phrase qualified is the subject or object, e.g. in *The Data Centre, which processes in excess of 1200 jobs per week*.

expect (1) in the sense 'suppose, think' is informal; (2) see **anticipate**.

explicit, express. *Explicit,* distinctly expressing all that is meant, leaving nothing implied, e.g. *I had been too tactful, .. too vague .. But I now saw that I ought to have been more explicit* (Iris Murdoch); *express*, definite, unmistakable in import, e.g. *Idolatry fulsome enough to irritate Jonson into an express disavowal of it* (G. B. Shaw).

exposure (to) may be used figuratively to mean 'being made subject (to an influence, etc.)' but should not be used for *experience (of)*, e.g. in *Candidates who have had exposure to North American markets*.

express (adjective): see **explicit**.

facility in the sense 'ease in doing something', e.g. *I knew that I had a facility with words* (George Orwell), should not be confused with a similar sense of *faculty*, viz. 'a particular kind of ability', e.g. *Hess .. had that odd faculty, peculiar to lunatics, of falling into strained positions* (Rebecca West).

factious: see **fractious**.

factitious, made for a special purpose; not natural; artificial; e.g. *Heroic tragedy is decadent because it is factitious; it substitutes violent emotionalism for emotion* (and) *the purple patch for poetry* (L. C. Knights); *fictitious,* feigned, simulated; imaginary, e.g. *Rumours of false accounting and fictitious loans surrounded the bank for years* (*Economist*).

farther, farthest: though originally interchangeable with *further, furthest,* these words are now only used where the sense of 'distance' is involved, e.g. *One whose actual dwelling lay presumably amid the farther mysteries of the cosmos* (J. I. M. Stewart).

● Even in this sense many people prefer *further, furthest.*

feasible, capable of being done, achieved, or dealt with, e.g. *Young people believing that niceness and innocence are politically as well as morally feasible* (J. I. M. Stewart).

● It is sometimes used to mean 'possible' or 'probable', but whichever of these two words is appropriate should be used instead.

fewer: see **less.**

fictitious: see **factitious.**

flammable, easily set on fire; preferable as a warning of danger to *inflammable,* which may be mistaken for a negative (= not easily set on fire). The real negatives are *non-flammable* and *non-inflammable.*

flaunt, to display proudly or ostentatiously, e.g. *He's unemployed by the way, so don't flaunt your fabulous wealth in front of him* (Joseph O'Connor); *Shops flaunted luxurious temptations after the austere essentials of wartime* (Juliette Huxley).

● Do not confuse with *flout* 'to disobey openly and scornfully', e.g. *His deliberate flouting of one still supposedly iron rule* (Frederic Raphael): *flout* should have been used by the public figure reported as having said *Those wanting to flaunt the policy would recognize that public opinion was not behind them.* Do not try to combine the uses, as in *She posed Marilyn Monroe style over a wind machine flaunting her skirts and old-fashioned sensibilities.*

following, as a sequel to, consequent on, is used in two ways. (1) Properly, as an adjective, dependent on a preceding noun, e.g. *During demonstrations following the hanging of two British soldiers.* (2) By extension, as an independent quasi-preposition, e.g. *The prologue was written by the company following an incident witnessed by them.*

● Many people regard use (2) as erroneous (cf. **due to** (3)). It can also give rise to ambiguity, e.g. *Police arrested a man following the hunt.* In any case, *following* should not be used as a mere synonym for *after* (e.g. *Following supper they went to bed*).

for: The subject of a clause of which the verb is the *to*-infinitive is normally preceded by *for*, e.g. *For him to stay elsewhere is unthinkable* (contrast *that he should stay elsewhere ..*). But if the clause is a direct object in a main sentence, *for* is omitted: hence *I could not bear for him to stay elsewhere* is non-standard.

forbid can be followed by a personal object and a *to*-infinitive, e.g. *My means forbade me to indulge in such delightful fantasies* (Lawrence Durrell) or by an *-ing* form (see pp. 193 ff.), e.g. *Politeness .. forbade my doubting them* (Dickens); *The law that forbade the evidence in divorce cases being published* (Graham Greene).

● Do not use with *from* as in *She has an injunction forbidding him from calling her on the telephone.*

forensic (1) of or used in courts of law, e.g. *forensic medicine, forensic science*; (2) of or involving forensic science, e.g. *An object which has been sent for forensic examination.*

● Sense (2) is often deplored as an illogical extension of sense (1), but is widespread.

former (latter). When referring to the first (last) of three or more, *the first* (*the last*) should be used, not *the former* (*the latter*).

fortuitous means 'happening by chance, accidental', e.g. *His presence is not fortuitous. He has a role to play* (André Brink).

● It does not mean either 'fortunate' or 'timely', as (incorrectly) in *He could not believe it. It was too fortuitous to be chance.*

fractious, unruly; peevish; e.g. *Christina was the more fractious of the two, passionate and given to terrible tantrums* (Kathleen Jones).

• Do not confuse with *factious* 'given to, or proceeding from, faction', e.g. *In spite of such a divisive past and a fractious* (correctly, *factious*) *present.*

fruition, fulfilment, especially in the phrase *be brought to, come to, grow to, reach,* etc. *fruition,* once stigmatized as a misuse, is now standard.

fulsome is a pejorative term, applied to nouns such as *flattery, praise, servility, affection,* etc., and means 'cloying, excessive, disgusting by excess', e.g. *They listened to fulsome speeches, doggedly translated by a wilting Olga Fiodorovna* (Beryl Bainbridge).

• *Fulsome* is not now regarded as a synonym of *copious,* though this was its original meaning.

further, furthest: see **farther, farthest.**

geriatric means 'pertaining to the health and welfare of the elderly'; it is very informal (and may in some circumstances be offensive) to use it as a synonym of *old* or *outdated,* or as a noun meaning 'old, outdated, or senile person'.

gourmand, glutton; *gourmet,* connoisseur of good food.

graffiti is strictly speaking the plural of *graffito.* The use of *graffiti* as a singular or mass noun is regarded as incorrect by some people but is frequently found, e.g. in *Graffiti is a destructive eyesore.*

half. The use of *half* in expressions of time to mean *half-past* is indigenous to Britain and has been remarked on since the 1930s, e.g. *We'd easily get the half-five bus* (William Trevor); it is to be distinguished from the use of *half* + the succeeding hour (i.e. *half-nine* = half-past eight) in parts of Scotland and Ireland. It remains non-standard.

hardly. (1) *Hardly* is not used with negative constructions.

• Expressions like *Without hardly a word of comment* (substitute *with hardly* or *almost without a word* . .) and *I couldn't hardly tell what he meant* (substitute *I could hardly tell* . .) are non-standard.

(2) *Hardly* and *scarcely* are followed by *when* or *before,* not *than,* e.g. *Hardly had Grimes left the house when a tall young man* . . *presented himself at the front door* (Evelyn Waugh).

heir apparent, one whose right of inheritance cannot be superseded by the birth of another heir; as opposed to an *heir presumptive,* whose right can be so superseded.

• *Heir apparent* does not mean 'seeming heir'.

help. *More than,* or *as little as, one can help* are illogical but established idioms, e.g. *They will not respect more than they can help treaties extracted from them under duress* (Winston Churchill).

hoi polloi can be preceded by *the,* even though *hoi* represents the Greek definite article, e.g. *The screens with which working archaeologists baffle the* hoi polloi (Frederic Raphael).

• **homogenous** is a frequent error for *homogeneous,* and is probably due partly to the form of the related verb *homogenize.* A word *homogenous* exists, but has a technical meaning in biology that is quite different and very restricted in its use. *Homogeneous* means 'of the same kind, uniform', e.g. *The style throughout was homogeneous but the authors' names were multiform* (Evelyn Waugh).

hopefully, thankfully. These adverbs are used in two ways: (1) As adverbs of manner = 'in a hopeful/thankful way', 'with hope/gratitude', e.g. *The prevailing mentality of that deluded time was still hopefully parliamentary* (G. B. Shaw); *I moved to the East Coast, and in 1938 hopefully built another boat* (Arthur Ransome); *When it thankfully dawned on her that the travel agency .. would be open* (Muriel Spark). (2) As sentence adverbs, outside the clause structure and conveying the speaker's comment on the statement, e.g. *Hopefully they will be available in the autumn (Guardian); The editor, thankfully, has left them as they were written* (TLS).

• Use (2) is very common but regarded by many people as unacceptable. The main reason is that other commenting sentence adverbs, such as *regrettably, fortunately,* etc., can be converted to the form *it is regrettable, fortunate,* etc., that —, but these are to be resolved as *it is to be hoped* or *one hopes that —* and *one is thankful that —.* (The same objection could be, but is not, made to *happily* and *unhappily* which mean *one is (un)happy* not *it is (un)happy that —,* e.g. in *Unhappily children do hurt flies* (Jean Rhys).) A further objection is that absurdity or ambiguity can arise from the interplay of senses (1) and (2), e.g. *There is also a screen, hopefully forming a backdrop to the*

whole stage (Tom Stoppard); *Any decision to trust Egypt
.. and move forward hopefully toward peace .. in the
Middle East* (*Guardian Weekly*). This use of *hopefully*
probably arose as a translation of German *hoffentlich*,
used in the same way, and first became popular in
America in the late 1960s; the same American provenance, but not the German, holds good for *thankfully*. It
is recommended that sense (2) should be restricted to
informal contexts.

i.e.: see **e.g., i.e.**

if in certain constructions (usually linking two adjectives or
adverbs that qualify the same noun or verb) can be
ambiguous, e.g. *A great play, if not the greatest, by this
author*.

 • It is best to paraphrase such sentences as, e.g., either *A
great play, though not the greatest by this author* or *A great
play, perhaps* (or *very nearly*) *the greatest by this author*.

ignorant is better followed by *of* than by *about*, e.g. *The
residents are either too apathetic or too ignorant of their
rights .. to break free* (*Independent*).

ilk. *Of that ilk* is a Scots term, meaning 'of the same place,
territorial designation, or name', e.g. *Wemyss of that ilk*
= Wemyss of Wemyss.

 • By a misunderstanding *ilk* has come to mean 'sort, lot'
(usually pejorative), e.g. *Joan Baez and other vocalists of
that ilk* (David Lodge). This should be avoided in formal
English.

ill used predicatively = 'unwell'; *sick* used predicatively =
'about to or likely to vomit, in the act of vomiting', e.g.
I felt sick; I was violently sick; used attributively =
'unwell', e.g. *a sick man*, except in collocations like *sick
bay, sick leave*.

 • It is non-standard to use *ill* predicatively for 'in the act
of vomiting' or *sick* predicatively for 'unwell' (though the
latter is standard Amer.), except in the phrase *off sick*
'away on sick leave'.

illusion: see **delusion**.

illusory: see **elusive**.

impact, used figuratively, is best confined to contexts in which
someone or something is imagined as striking another,

e.g. *The most dynamic colour combination if used too often loses its impact* (i.e., on the eye). It is weakened if used as a mere synonym for *effect, impression,* or *influence.*

impedance, the total effective resistance of an electric circuit to the flow of alternating current.

● Do not confuse with *impediment,* a hindrance, a defect (in speech, etc.), e.g. *Convinced of the existence of a serious impediment to his marriage* (Evelyn Waugh).

imply, infer. *Imply* (1) to involve the truth or existence of; (2) to express indirectly, insinuate, hint at. *Infer* (1) to reach (an opinion), deduce, from facts and reasoning, e.g. *She left it to my intelligence to infer her meaning. I inferred it all right* (W. Somerset Maugham); *He is a philosopher's God, logically inferred from self-evident premises* (Tom Stoppard).

(2) = *imply,* sense (2), e.g. *I have inferred once, and I repeat, that Limehouse is the most overrated excitement in London* (H. V. Morton).

● Sense (2) of *infer* is generally unacceptable, since it is the reverse of the primary sense of the verb.

imprimatur, official licence to print.

● Do not confuse with *imprint,* the name of the publisher/printer, place of publication/printing, etc., on the title-page or at the end of a book.

inapt, inept. *Inapt* = 'not apt', 'unsuitable'; *inept* = (1) without aptitude, unskilful, e.g. *Fox-trots and quicksteps, at which he had been so inept* (David Lodge); (2) inappropriate, out of place, e.g. *Not much less than famous for looking ineptly dressed* (Anthony Powell); (3) absurd, silly, e.g. *Here I was, awkward and tongue-tied, and all the time in danger of saying something inept or even rude* (Siegfried Sassoon).

inchoate means 'just begun, underdeveloped', e.g. *Trying to give his work a finished look—and all the time it's pathetically obvious .. that the stuff's fatally inchoate* (John Wain).

● It does not mean *chaotic* or *incoherent.* The form *choate* is erroneous.

include: see **comprise** (1).

infer: see **imply**.

inflammable: see **flammable**.

inflict, afflict. One *inflicts* something *on* someone or *afflicts* someone *with* something; something is *inflicted on* one, or one is *afflicted with* something.

- Do not use *inflict with* where *afflict with* is meant, e.g. in *The miners are still out, and industry is inflicted* (correctly, *afflicted*) *with a kind of creeping paralysis.*

ingenious, clever at inventing, etc.; noun *ingenuity*; *ingenuous* open, frank, innocent; noun *ingenuousness.*

insignia is, in origin, a plural noun, e.g. *Fourteen different airline insignia* (David Lodge); its singular, rarely encountered, is *insigne.* It can be used collectively, e.g. *The most important insignia of Croatian statehood, . . the coat of arms of the . . Croat kingdom.*

- Use as a countable noun is non-standard, e.g. in *One of the insignias that immune system cells use to tell friend from foe.*

intense, existing, having some quality, in a high degree, e.g. *The intense evening sunshine* (Iris Murdoch); *intensive* employing much effort, concentrated, e.g. *Intensive care*; *The intensive geological surveys of the Sahara* (Margaret Drabble).

interface (noun) (1) A surface forming a common boundary between two regions, e.g. *The concepts of surface tension apply to the interfaces between solid and solid, solid and liquid,* (etc.). (2) A piece of equipment in which interaction occurs between two systems, processes, etc., e.g. *Modular interfaces can easily be designed to adapt the general-purpose computer to the equipment.* (3) A point or area of interaction between two systems, organizations, or disciplines, e.g. *The interface between physics and music is of direct relevance to . . the psychological effects of hearing* (Nature).

- Sense (3) is deplored by many people, since it is often debased into a high-sounding synonym for *boundary*, *meeting-point, interaction, liaison, link*, etc., e.g. *The need for the interface of lecturer and student will diminish.*

interface (verb), to connect (equipment) with (equipment) by means of an interface; (of equipment) to be connected by an interface; e.g. *Using the Kontron image analyser interfaced to the computer* (Brain).

● *Interface* is nowadays overused as a synonym for *interact* (*with*), as, e.g., in *The ideal candidate will have the ability to interface effectively with the heads of staff of various departments*. This use should be avoided.

internment, confinement (from verb *intern*).

● Do not confuse with *interment*, burial (from verb *inter*).

invite (noun = 'invitation'), although over three centuries old, remains informal only.

ironic, ironical, ironically. The noun *irony* can mean (1) a way of speaking in which the intended meaning (for those with insight) is the opposite to, or very different from, that expressed by the words used (and apprehended by the victim of the irony); or (2) a condition of affairs or events that is the opposite of what might be expected, especially when the outcome of an action appears as if it is in mockery of the agent's intention.

The adjectives *ironic, ironical*, and the adverb *ironically* are commonly used in sense (1) of *irony*, e.g. *Ironical silent apology for the absence of naked women and tanks of gin from the amenities* (Kingsley Amis). They are also frequently found in sense (2), e.g. *The outcome was ironic. The expenditure of British treasure served to rearm the United States rather than to strengthen Great Britain* (A. J. P. Taylor); *The fact that after all she had been faithful to me was ironic* (Graham Greene).

● Some people object to this use, especially when *ironic* or *ironically* is used to introduce a trivial oddity, e.g. *It was ironic that he thought himself locked out when the key was in his pocket all the time.*

kind of, sort of (1) *A kind of, a sort of* should not be followed by *a* before the noun, e.g. *a kind of shock*, not *a kind of a shock*. (2) *Kind of, sort of*, etc., followed by a plural noun, are often treated as plural and qualified by plural words like *these, those*, or followed by a plural verb, e.g. *They would be on those sort of terms* (Anthony Powell). This is widely regarded as incorrect except in informal use: substitute *that* (etc.) *kind* (or *sort*) *of* or *of that kind* (or *sort*), e.g. *this kind of car is unpopular* or *cars of this kind are unpopular*. (3) *Kind of, sort of* used adverbially, e.g. *I kind of expected it*, are informal only.

kudos is a mass noun like *glory* or *fame*, e.g. *He's made a lot of kudos out of the strike* (Evelyn Waugh).

● It is not a plural noun and there is no singular *kudo*.

latter: see **former**.

laudable, praiseworthy, e.g. *I saw clearly . . her own laudable cleanliness of mind, where all was what it seemed* (Candia McWilliam); *laudatory*, expressing praise, e.g. *The concept of travel 'junkets' as a means of generating strictly laudatory travel news . . is improper* (*Public Relations Journal*).

lay (verb), past *laid*, = 'put down, arrange', etc. is only transitive, e.g. *Lay her on the bed*; *They laid her on the bed*; (reflexive, somewhat literary) *Once she had . . laid herself down to sleep untroubled* (Sara Maitland).

● To use *lay* intransitively, to mean 'lie', e.g. *She wants to lay down*; *She was laying on the bed*, is non-standard, even though fairly common in spoken English. Cf. *lie*.

leading question, in Law, is a question so worded that it prompts a person to give the desired answer, e.g. *The solicitor . . at once asked me some leading questions . . I had to try to be both forthcoming and discreet* (C. P. Snow).

● It does not mean a 'principal (or loaded or searching) question'.

learn with a person as the object, = 'teach', is non-standard, or occasionally jocular as in *I'll learn you*.

less (adjective) is the comparative of (*a*) *little*, and, like the latter, is used with mass nouns, e.g. *I owe him little duty and less love* (Shakespeare); *fewer* is the comparative of (*a*) *few*, and both are used with plural countable nouns, e.g. *Few people have their houses broken into; and fewer still have them burnt* (G. B. Shaw).

● *Less* is quite often used informally as the comparative of *few*, probably on the analogy of *more*, which is the comparative both of *much* (with mass nouns) and *many* (with plural countable nouns), e.g. *I wish that they would send less delicacies and frills and some more plain and substantial things* (Susan Hill); *Our copiers have less parts inside them so there's less to go wrong* (*Office Magazine*). This is regarded as incorrect in formal English.

- *Less* should not be used as the comparative of *small* (or some similar adjective such as *low*), e.g. *a lower price* not *a less price*.

lesser, not so great as the other or the rest, e.g. *He opened* The Times *with the rich crackle that drowns all lesser sounds* (John Galsworthy).

- *Lesser* should not be used when the meaning is 'not so big' or 'not so large': its opposition to *greater* is essential. It cannot replace *smaller* in *A smaller prize will probably be offered.*

lest is very formal (in ordinary English, *so that . . not* or *in case* is used); it is followed by *should* or (in exalted style) the subjunctive, e.g. *Lest the eye wander aimlessly, a Doric temple stood by the water's edge* (Evelyn Waugh); *Lest some too sudden gesture or burst of emotion should turn the petals brown* (Patrick White).

let, to allow (followed by the bare infinitive) is rarely used in the passive: the effect is usually unidiomatic, e.g. *Halfdan's two sons . . are let owe their lives to a trick* (Gwyn Jones). *Allowed to* is usual.

liable (1) can be followed by *to* + a noun or noun phrase in the sense 'subject to, likely to suffer from', or by an infinitive; (2) carries the implication that the action or experience expressed by the infinitive is undesirable, e.g. *Receiving in the bedroom is liable to get a woman talked about* (Tom Stoppard); (3) can indicate either the mere possibility, or the habituality, of what is expressed by the verb, e.g. *The cruellest question which a novelist is liable . . to be asked* (Frederic Raphael); *The kind of point that one is always liable to miss* (George Orwell).

- The sense 'likely to' is American, e.g. *Boston is liable to be the ultimate place for holding the convention.*
Contrast **apt**.

lie (verb) past *lay*, *lain*, = 'recline', 'be situated', is only intransitive, e.g. *Lie down on the bed*; *The ship lay at anchor until yesterday*; *Her left arm, on which she had lain all night, was numb.* Although correct, *lain* can sound somewhat stilted, and *been lying* is often preferred.

- To use *lie* transitively, to mean 'lay', e.g. *Lie her on the bed*, is non-standard. The past *lay* and participle *lain* are quite often wrongly used for *laid* out of over-correctness, e.g. *He had lain this peer's honour in the dust.* Cf. **lay**.

ligature: see **digraph**.

like, indicating resemblance between two things: (1) It is normally used as an adjective followed by a noun, noun phrase, or pronoun (in the objective case), e.g. *There can't be many fellows about with brains like yours* (P. G. Wodehouse); *He loathes people like you and me* (not . . *and I*). It can be used to mean 'such as' (introducing a particular example of a class about which something is said), e.g. *With a strongly patterned dress like that you shouldn't really wear any jewellery* (Iris Murdoch).

● In formal contexts some people prefer *such as* to be used if more than one example is mentioned, e.g. *He dealt in types, such as the rich bitch, the honest whore, the socializing snob* (*London Magazine*).

(2) It is often used as a conjunction with a dependent clause, e.g. *Everything went wrong . . like it does in dreams* (Iris Murdoch); *Not with a starched apron like the others had* (Jean Rhys), or with an adverbial phrase, e.g. *With glossy hair, black, and a nose like on someone historical* (Patrick White); *It was as if I saw myself. Like in a looking-glass* (Jean Rhys).

● Although this use of *like* as a conjunction is not uncommon in formal writing, it is often 'condemned as vulgar or slovenly' (*OED*), and is best avoided, except informally. Use *as*, e.g. *Do you mean to murder me as you murdered the Egyptian?* (*Revised English Bible*), or recast the sentence, e.g. *A costume like those that the others wore.*

(3) It is often informally used to mean 'as if', e.g. *The light at either end of the tunnel was like you were looking through a sheet of yellow cellophane* (Patrick White); *You wake like someone hit you on the head* (T. S. Eliot).

● This use is very informal.

likely (adverb), in the sense 'probably', must be preceded by *more, most,* or *very,* e.g. *Its inhabitants . . very likely do make that claim for it* (George Orwell).

● The use without the qualifying adverb is standard only in American English, e.g. *They'll likely turn ugly* (Eugene O'Neill).

linguist means 'one whose subject is linguistics' as well as 'one skilled in the use of languages'; there is no other suitable term (*linguistician* exists but is not commonly used).

literally. In very informal speech, *literally* is used as an intensifying adverb without meaning apart from its emotive force.

• This use should be avoided in writing or formal speech, since it almost invariably involves absurdity, e.g. *The dwarfs mentioned here are literally within a stone's throw of the Milky Way* (*New Scientist*). The appropriate use is seen in *She emerged, fully armed, from the head of Zeus who was suffering from a literally splitting headache* (Frederic Raphael).

loan (verb) has some justification where a businesslike loan is in question, e.g. *The gas industry is using a major part of its profits to benefit the PSBR by loaning money to Government* (*Observer*). It should not be used merely as a variant for *lend*.

locate can mean 'discover the place where someone or somebody is', e.g. *She had located and could usefully excavate her Saharan highland emporium* (Margaret Drabble); it should not be used to mean merely 'find'.

lot. *A lot of*, though somewhat informal, is acceptable in serious writing; *lots of* is not.

luncheon is an especially formal variant of *lunch*; the latter should normally be used, except in fixed expressions like *luncheon voucher*.

luxuriant, growing profusely, prolific, profuse, exuberant, e.g. *His hair . . does not seem to have been luxuriant even in its best days* (G. B. Shaw).

• Do not confuse with *luxurious* (the adjective relating to *luxury*), e.g. *The food, which had always been good, was now luxurious* (C. P. Snow).

majority can mean 'the greater number of a countable set', and is then followed by the plural, e.g. *The majority of the plays produced were failures* (G. B. Shaw).

• *Great* (or *huge*, *vast*, etc.) can precede *majority* in this sense, e.g. *The first thing you gather from the vast majority of the speakers* (C. S. Lewis); but not *greater*, *greatest* (since 'more' is already contained in the word).

• *Majority* is not used to mean 'the greater part of an

uncountable mass', e.g. *I was doing most* (or *the greater part) of the cooking* (not *the majority of the cooking*).

malignant: see **benign.**

masterful, domineering, e.g. *People might say she was tyrannical, domineering, masterful* (Virginia Woolf).

• Do not confuse with *masterly*, very skilful, e.g. *A masterly compound of friendly argumentation and menace* (Iris Murdoch).

maximize, to make as great as possible.

• It should not be used for 'to make as good, easy, (etc). as possible' or 'to make the most of' as in *To maximize customer service*; *To maximize this situation.*

means (1) Money resources: a plural noun, e.g. *You might find out from Larry . . what his means are* (G. B. Shaw).

(2) That by which a result is brought about. It may be used either as a singular noun or as a plural one, without any change in form, e.g. (singular) *The press was, at this time, the only means . . of influencing opinion at home* (A. J. P. Taylor); (plural) *All the time-honoured means of meeting the opposite sex* (Frederic Raphael).

• Beware of mixing singular and plural, as in *The right to resist by every* (singular) *means that are* (plural) *consonant with the law of God.*

media, agency, means (of communication etc.), is a plural noun, e.g. *The communication media inflate language because they dare not be honest* (Anthony Burgess). Its singular is *medium* (rare except in *mass medium*).

• Although *media* is commonly treated as a singular noun, this use is disapproved of by many people and should be avoided. The plural form *medias* should also be avoided. *Medium* (in Spiritualism) forms its plural in *-s*.

militate: see **mitigate.**

milliard: see **billion.**

minimize, to reduce to, or estimate at, the smallest possible amount or degree, e.g. *Each side was inclined to minimize its own losses in battle.*

• It does not mean *lessen* and therefore cannot be qualified by adverbs like *greatly*.

minority. *Large, vast*, etc. *minority* can mean either 'a considerable number who are yet less than half', or 'a number who are very much the minority': although the expression is more commonly used to mean the former, it is best to avoid the ambiguity.

mitigate, appease, alleviate, moderate (usually transitive), e.g. *Its heat mitigated by the strong sea-wind* (Anthony Burgess).

● Do not confuse with *militate* (intransitive) *against*, to serve as a strong influence against, e.g. *The very fact that Leamas was a professional could militate against his interests* (John le Carré): it is only the idea of countering that they have in common.

momentum, impetus.

● Do not confuse with *moment* 'importance', e.g. *He has marked his entrance with an error of some moment* (not *momentum*).

more than one is followed by a singular verb and is referred back to by singular pronouns, e.g. *More than one popular dancing man inquired anxiously at his bank* (Evelyn Waugh).

motif, motive. *Motif* (1) theme repeated and developed in an artistic work, (2) decorative design or pattern, (3) ornament sewn separately on a garment.

Motive, what induces a person to act in a particular way. *Motive* might have been a better choice in the following where *motif* is perhaps meant metaphorically: *Fear of failure is a strong motif in men's lives.*

motivate, to cause (a person) to act in a particular way, be the motive of (an action), e.g. *A . . tax grab motivated by the politics of envy* (*Daily Express*).

● It does not mean 'supply a motive, justify', e.g. (wrongly) in *The publisher motivates the slim size of these volumes by claiming it makes them more likely to be read.*

mutual (1) Felt, done, etc., by each to(wards) the other, e.g. *The mutual affection of father and son was rather touching* (W. Somerset Maugham). (2) Standing in a (specified) relation to each other, e.g. *Kings and subjects, mutual foes* (Shelley). This sense is now rare.

(3) Common to two (or more) parties, e.g. *a mutual friend* or *acquaintance*.

● Sense (3) is acceptable in a small number of collocations, such as the two indicated, in which *common* might be ambiguous; cf. *They had already formed a small island of mutual Englishness* (Muriel Spark): *common English-ness* might imply vulgarity. Otherwise *common* is prefer-able, e.g. in *By common* (rather than *mutual*) *agreement they finished the card-game at nine every night.*

naturalist, expert in natural history; *naturist,* nudist.

nature. ● Avoid using adjective + *nature* as a periphrasis for an abstract noun, e.g. write *The dangerousness of the spot,* not *The dangerous nature of the spot.*

need (*this needs changing,* etc.): see **want.**

neighbourhood. *In the neighbourhood of* is an unnecessarily cumbersome periphrasis for *round about, approximately.*

neither (adverb). ● It is non-standard to use it instead of *either* to strengthen a preceding negative, e.g. *There were no books either* (not *neither*).

non-flammable: see **flammable.**

normalcy is chiefly Amer.
    ● Prefer *normality.*

not only: see **only** (4).

no way (1) (Initially, followed by inversion of verb and subject) = 'not at all, by no means', e.g. *No way will you stop prices or unemployment going up again* (James Cal-laghan). ● Informal only. (2) (Emphatic) = 'certainly not', e.g. *'Did you go up in the elevator?' 'No way.'* ● Chiefly Amer.; informal only.

number. *A number* (*of*) is constructed with the plural, *the number* (*of*) the singular, e.g. *A number of people around us were unashamedly staring* (Bruce Arnold); *The number of men who make a definite contribution to anything whatsoever is small* (Virginia Woolf).

obligate (verb) is in Britain only used in Law.
    ● There is no gain in using it (as often in Amer. usage) for *oblige.*

oblivious, in the sense 'unaware of, unconscious of', may be followed by *of* or *to,* e.g. *'When the summer comes,' said Lord Marchmain, oblivious of the deep corn and swelling fruit . . outside his windows* (Evelyn Waugh); *Rose seemed oblivious to individuals* (Angus Wilson).
    ● This sense, which developed from the older sense 'forgetful', is sometimes censured, but is now fully estab-lished in the language.

obscene is sometimes used informally as a general term of disapproval meaning 'highly offensive, objectionable, outrageous', e.g. *TV's claim to 'show it like it is' in 1990 appears as obscene as it did in the Falklands War.*
● The word is overused in this sense and should be avoided.

of used for *have*: see **of,** p. 59, and **have,** p. 102.

off of used for the preposition *off*, e.g. *Picked him off of the floor*, is non-standard.

one (pronoun) (1) = 'any person, the speaker or writer as representing people in general' has *one, one's,* and *oneself* as objective, possessive, and reflexive forms.
● These forms should be used to point back to a previous use of *one*, e.g. *One always did, in foreign parts, become friendly with one's fellow-countrymen more quickly than one did at home* (Muriel Spark). *One* should not be mixed with *he* (*him, his,* etc.) (acceptable Amer. usage) or *we, you,* etc.
(2) = single thing or person, following *any* and *every*; the resulting phrase is written as two words and is distinct from *anyone, everyone* (= anybody, everybody), e.g. *Any one (of these) will do; Perhaps every one of my conclusions would be negatived by other observers* (George Orwell).

ongoing has a valid use as an adjective meaning 'that goes on', i.e. 'that is happening and will continue' (just as *oncoming* means 'that comes on'), e.g. *The refugee problem in our time is an ongoing problem* (Robert Kee).
● The vague or tautologous use of *ongoing* should be avoided, as in the cliché *ongoing situation*, or in *We have an ongoing military relationship which we are continuing* (*Guardian*).

only (1) In spoken English, it is usual to place *only* between subject and verb, e.g. *He only saw Bill yesterday*: intonation is used to show whether *only* limits *he, saw, Bill,* or *yesterday*.
(2) It is an established idiom that, in a sentence containing *only* + verb + another item, in the absence of special intonation, *only* is understood as limiting, not the subject or verb, but the other item. *I only want some water* is the natural way of saying *I want only some water*. If there is

more than one item following the verb, *only* often limits the item nearest the end of the sentence, e.g. *A type of mind that can only accept ideas if they are put in the language he would use himself* (Doris Lessing) (= only if . .); but not always, e.g. *The captain was a thin unapproachable man . . who only appeared once at table* (Graham Greene) (= only once). This idiom is tacitly recognized by all good writers, e.g. *They only met on the most formal occasions* (C. P. Snow); *The contractors were only waiting for the final signature to start their work of destruction* (Evelyn Waugh); *The Nonconformist sects only influenced minorities* (George Orwell).

(3) Despite the idiom described under (2), there are often sentences in which confusion can arise, e.g. *Patrick only talked as much as he did, which was not as much as all that, to keep the ball in the air* (Kingsley Amis), where at first sight *only* might appear to limit *he* (referring to some other person) but really limits *to keep . . air*. If confusion or ambiguity is likely to arise, *only* should be placed before the item which it limits, e.g. *They sought to convert others only by the fervour of their sentiments and the earnestness of their example* (Frederic Raphael); *The coalminer is second in importance only to the man who ploughs the soil* (George Orwell).

(4) *Not only* should always be placed next to the item which it qualifies, and not in the position before the verb. This is a fairly common slip, e.g. *Katherine's marriage not only kept her away, but at least two of Mr. March's cousins* (C. P. Snow); *kept not only her* would be better. If placing it before the verb is inevitable, the verb should be repeated after *but* (*also*), e.g. *It not only brings the coal out but brings the roof down as well* (George Orwell).

ordinance, (1) authoritative order, decree; (2) religious rite.
  ● Do not confuse with *ordnance*, (1) mounted guns, (2) government service dealing with military stores and materials. Note also *Ordnance Survey*.
orient, orientate. In meaning the two words are virtually synonymous. In general, as opposed to technical, use, *orientate* seems to be predominant, but either is acceptable.

other than can be used where *other* is an adjective or pronoun, e.g. *He was no other than the rightful lord*; *The acts of any person other than myself.*

● *Other* cannot be treated as an adverb: *otherwise than* should be used instead, e.g. in *It is impossible to refer to them other than very cursorily.*

out used as a preposition instead of *out of,* e.g. *You should of* [sic] *pushed him out the nest long ago* (character in work by Muriel Spark), is non-standard.

outside of (1) = apart from (a sense *outside* cannot have) is informal only, e.g. *The need of some big belief outside of art* (Roger Fry, in a letter).

(2) = beyond the limits of, e.g. *The most important such facility outside of Japan* (*Gramophone*).

● In sense (2) *outside* alone is preferable: the *of* is redundant.

outstanding. ● Do not use in the sense 'remaining undetermined, unpaid, etc.' in contexts where ambiguity with the sense 'eminent, striking' can arise, e.g. *In a moment we'll give you the other outstanding results* (in a sports commentary).

overly, excessively, too, is still regarded as an unassimilated Americanism, e.g. *Those overly rationalistic readers* (TLS).

● Use *excessively, too,* or *over-* instead; for *not overly, not very* or *none too* make satisfactory replacements.

overseas (adjective and adverb) is now more usual than *oversea.*

owing to, unlike **due to,** has for long been established as a compound preposition meaning 'because of', e.g. *My rooms became uninhabitable, owing to a burst gas-pipe* (C. P. Snow).

● *Owing to the fact that* should be avoided: use a conjunction like *because.*

pace means 'despite (someone)'s opinion', e.g. *Our civilization, pace Chesterton, is founded on coal* (George Orwell).

● It does not mean 'according to (someone)' or 'notwithstanding (something)'.

parameter. (1) (In technical use, especially in Mathematics and Computing) a quantity constant in the case considered, but varying in different cases.

(2) (In extended use) a defining characteristic, especially

one that can be measured, e.g. *The three major parameters of colour—brightness, hue, and saturation.*

(3) (Loosely) a limit or boundary, e.g. *The considerable element of indeterminacy which exists within the parameters of the parole system* (*The Times*); an aspect or feature, e.g. *The main parameters of the problem.*

● Use (3) is a popular dilution of the word's meaning, probably influenced (at least in the first quotation) by *perimeter*; it should be avoided.

parricide refers to the killing of a near relative, especially of a parent; *patricide* only to the killing of one's father.

part (on the part of): see **behalf**.

partially, partly. Apart from the (rare) use of *partially* to mean 'in a partial or biased way', these two words are largely interchangeable. Note, however, that *partly .. partly* is more usual than *partially .. partially*, e.g. *Partly in verse and partly in prose.*

peer, as in *to have no peer*, means 'equal', not 'superior'.

pence is sometimes informally used as a singular, e.g. *How Fine Fare, on lard, is one pence up on Sainsbury's* (Malcolm Bradbury).

● This use is very informal. Normally *penny* should be used in the singular.

perquisite (informal abbreviation *perk*) extra profit or allowance additional to main income, incidental benefit attached to employment, e.g. *The dead man's clothes are the perquisites of the layer-out* (Lawrence Durrell).

● Do not confuse with *prerequisite* 'something required as a previous condition (*for*, *of*, or *to* something)', e.g. *Her mere comforting presence beside me which was already a prerequisite to peaceful sleep* (Lynne Reid Banks).

persistency is limited in sense to 'the action of persisting in one's course', e.g. *They made repeated requests for compensation, but an official apology was the only reward for their persistency*; *persistence* is sometimes used in that sense, e.g. *Phil Davies' try .. was just reward for the flanker's persistence* (*Independent on Sunday*), but more often for 'continued existence', e.g. *One of the more surprising things about the life-ways of primitive societies is their persistence* (Sean O'Faolain).

perspicuous, easily understood, clearly expressed; expressing things clearly; similarly *perspicuity*; e.g. *There is nothing more desirable in composition than perspicuity* (Southey).
● Do not confuse with *perspicacious*, having or showing insight, and *perspicacity*, e.g. *Her perspicacity at having guessed his passion* (Vita Sackville-West).

petit bourgeois, **petty bourgeois.** The meaning (and with many people, the pronunciation) of these is the same. If the former is used, the correct French inflections should be added: *petits bourgeois* (plural), *petite(s) bourgeoise(s)* (feminine (plural)); also *petite bourgeoisie*. With *petty bourgeois* it should be remembered that the sense of the original French *petit* is not English *petty*, although that may be one of its main connotations.

phenomena is the plural of *phenomenon*.
● It cannot be used as a singular and cannot form a plural *phenomenas*.

picaresque (of a style of fiction) dealing with the episodic adventures of rogues.
● It does not mean 'transitory' or 'roaming'.

pivotal, being that on which anything pivots or turns, e.g. *The pardon of Richard Nixon was pivotal to those who made up their minds at the last minute.*
● Do not use it merely to mean *vital*.

plaid, shawl-like garment; *tartan*, woollen cloth with distinctive pattern; the pattern itself.
● **plus** (conjunction), = 'and in addition', is an Amer. colloquialism that is not generally acceptable in Standard English, e.g. *The School . . sounds like a POW camp.* (*Plus I knew one of the kids was trying to escape all the time.*)

polity, a form of civil government, e.g. *A republican polity*; a state.
● It does not mean *policy* or *politics*.

portentous can mean: (1) Like a portent, ominous, e.g. *Fiery-eyed with a sense of portentous utterance* (Muriel Spark). (2) Prodigious, e.g. *Every movement of his portentous frame* (James Joyce). (3) Solemn, ponderous, and somewhat pompous, e.g. *Our last conversation must have sounded to you rather portentous* (Iris Murdoch); *A portentous commentary on Holy Scripture* (Lord Hailsham).

● Sense (3) is sometimes criticized, but is an established, slightly jocular use.

● The form *portentious* (due to the influence of *pretentious*) is erroneous.

post, pre. Their use as full words (not prefixes) to mean 'after' and 'before' is unnecessary and should be avoided, e.g. in *Post the Geneva meeting of Opec* (*Daily Telegraph*); *Pre my being in office* (Henry Kissinger).

practicable, practical. When applied to things, *practicable* means 'able to be done, possible in practice', e.g. (with the negative *impracticable*), *Schemes which look very fine on paper, but which, as we well know, are impracticable* (C. S. Lewis); *practical* 'concerned with practice, suitable for use, suited to the conditions', e.g. *Having considered the problem, he came up with several practical suggestions*; *It is essential that the plan should cover all the practical details.*

pre: see **post, pre.**

precipitous, like a precipice, e.g. *Our rooms were . . reached by a precipitous marble staircase* (Evelyn Waugh).

● Do not confuse with *precipitate*, hasty, rash, e.g. *They were all a little out of breath from precipitate arrival* (Patrick White).

predicate (verb) (1) (Followed by *of*) to assert as a property of, e.g. *That easy Bohemianism—conventionally predicated of the 'artistic' temperament* (J. I. M. Stewart). (2) (Followed by *on*) to found or base (something) on, e.g. *A new conception of reality . . predicated on dissatisfaction with formalist literature* (TLS)

● Sense (2) tends to sound pretentious. Use *found*, or *base, on.*

pre-empt (1) To obtain beforehand, secure for oneself in advance, e.g. *Sound allows the mind an inventive role systematically pre-empted by the cinema* (Frederic Raphael). (2) To preclude, forestall, e.g. *The Nazi régime by its own grotesque vileness pre-empted fictional effort* (Listener).

● Sense (2) is better expressed by a verb such as *preclude* or *forestall.*

● *Pre-empt* is not a synonym for *prevent.*

prefer. The rejected alternative is introduced by *to*, e.g. *People preferred darkness to light* (*Revised English Bible*). But when the rejected alternative is an infinitive, it is preceded by *rather than* (not *than* alone), e.g. *I'd prefer to be stung to death rather than to wake up .. with half of me shot away* (John Osborne).

● *Prefer .. over* is chiefly Amer., e.g. *An electorate that prefers style over substance* (*New York Times*).

preferable to means 'more desirable than' and is therefore intensified by *far, greatly*, or *much*, not *more*, e.g. *After a hundred and eighty* (skips) *an unclear head seemed much preferable to more skips* (Kingsley Amis).

preference. The alternatives are introduced by *for* and *over*, e.g. *The preference for a single word over a phrase or clause* (Anthony Burgess); but *in preference* is followed by *to*, e.g. *Both were sensitive to artistic impressions musical in preference to plastic or pictorial* (James Joyce).

prejudice (1) = bias, is followed by *against* or *in favour of*; (2) = detriment, is followed by *to*; (3) = injury, is followed by *of* (in the phrase *to the prejudice of*).

prepared: *to be prepared to*, to be willing to, has been criticized as officialese by some authorities, but is now established usage, e.g. *One should kill oneself, which, of course, I was not prepared to do* (Cyril Connolly).

prerequisite: see **perquisite.**

prescribe, to lay down as a rule to be followed; *proscribe*, to forbid by law.

presently (1) After a short time, e.g. *Presently we left the table and sat in the garden-room* (Evelyn Waugh). (2) At present, currently, e.g. *The praise presently being heaped upon him* (*The Economist*).

● Sense (2) (for long current in American English) is regarded as incorrect by some people but is widely used and often sounds more natural than *at present*.

prestigious (1) Characterized by juggling or magic, delusive, deceptive, e.g. *The prestigious balancing act which he was constantly obliged to perform* (TLS): now rare. (2) Having or showing prestige, e.g. *A career in pure science is still more socially prestigious .. than one in engineering* (*The Times*): a fully acceptable sense.

prevaricate, to speak or act evasively or misleadingly, e.g. *I never have told a lie . . On many occasions I have resorted to prevarication; but on great occasions I have always told the truth* (G. B. Shaw); *procrastinate*, to postpone action, e.g. *Hamlet . . pronounces himself a procrastinator, an undecided man, even a coward* (C. S. Lewis).

prevent is followed by the objective case and *from* + the gerund, or by the possessive case + the gerund, e.g. *prevent me from going* or *prevent my going.*

● *Prevent me going* is informal only.

● **pre-war** as an adverb, in, e.g., *Some time pre-war there was a large contract out for tender* (*Daily Telegraph*): prefer *before the war.*

pristine (1) Ancient, original, e.g. *Stone which faithfully reproduced its pristine alternations of milk and cream* (J. I. M. Stewart). (2) Having its original, unspoilt condition, e.g. *Pristine snow reflects about 90 per cent of incident sunlight* (Fred Hoyle).

● *Pristine* does not mean 'spotless', 'pure', or 'fresh'.

procrastinate: see **prevaricate.**

prone (followed by *to*) is used like, and means much the same as, **liable,** except that it usually qualifies a personal subject, e.g. *My literary temperament rendering me especially prone to 'all that kind of poisonous nonsense'* (Cyril Connolly).

proportion means 'a comparative part, share, or ratio'; it is not a mere synonym for *part.*

proscribe: see **prescribe.**

protagonist, the leading character in a story or incident.

● In Greek drama there was only one protagonist, but this is no reason to debar the use of the word in the plural, e.g. *We . . sometimes mistook a mere supernumerary in a fine dress for one of the protagonists* (C. S. Lewis).

● Do not confuse with *proponent*: the word contains the Greek prefix *prot-* 'first', not the prefix *pro-* 'in favour of', and does not mean 'champion, advocate'.

protest (verb, transitive) to affirm solemnly, e.g. *He barely attempted to protest his innocence* (George Orwell).

● The sense 'protest against, object to', e.g. in *The residents have protested the sale*, is Amer. only.

proven. It is not standard to use this as the ordinary past participle of *prove* in British English (it is standard Scots and Amer.); it is, however, common attributively in certain expressions, such as *of proven ability*.

provenance, origin, place of origin, is used in Britain; the form *provenience* is its usual Amer. equivalent.

prudent, showing carefulness and foresight, e.g. *What is the difference in matrimonial affairs, between the mercenary and the prudent move? Where does discretion end, and avarice begin?* (Jane Austen); *prudential*, involving or marked by prudence, e.g. *The humble little outfit of prudential maxims which really underlay much of the talk about Shakespeare's characters* (C. S. Lewis).

pry, to prise (open, etc.): chiefly Amer., but occasionally in British literary use, e.g. *For her to pry his fingers open* (David Garnett). The normal sense is 'peer' or 'inquire'.

quadrillion: see **billion**.

question: (1) *No question that* (sometimes *but*), no doubt that, e.g. *There can be no question that the burning of Joan of Arc must have been a most instructive and interesting experiment* (G. B. Shaw); *There is no question but Leslie was an unusually handsome boy* (Anthony Powell).

(2) *No question of*, no possibility of, e.g. *There can be no question of tabulating successes and failures and trying to decide whether the successes are too numerous to be accounted for by chance* (C. S. Lewis). See also **beg the question, leading question**.

quote (noun = quotation) is informal only (except in Printing and Commerce).

● **re** (in the matter of, referring to) is better avoided and should not be used for 'about, concerning'.

reason. *The reason* (*why*) . . *is* . . should be followed by *that*, not *because*, e.g. *The reason why such a suggestion sounds hopeless* . . *is that few people are able to imagine the radio being used for the dissemination of anything except tripe* (George Orwell).

recoup (1) (transitive) to recompense (oneself or a person) *for* (a loss or expenditure), e.g. *Dixon felt he could recoup himself a little for the expensiveness of the drinks* (Kingsley Amis); also *to recoup one's losses*; (2) (intransitive) to make good one's loss, e.g. *I had .. acquired so many debts that if I didn't return to England to recoup, we might have to run for it* (Chaim Bermant).

● This word is not synonymous with *recuperate* except partly in sense (2) above ('to make good one's loss').

recuperate (1) (intransitive) to recover from exhaustion, ill-health, financial loss, etc., e.g. *I've got a good mind .. to put all my winnings on red and give him a chance to recuperate* (Graham Greene); (2) (transitive) to recover (health, a loss, material). In sense (2) *recover* is preferable.

redolent, smelling *of* something, e.g. *Corley's breath redolent of rotten cornjuice* (James Joyce); also used figuratively to mean 'strongly suggestive or reminiscent of', e.g. *The missive most redolent of money and sex* (Martin Amis).

referendum. ● For the plural, *referendums* is preferable to *referenda*.

refute, to prove (a statement, opinion, accusation, etc.) to be false, e.g. *The case against most of them must have been so easily refuted that they could hardly rank as suspects* (Rebecca West); to prove (a person) to be in error, e.g. *One of those German scholars whose function is to be refuted in a footnote* (Frederic Raphael).

● *Refute* does not mean 'deny' or 'repudiate' (an allegation etc.).

regalia is a plural noun, meaning 'emblems of royalty or of an order'. It has no singular in ordinary English.

region: *in the region of*, an unwieldy periphrasis for *round about, approximately*, is better avoided.

register office is the official term for the institution informally often called the *registry office*.

regretfully, in a regretful manner; *regrettably*, it is to be regretted (that).

● *Regretfully* should not be used where *regrettably* is intended: *The investigators, who must regretfully remain anonymous* (TLS), reads as a guess at the investigators' feelings instead of an expression of the writer's opinion, which was what was intended. The influence of **hopefully** (2) may be discernible here.

renege (intransitive), to fail to fulfil an agreement or undertaking, is usually constructed with *on*, e.g. *It .. reneged on*

Britain's commitment to the East African Asians (The Times).

resource is often confused with *recourse* and *resort*. *Resource* means (1) a reserve upon which one can draw (often used in the plural); (2) an action or procedure to which one can turn in difficulty, an expedient; (3) mental capabilities for amusing oneself, etc. (often used in the plural, e.g. *Left to his own resources*); (4) ability to deal with a crisis, e.g. *A man of infinite resource*. *Recourse* means the action of turning to a possible source of help; frequently in the phrases *have recourse to, without recourse to*. *Resort* means (1) the action of turning to a possible source of help (= *recourse*; but *resorting* is more usual than *resort* after *without*); frequently in the phrase *in the last resort*, as a last expedient, in the end; (2) a thing to which one can turn in difficulty.

responsible for (1) Liable to be called to account for, e.g. *I'm not responsible for what uncle Percy does* (E. M. Forster).
(2) Obliged to take care of or carry out, e.g. *Until 1952 the Prime Minister was directly responsible for the security service* (Harold Wilson).
(3) Being the cause of, e.g. *A war-criminal responsible for so many unidentified deaths* (Graham Greene).
● Beware of using senses (1) or (2) in expressions in which sense (3) can be understood, with absurd results, e.g. *Now, as Secretary for Trade, he is directly responsible for pollution* (*The Times*).

restive (1) Unmanageable, rejecting control, obstinate, e.g. *The I.L.P .. had been increasingly restive during the second Labour government, and now, refusing to accept Labour-party discipline in the house of commons, voluntarily disaffiliated from the Labour party* (A. J. P. Taylor).
(2) Restless, fidgety, e.g. *The audiences were not bad, though apt to be restive and noisy at the back* (J. B. Priestley).
● Sense (2) is objected to by some authorities but is quite commonly used by good writers.

revenge: one revenges oneself or a wrong (*on* an offender); one is revenged (*for* a wrong): the noun is *revenge* (*on*), and the idea is usually of satisfaction of the offended party's resentment. Cf. **avenge.**

reverend, deserving reverence; *reverent,* showing reverence. (*The*) *Revd,* plural *Revds,* is the abbreviation of *Reverend* as a clergy title and should be used in preference to *Rev.*

reversal is the noun corresponding to the verb *reverse; reversion* is the noun corresponding to the verb *revert.*

same. ● It is non-standard to use the phrase *same as* as a kind of conjunction meaning 'in the same way as, just as', e.g. *But I shouldn't be able to serve them personally, same as I do now* (L. P. Hartley).

sanction (verb) to give approval to, to authorize, e.g. *This council sanctioned the proclamation of a state of war with Germany from 11 p.m.* (A. J. P. Taylor).

● It does not mean 'impose sanctions on'.

sc. (short for Latin *scilicet = scire licet* one is permitted to know) introduces (1) a word to be supplied, e.g. *He asserted that he had met him* (*sc. the defendant*) *on that evening,* or (2) a word to be substituted for one already used, in order to render an expression intelligible, e.g. *'I wouldn't of* (*sc. have*) *done' was her answer.*

scabrous (1) (In Botany and Zoology) having a rough surface, scaly. (2) Risqué, salacious, indecent, e.g. *Silly and scabrous titters about Greek pederasty* (C. S. Lewis).

● *Scabrous* does not mean 'scathing, abusive, scurrilous'.

scarify, to loosen the surface of (soil, etc.); to make slight cuts in (skin, tissue) surgically.

● The verb *scarify* (pronounced scare-ify) 'scare, terrify', e.g. *To be on the brink of a great happiness is a scarifying feeling* (Noel Coward), is informal only.

scenario (1) An outline of the plot of a play. (2) A film script giving details of scenes, stage-directions, etc. (3) An outline of an imagined (usually future) sequence of events, e.g. *Several of the computer 'scenarios' include a catastrophic and sudden collapse of population* (*Observer*).

● Sense (3) is valid when a detailed narrative of events that might happen under certain conditions is denoted. The word should not be used as a loose synonym for *scene, situation, circumstance,* etc.

scilicet: see **sc.**

Scottish is now the usual adjective; *Scotch* is restricted to a fairly large number of fixed expressions, e.g. *Scotch broth,* *egg, whisky*; *Scots* is used mainly for the Scottish variety of English, in the names of regiments, and in *Scotsman, Scotswoman* (*Scotchman, -woman* are old-fashioned). To designate the inhabitants of Scotland, the plural noun *Scots* is normal.

seasonable, suitable for the time of year, occurring at the right time or season, opportune; *unseasonable* occurring at the wrong time or season, e.g. *You are apt to be pressed to drink a glass of vinegary port at an unseasonable hour* (Somerset Maugham).

● Do not confuse with *seasonal*, occurring at or associated with a particular season, e.g. *There is a certain seasonal tendency to think better of the Government .. in spring* (*The Economist*).

senior, superior are followed by *to*. They contain the idea of 'more' (advanced in years, exalted in position, etc.) and so cannot be constructed with *more .. than*, e.g. *There are several officers senior*, or *superior in rank, to him*, not *.. more senior*, or *more superior in rank, than him*.

sensibility, ability to feel, sensitiveness, delicacy of feeling, e.g. *The man's moving fingers .. showed no sign of acute sensibility* (Graham Greene).

● *Sensibility* is not the noun corresponding to *sensible* meaning 'having good sense'; i.e. it does not mean 'possession of good sense'.

sensual, gratifying to the body; indulging oneself with physical pleasures, showing that one does this, e.g. *His sensual eye took in her slim feminine figure* (Angus Wilson); *sensuous*, affecting or appealing to the senses (without the pejorative implications of *sensual*), e.g. *I got up and ran about the .. meadow in my bare feet. I remember the sensuous pleasure of it* (C. Day Lewis); *sensory*, of sensation or the senses, e.g. *When the external facts, which must terminate in sensory experience, are given, the emotion is immediately evoked* (T. S. Eliot).

serendipity, the making of pleasant discoveries by accident, or the knack or fact of doing this; the adjective (usually applied to a discovery, event, fact, etc.) is *serendipitous*.

● *Serendipitous* does not mean merely 'fortunate'.

sic (Latin for *thus*) is placed in brackets after a word that appears odd or erroneous to show that the word is quoted exactly as it stands in the original, e.g. *Daisy Ashford's novel* The Young Visiters (*sic*).

sick: see **ill**.

similar should be followed by *to*, not *as*. The following is non-standard: *Wolverton Seconds showed similar form as their seniors in their two home games.*

● **sit, stand.** The use of the past participle *sat, stood* with the verb *to be*, meaning *to be sitting, standing*, is non-standard, e.g. *No really, I'd be sat there falling asleep if I did come* (Kingsley Amis).

situation. A useful noun for expressing the sense 'position of affairs, combination of circumstances' which may validly be preceded by a defining adjective, e.g. *the financial, industrial, military, political, situation.*

● The substitution of an attributive noun for an adjective before *situation* should be carefully considered. It should not be used when the resulting phrase will be tautologous (e.g. *a crisis situation, people in work situations*: *crises* and *work* are themselves *situations*). The placing of an attributive phrase before *situation* is nearly always ugly and should be avoided, e.g. *The deep space situation, a balance-of-terror situation, a standing credit situation.*

● The combination of **ongoing** with *situation* is a cliché to be avoided.

sled is Amer. for *sledge*; *sleigh* is a sledge for passengers that is drawn by horses (or reindeer).

so used adverbially as a means of linking two clauses and meaning 'therefore' may be preceded by *and* but need not be; e.g. *Leopold Bloom is a modern Ulysses, so he has to encounter Sirens and a Cyclops* (Anthony Burgess); *I had received no word from Martha all day, so I was drawn back to the casino* (Graham Greene).

so-called (1) has long been used in the sense 'called by this term, but not entitled to it'; (2) is now often used quite neutrally, without implication of incorrectness, especially in Science.

sort of: see **kind of**.

specialty, except for its use in Law, is an equivalent of *speciality* restricted to North America.

spectate, to be a spectator, is informal only.

• *Watch* is usually an adequate substitute, e.g. in *A spectating, as opposed to a reading, audience* (*Listener*).

strata is the plural of *stratum*.

• It is incorrect to treat it as a singular noun, e.g. in *The movement has .. sunk to a wider and more anonymous strata.*

style. (1) Adjective + -*style* used to qualify a noun, e.g. *European-style clothing, contemporary-style dancing,* is acceptable.

(2) Adjective or noun + -*style,* forming an adverb, is somewhat informal, e.g. *A revolution, British-style* (A. J. P. Taylor).

substantial, actually existing; of real value; of solid material; having much property; in essentials; e.g. *substantial damages, progress; a substantial house, yeoman; substantial agreement.*

• It is not merely a synonym of *large.*

substantive (adjective) is used mainly in technical senses; e.g. *substantive rank,* in the services, is permanent, not acting or temporary.

substitute (verb) to put (someone or something) in place of another: constructed with *for*; e.g. *Democracy substitutes election by the incompetent many for appointment by the corrupt few* (G. B. Shaw).

• The sense 'replace (someone or something) *by* or *with* another' is incorrect, or at best highly informal, e.g. in *Having substituted her hat with a steel safety helmet, she went on a tour of the site* (better, *Having replaced her hat with ..* or *Having substituted a steel safety helmet for ..*).

such as: see **like.**

superior: see **senior.**

supposititious, hypothetical, conjectural, e.g. *We might take a small cottage .. Not that .. the atmosphere of our suppositious cottage could .. become .. unpleasant* (James Joyce); *supposititious,* fraudulently substituted (especially of a child displacing a real heir), e.g. *Russia .. is the* *supposititious child of necessity in the household of theory* (H. G. Wells).

synchronize (transitive), to cause to occur at the same time, e.g. *Everyday cordialities would be synchronized with gazes of rapt ardour* (Martin Amis).

● It is not a synonym for *combine* or *coordinate*.

than: see **different, other than, prefer, senior.**

thankfully: see **hopefully.**

the (article). When a name like *The Times* or *The Hague* is used attributively, *The* is dropped, e.g. *A* Times *correspondent, Last year's* Hague *conference.* If *the* precedes the name in such a construction, it belongs to the succeeding noun, not to the name, and is therefore not given a capital initial (or italics), e.g. *A report from the* Times *correspondent.*

the (adverb) prefixed to a comparative means 'thereby' or 'by so much', e.g. *What student is the better for mastering these futile distinctions?* This combination can enter into the further construction seen in *The more the merrier* (i.e. 'by how much more, by that much merrier'). It cannot enter into a construction with *than*: the tendency to insert it before *more* and *less* (putting *any the more, none the less* for *any more, no less*) should be resisted, e.g. in *The intellectual release had been no less* (not *none the less*) *marked than the physical.*

then may be used as an adjective preceding a noun as a neat alternative to *at that time* and similar phrases, e.g. *Hearing that they were on personal terms with the then Prime Minister* (Frederic Raphael).

● It should not be placed before the noun if it would sound equally well in its usual position, e.g. *Harold Macmillan was the then Prime Minister* could equally well be . . *was then the Prime Minister.* The same applies to an adverbial use of *then* before attributive adjectives, e.g. *The then existing constitution*: write *The constitution then existing.*

there- adverbs, e.g. *therein, thereon, thereof,* etc., belong mainly to very formal diction and should be avoided in ordinary writing (apart from certain idiomatic adverbs, e.g. *thereabouts, thereby, thereupon*); e.g. *We did not* *question this reasoning, and there lay our mistake* (Evelyn Waugh): a lesser writer might have written *therein*. But such adverbs can be employed for special effectiveness, e.g. *This idea brought him rocketing back to earth. But he stood thereupon like a giant* (Iris Murdoch).

through, up to and including, e.g. *Friday through Tuesday*, though useful, is Amer. only.

too followed by an adjective used attributively should be confined to poetry or special effects in prose, e.g. *Metropolis, that too-great city* (W. H. Auden); *A small too-pretty house* (Graham Greene).

● In normal prose it is a clumsy construction, e.g. *The crash came during a too-tight loop.*

tooth-comb and *fine tooth-comb*, arising from a misapprehension of *fine-tooth comb*, are now established expressions whose illogicality it is pedantic to object to.

tortuous, torturous. Do not confuse: *tortuous* means (1) twisting, e.g. *Through tortuous lanes where the overhanging boughs whipped the windscreen* (Evelyn Waugh); (2) devious, e.g. *Control had his reasons; they were usually so bloody tortuous it took you a week to work them out* (John le Carré). *Torturous* means 'involving torture, excruciating', e.g. *There is no difference between unbearable pain and torturous pleasure* (Edward Dahlberg).

transcendent, surpassing others (e.g. *Of transcendent importance*), (of God) above and distinct from the universe, e.g. *The theist claims that in asserting the existence of a transcendent god he is expressing a genuine proposition* (A. J. Ayer); *transcendental*, visionary, idealistic, beyond experience, etc., e.g. *Most of those who have been near death have also described some kind of mystical or transcendental experience* (*British Medical Journal*). (Other more technical senses of each word are ignored here.)

transpire (figuratively): (1) To leak out, come to be known, e.g. *What had transpired concerning that father was not so reassuring* (John Galsworthy). (2) To come about, take place, e.g. *What transpired between them is unknown* (David Cecil).

● Sense (2), probably arising from the misunderstanding of sentences like 'What had transpired during his absence he did not know', is chiefly informal. It is regarded by many people as unacceptable, especially if the idea of something emerging from ignorance is absent: it should therefore not be used in sentences like *A storm transpired.*

trillion: see **billion.**

triumphal, of or celebrating a triumph, e.g. *A triumphal arch*; *triumphant*, victorious, exultant.

try (verb) in writing normally followed by the *to*-infinitive: *try and* + bare infinitive is informal. This latter construction is uncommon in negative contexts (except in the imperative, e.g. *Don't try and pull the wool over my eyes*) and in the past tense.

turbid (1) muddy, thick; (2) confused, disordered, e.g. *In an access of despair had sought death in the turbid Seine* (W. Somerset Maugham).
Turgid (1) swollen; (2) (of language) inflated, pompous, e.g. *Some of them are turgid, swollen with that kind of intellectual bombast which never rises to gusto* (G. H. Vallins).

underlay (verb) (past *underlaid*) to lay something under (a thing), e.g. *Underlaid the tiles with felt*: a somewhat rare verb; *underlie* (past tense *underlay*, past participle *underlain*) to lie under; to be the basis of; to exist beneath the surface of, e.g. *The arrogance that underlay their cool good manners* (Doris Lessing).

unequivocal, not ambiguous, unmistakable, e.g. *His refusal . . was unequivocal. 'Not in a million years' was the expression he used* (P. G. Wodehouse); similarly *unequivocally* adverb, e.g. *In private conversation business men will unequivocally express disapproval of the course of events* (*The Times*).
• The forms *unequivocable, -ably*, sometimes seen, are erroneous.

unexceptionable, -al: see **exceptionable.**

unique: (1) Being the only one of its kind, e.g. *The fighting quality that gives war its unique power over the imagination* (G. B. Shaw): in this sense *unique* cannot be qualified by adverbs like *absolutely, most, quite, so, thoroughly*, etc. (2) Unusual, remarkable, singular, e.g. *A passionate human insight so unique in her experience that she felt it to be unique in human experience* (Muriel Spark).

- Sense (2) is regarded by many people as incorrect. Substitute one of the synonyms given above, or whatever other adjective is appropriate.

unlike (adverb) may govern a noun, noun phrase, or pronoun, just as *like* may, e.g. *A sarcasm unlike ordinary sarcasm* (V. S. Pritchett).

- It may not govern a clause with or without ellipsis of the verb, e.g. *He was unlike he had ever been*; *Unlike in countries of lesser economic importance.*

- **various** cannot be used as a pronoun followed by *of* (as, for example, *several* can), as (wrongly) in *The two ministers concerned . . have been paying private visits to various of the Commonwealth representatives.*

venal, able to be bribed, influenced by bribery; *venial*, pardonable.

vengeance: see **avenge.**

verbal (1) of or in words; (2) of a verb; (3) spoken rather than written.

- Some people reject sense (3) as illogical and prefer *oral*. However, *verbal* is the usual term in a number of idioms, such as *verbal communication, contract, evidence.*

verge (verb) in *verge on, upon,* to border on, e.g. *He told two or three stories verging on the improper* (John Galsworthy), is in origin a different word from *verge* in *verge to, towards* to incline towards, approach, e.g. *The London docks, where industrial disputes always verged towards violence* (A. J. P. Taylor). Both are acceptable.

vermin is usually treated as plural, e.g. *A lot of parasites, vermin who feed on God's love and charity* (Joyce Cary).

via (1) By way of (a place), e.g. *To London via Reading.* (2) By means of, through the agency of, e.g. *Other things can . . be taught . . via the air, via television, via teaching machines, and so on* (E. F. Schumacher); *They had sent a photo of Tina as a baby to the . . mother via a social worker* (*Independent*).

- Sense (2) is sometimes criticized, but is certainly acceptable in informal use.

waive to refrain from using or insisting on, to forgo or dispense with, e.g. *Only too willing to waive the formalities in return for services rendered* (P. G. Wodehouse).

• Do not confuse this with *wave*, chiefly in conjunction with *aside*, *away*, as (wrongly) in *But the Earl simply waived the subject away with his hand* (Trollope).

want, need (verbs) in the sense 'require' can be followed (1) by a gerund as object, e.g. *Your hair needs* or *wants cutting* or (2) by an object and a past participle as complement to the object (with the verb 'to be' omitted), e.g. *We want* or *need this changed.*

• The idiom *We want* or *need this changing* (perhaps a mixture of the two constructions, but having the sense of (2)) is informal only.

well is joined by a hyphen to a following participle when the combination is used attributively, e.g. *A well-worn argument*. Predicatively a hyphen is not necessary unless the combintion is to be distinguished in meaning from the two words written separately, e.g. *He is well-spoken* but *The words were well spoken.*

what ever, when ever, where ever: see **ever**.

whence meaning 'from where', does not need to be preceded by *from*.

who ever: see **ever**.

whoever, any one who, no matter who: use *whoever* for the objective case as well as the subjective, rather than *whomever*, which is rather stilted; e.g. *Whoever he painted now was transfigured into that image on the canvas* (Kathleen Jones).

• Beware of introducing the objective *whomever* incorrectly, as in *A black mark for whomever it was that ordered the verges to be shorn* (*Daily Telegraph*).

-wise (suffix) added to nouns (1) forming adverbs of manner, is very well established, but is now, except in fixed expressions like *clockwise*, rather literary or poetic, e.g. *The Saint wears tight yellow trousers . . and is silkily shaven Romanwise* (TLS); (2) forming viewpoint adverbs (meaning 'as regards —'), e.g. *I can eat only Cox's Orange Pippins, and am in mourning applewise from April to October* (Iris Murdoch).

• (2) is widely regarded as unacceptable in formal usage and should be restricted to informal contexts.

- Adverbs of type (2) are formed on nouns only, not on adjectives: hence sentences like *The ratepayers would have to shoulder an extra burden financial-wise* are incorrect (substitute . . *burden finance-wise* or *financial burden*).
- **without** = 'unless' is non-standard, e.g. *Without you have a bit of class already, your town gets no new theatre* (*Listener*).

  See also **hardly**.

womankind is better than *womenkind* (cf. *mankind*).

worth while is usually written as two words predicatively, but as one attributively, e.g. *He thought it worth while*, or *a worthwhile undertaking, to publish the method*.

write (to compose a letter) with indirect personal object, e.g. *I will write you about it*, is not acceptable British English (but is good Amer. English).

IV
GRAMMAR

Language is an instrument for communication. The language which can with the greatest ease make the finest and most numerous distinctions of meaning is the best.
(C. S. Lewis, *Studies in Words*)

THIS section deals with specific problems of grammar; it makes no attempt at a systematic exposition of English syntax.

It is notoriously difficult to find convenient labels for many of the topics on which guidance is needed. Wherever possible, the headings chosen for the entries are, or include, the words which actually cause grammatical problems (e.g. *as*, *may* or *might*). Some headings include the grammatical endings involved (e.g. *-ing*). But inevitably many entries have had to be given abstract labels (e.g. *double passive*, *subjunctive*). To compensate for this, a number of cross-references are included, by which the user can find a way to the required entry. The aim throughout is to tackle a particular problem immediately and to give a recommendation as soon as the problem has been identified. Explanations entailing wider grammatical principles are postponed or even omitted.

adverbial relative clauses

A relative clause, expressing time, manner, or place, can follow a noun governed by a preposition (*on the day* in the example below):

> *The town was shelled by heavy guns on the day* that we departed (Edmund Blunden)

It is possible for the relative clause to begin with the same preposition and *which*, e.g.

> *On the day* on which the books were opened *three hundred thousand pounds were subscribed* (Lord Macaulay)

But it is a perfectly acceptable idiom to use a relative clause introduced by *that* without repetition of the preposition, especially after the nouns *day, morning, night, time, year*, etc., *manner, sense, way* (see p. 226), *place*, e.g.

Envy in the consuming sense that certain persons display *the trait* (Anthony Powell)

It is, if anything, even more usual for *that* to be omitted:

He cannot have been more than thirty at the time we met him (Evelyn Waugh)
If he would take it in the sense she meant it (L. P. Hartley)
On the night he arrived in London, *he would get blind . . drunk* (W. Somerset Maugham)

adverbs without -ly

Most adverbs consist of an adjective + the ending *-ly*, e.g. *badly, differently*. For the changes in spelling that the addition of *-ly* may require, see p. 34. Normally the use of the ordinary adjective as an adverb, without *-ly*, is non-standard, e.g.

I was sent for special
The Americans speak different *from us*
They just put down their tools sudden *and cut and run*

There are, however, a number of words which are both adjective and adverb and cannot add the adverbial ending *-ly*, e.g.

alone	fast	low
early	further	much
enough	little	still
far	long	straight

Some other adjectives can be used as adverbs both with and without *-ly*. The two forms have different meanings, e.g.

deep	high	near
hard	late	

The forms without *-ly* are the adverbs more closely similar in meaning to the adjectives, as the following examples illustrate:

deep: *Still waters run deep*
He read deep into the night

hard: *They hit me hard in the chest*
      He lost his hard-earned money
      We will be hard put to it to be ready by
        Christmas
high: *It soared high above us*
      Don't fix your hopes too high
late: *I will stay up late to finish it*
      A drawing dated as late as 1960
near: *He won't come near me*
      As near as makes no difference
      Near-famine conditions

The forms with -*ly* have meanings more remote from those of the adjectives:

deeply is chiefly figurative, e.g. *Deeply in love*
hardly = 'scarcely', e.g. *He hardly earned his money*
highly is chiefly figurative, e.g. *Don't value possessions too highly*
lately = 'recently', e.g. *I have been very tired lately*
nearly = 'almost', e.g. *The conditions were nearly those of a famine*

● The forms with and without -*ly* are not interchangeable and should not be confused.

See also **-lily adverbs**.

article, omission of

To omit, or not to omit, *a* (*an*) and *the*?

Omission of the definite or indefinite article before a noun or noun phrase in apposition to a name is a journalistic device, e.g.

Clarissa, American business woman, comes to England (*Radio Times*)

Nansen, hero and humanitarian, moves among them (*The Times*)

It is more natural to write *an American business woman, the hero and humanitarian.*

Similarly, when the name is in apposition to the noun or noun phrase, and the article is omitted, the effect is of journalistic style, e.g.

NUM President Arthur Scargill
Best-selling novelist Barbara Cartland
Unemployed labourer William Smith

Preferably write: *The NUM President, The best-selling novelist, An unemployed labourer* (with a comma before and after the name which follows).

After *as* it is possible to omit *a* or *the*, e.g.

As manipulator of words, the author reminded me of X. Y.
The Soviet system could no longer be regarded as sole model for Communism everywhere

It is preferable not to omit these words, however, except where the noun or noun phrase following is treated as a kind of generic mass noun, e.g.

The vivid relation between himself, as man, and the sunflower, as sunflower (D. H. Lawrence)

as, case following

In the following sentences, formal usage requires the *subjective* case (*I, he, she, we, they*) because the pronoun would be the subject if a verb were supplied:

I am, my lord, as well deriv'd as he (Shakespeare) (in full, *as he is*)
Widmerpool . . might not have heard the motif so often as I (Anthony Powell) (in full, *as I had*)

Informal usage permits the objective case, e.g. *You are just as intelligent as* him.

Formal English uses the *objective* case (*me, him, her, us, them*) only when the pronoun would be the object if a verb were supplied:

I thought you preferred John to Mary, but I see that you like her just as much as him (which means . . *just as much as you like him*)

In real usage, sentences like this are rare and not very natural. It is more usual for the verb to be included in the sentence or for the thought to be expressed in a different construction.

as if, as though

For the tense following these see p. 120.

auxiliary verbs

There are sixteen auxiliary verbs in English, three primary auxiliaries (used in the compounding of ordinary verbs) and thirteen modal auxiliaries (used to express mood, and, to some extent, tense).

Primary: *be, do, have*

Modal:
can	*ought (to)*
could	*shall*
dare	*should*
may	*used (to)*
might	*will*
must	*would*
need	

Auxiliaries differ from regular verbs in the following ways:

(1) They can precede the negative *not*, instead of taking the *do not* construction, e.g. *I cannot* but *I do not know*;

(2) They can precede the subject in questions, instead of taking the *do* construction, e.g. *Can you hear* but *Do you know*.

The modal auxiliaries additionally differ from regular verbs in the following ways:

(3) They are invariable: they do not add -*s* for the third person present, and do not form a separate past tense in -*ed*; e.g. *He must go*; *he must have seen it*.

(4) They are usually followed by the bare infinitive; e.g. *He will go, he can go* (not 'to go' as with other verbs, e.g. *He intends to go, he is able to go*).

Use of auxiliaries

In reported speech and some other *that*-clauses *can, may, shall,* and *will* become *could, might, should,* and *would* for the past tense:

He said that he could *do it straight away*
I told you that I might *arrive unexpectedly*

> *I knew that when I grew up I* should *be a writer* (George Orwell)
> *Did you think that the money you brought* would *be enough?*

In clauses of this kind, the auxiliaries *must, need,* and *ought,* which normally refer to the present tense, can also be used for the past tense:

> *I had meant to return direct to Paris, but this business . .*
> *meant that I* must *go to London* (Evelyn Waugh)
> *To go to church had made her feel she* need *not reproach*
> *herself for impropriety* (V. S. Pritchett)
> *She was quite aware that she* ought *not to quarter Freddy*
> *there* (G. B. Shaw)

Note that this use is restricted to *that*-clauses. It would not be permissible to use *must, need,* or *ought* for the past tense in a main sentence; for example, one could not say: *Yesterday I must go.*

Further discussion of the use of auxiliary verbs will be found under **can and may, dare, have, need, ought, shall and will, should and would, used to, were or was.**

but, case following

The personal pronoun following *but* (= 'except') should be in the case it would have if a verb were supplied.

> *I walked through the mud of the main street. Who but I?*
> (Kipling)
> *Our uneducated brethren who have, under God, no defence but*
> us (C. S. Lewis)

In the Kipling example *I* is used because it would be the subject of *I walked.* In the Lewis example *us* is used because it would be the object of *who have* (i.e. 'who have *us* as their only defence').

can and *may*

The auxiliary verbs *can* and *may* are both used to express permission, but *may* is more formal and polite:

> *May I offer you a spot? . . I can recommend the Scotch*

Can I have a word with you? . . In private. Get lost, young Jane (both examples from **P. G.** Wodehouse)

collective nouns

Collective nouns are singular words that denote many individuals, e.g.

army	enemy	orchestra
audience	family	parliament
board (of	fleet	party (i.e.
directors,	flock	body of
examiners, etc.)	gang	persons)
choir	government	squad
clan	group	staff
class	herd	swarm
club	jury	team
committee	majority	tribe
company	militia	union (i.e.
congregation	nation	trade
crowd	navy	union)

the aristocracy	the laity
the bourgeoisie	the nobility
the Cabinet	the proletariat
the clergy	the public
the élite	the upper class
the gentry	the working class
the intelligentsia	

It is normal for collective nouns, being singular, to be followed by singular verbs and pronouns (*is, has, consists,* and *it* in the examples below):

The Government is *determined to beat inflation, as* it has *promised*
Their family is *huge:* it consists *of five boys and three girls*
The bourgeoisie is *despised for not being proletarian* (C. S. Lewis)

The singular verb and pronouns are preferable unless the collective is clearly and unmistakably used to refer to separate individuals rather than to a united body, e.g.

The Cabinet has made its decision, but
*The Cabinet are resuming their places around the table at
Number 10 Downing Street*
The Brigade of Guards is on parade, but
The Brigade of Guards are above average height

The singular should always be used if the collective noun is qualified by a singular word like *this, that, every,* etc.:

This family is divided
Every team has its chance to win

If a relative clause follows, it must be *which* + singular verb or *who* + plural verb, e.g.

It was not the intelligentsia, but just intellectual society,
which was *gathered there* (John Galsworthy)
The working party who had been preparing the decorations
(Evelyn Waugh)

• Do not mix singular and plural, as (wrongly) in

*The congregation were now dispersing. It tended to form
knots and groups*

comparison of adjectives and adverbs
Whether to use *-er, -est* or *more, most.*

The two ways of forming the comparative and superlative of adjectives and adverbs are:

(*a*) The addition of the comparative and superlative suffixes *-er* and *-est* (for spelling changes that may be required see p. 24). Monosyllabic adjectives and adverbs almost always require these suffixes, e.g. *big* (*bigger, biggest*), *soon* (*sooner, soonest*), and so normally do many adjectives of two syllables, e.g. *narrow* (*narrower, narrowest*), *silly* (*sillier, silliest*).

(b) The placing of the comparative and superlative adverbs *more* and *most* before the adjective or adverb. These are used with adjectives of three syllables or more (e.g. *difficult, memorable*), participles (e.g. *bored, boring*), many adjectives of two syllables (e.g. *afraid, widespread*), adjectives containing any suffix except *-ly* or *-y* (e.g. *awful, childish, harmless, static*), and adverbs ending in *-ly* (e.g. *highly, slowly*).

Adjectives with two syllables vary between the use of the suffixes and of the adverbs.

There are many which never take the suffixes, e.g.

antique	*constant*	*steadfast*
bizarre	*devoid*	*upright*

There are also many adjectives which are acceptable with either, e.g.

clever	*handsome*	*polite*
common	*honest*	*solemn*
cruel	*pleasant*	*tranquil*
extreme		

The choice is largely a matter of style. Some examples will show how much variation there is in literary English.

With the suffixes:

An attitude of completest *indifference* (George Orwell).
The extremest *forms of anti-Semitism* (Lewis Namier)
You are so much honester *than I am* (Iris Murdoch)
Now the stupidest *of us knows* (C. S. Lewis)

With the adverbs:

I was a bit more clever *than the other lads* (Angus Wilson)
The most solemn *of Jane Austen's beaux* (Iris Murdoch)
Those periods which we think most tranquil (C. S. Lewis)

With a mixture in one sentence:

Only the dirtiest *and* most tipsy *of cooks* (Evelyn Waugh)

Even monosyllabic adjectives can sometimes take *more* and *most*:

(i) When two adjectives are compared with each other, e.g.
    More dead than alive
    More good than bad
    More well-known than popular
    This is standard (we would not say 'better than bad' or 'better-known than popular').

(ii) Occasionally, for stylistic reasons, e.g.
    I am the more bad because I realize where my badness lies (L. P. Hartley)

>*This was never more true than at present*

(iii) Thoughtlessly, e.g.

>*Facts that should be more well known*
>*The most well-dressed man in town*
>*Wimbledon will be yet more hot tomorrow*

● These are not acceptable: substitute *better known*, *best-dressed*, and *hotter*.

comparisons

Comparisons between two persons or things require the comparative (*-er* or *more*) in constructions like the following:

>*I cannot tell which of the two is the* elder (not *eldest*)
>*Which of the two is more likely to win?* (not *most likely*)
>*Of the two teams, they are the* slower-moving (not *slowest-moving*)

The superlative is of course used when more than two are compared.

compound subject

A subject consisting of two singular nouns or noun phrases joined by *and* normally takes a plural verb:

>*My son and daughter* are *twins*
>*Where to go and what to see* were *my main concern*

If one half of the subject is the pronoun *I* or the pronoun *you*, and the other is a noun or third person singular pronoun (*he*, *she*, or *it*), or if the subject is *you and I*, the verb must be plural.

>*He and I* are *good friends*
>Do *my sister and I look alike?*
>*You and your mother* have *similar talents*
>*You and I* are *hardly acquainted*

But if the phrase containing *and* represents a single item, it is followed by a singular verb:

>*The bread and butter* was *scattered on the floor* (W. Somerset Maugham)
>*The Stars and Stripes* was *flying at half-mast*

And similarly if the two parts of the subject refer to a single individual:

> *His friend and legal adviser, John Smith,* was *present*
> *My son and heir* is *safe!*

See also **neither . . nor** and **subjects joined by** (**either . .**) **or.**

coordination

The linking of two main clauses by a comma alone, without any connecting conjunction, is sometimes said to be incorrect. It is on occasion used by good writers, however, as the examples show. It should be regarded as acceptable if used sparingly.

> *The peasants possess no harrows, they merely plough the soil several times over* (George Orwell)
> *Charles carried a mackintosh over his arm, he was stooping a little* (C. P. Snow)
> *I began to wonder when the Presidential Candidate would appear, he must have had a heavy handicap* (Graham Greene)

correlative conjunctions

The correct placing of the pairs

> *both . . and*   *neither . . nor*
> *either . . or*   *not only . . but* (*also*)

A sentence containing any of these pairs must be so constructed that the part of the sentence introduced by the first member of the pair (*both, either, neither,* or *not only*) is parallel in structure to the part introduced by the second member (*and, or, neither,* or *but* (*also*)).

The rule is that if one covers up the two correlative words and all the words between them, the remaining sentence should still be grammatical.

The following sentence from a typical newspaper advertisement illustrates this rule:

> *Candidates will have a background in* either commercial electronics or *university research*

Because *in* precedes *either*, it need not be repeated after *or*. If it had followed *either*, it would have had to be inserted after *or* as well. But the sentence as given is the most economical structure possible.

In the following example the preposition *of* comes after *either* and must therefore be repeated after *or*:

> *He did not wish to pay the price* either *of peace* or *of war* (George Orwell)

This conforms with the rule stated above, while perhaps sounding better than *of either peace or war* (which would be as good grammatically).

It is, however, not uncommon for the conjunctions to be placed so that the two halves are not quite parallel, even in the writings of careful authors, e.g.

> *I end* neither *with a death* nor *a marriage* (W. Somerset Maugham)
> *People who* either *hadn't been asked to pay* or *who were simply not troubling themselves* (V. S. Pritchett)

In the first example, *with* belongs to both halves and needs to be repeated after *nor*. In the second, *who* precedes *either* and strictly need not be repeated after *or*.

These sentences exhibit fairly trivial slips that rarely cause difficulty (except in the case of *not only*: see p. 153).

● A more serious error is the placing of the first correlative conjunction too late, so that words belonging only to the first half are carried over to the second, resulting in a grammatical muddle, e.g.

> *The other Exocet was either destroyed or blew up* (BBC News)

This should be carefully avoided.

dangling participles: see **participles**

dare

The verb *to dare* can be used either like a regular verb or like an auxiliary verb. Either use is entirely acceptable (though in a particular context, one may sound better than the other).

As an ordinary verb it forms such parts as:

I dare	*I do not dare*	*do I dare?*
he dares	*he does not dare*	*does he dare?*
he dared	*he did not dare*	*did he dare?*
I would dare	*I have dared*	

As an auxiliary verb it forms:

I dare not	*he dared not*
he dare not	*dared he?*
dare he?	

The first use, as an ordinary verb, is always acceptably followed by the *to*-infinitive, e.g.

I knew what I would find if I dared to look (Jean Rhys)
James did not dare to carry out the sentence (Frederic Raphael)

But many of the forms can also be followed by the bare infinitive. This sometimes sounds more natural:

None of which they'd dare go near (John Osborne)
Don't you dare put that light on (Shelagh Delaney)

The second use, as an auxiliary verb, normally requires the bare infinitive, e.g.

How dare he keep secrets from me? (G. B. Shaw)
He dared not risk being carried past his destination (C. S. Forester)

double passive

The construction whereby a passive infinitive directly follows a passive verb is correctly used in the following:

The prisoners were ordered to be shot
This music is intended to be played on a piano

The rule is that if the subject and the first passive verb can be changed into the active, leaving the passive infinitive intact, the sentence is correctly formed. The examples above (if a subject, say *he*, is supplied) can be changed back to:

He ordered the prisoners *to be shot*
He intends this music *to be played on a piano*

In other words, the passive infinitive is not part of the passive construction. An active infinitive could equally well be part of the sentence, e.g.

The prisoners were ordered to march

The examples below violate the rule because both the passive verb and the passive infinitive have to be made active in order to form a grammatical sentence:

The order was attempted to be carried out
(active: *He attempted to carry out the order*)
A new definition was sought to be inserted in the Bill
(active: *He sought to insert a new definition in the Bill*)

This 'double passive' construction is unacceptable.

The passive of the verbs *to fear* and *to say* can be followed by either an active or a passive infinitive, e.g.

 (i) *The passengers are feared* to have drowned
 The escaped prisoner is said to be very dangerous

or

(ii) *The passengers are feared* to have been killed
 The escaped prisoner is said to have been sighted

The construction at (ii) is not the double passive and is entirely acceptable. Both constructions are sometimes found with other verbs of saying (e.g. *to allege, to assert, to imply*):

Morris demonstrated that Mr Elton was obviously implied to be impotent (David Lodge)

either .. or: see **subjects joined by (*either ..*) or.**

either (pronoun)

Either is a singular pronoun and should be followed by a singular verb:

Enormous evils, either of which depends on *somebody else's voice* (Louis MacNeice)

In the following example the plural verb accords with the notional meaning 'both parents were not'.

It was improbable that either of our parents were *giving
thought to the matter* (J. I. M. Stewart)

This is quite common in informal usage, but should not be
carried over into formal prose.

gender of indefinite expressions

It is often uncertain what personal pronoun should be used to
refer back to the indefinite pronouns and adjectives in the
following list:

any	*no* (+ noun)
anybody	*nobody*
anyone	*none*
each	*no one*
every (+ noun)	*some* (+ noun)
everybody	*somebody*
everyone	*someone*

and also to refer back to (*a*) *person*, used indefinitely, or a male
and female noun linked by (*either* . .) *or* or *neither* . . *nor*, e.g.

Has anybody eaten his/their *lunch yet?*
A person who is upset may vent his/their *feelings on* his/their
family
Neither John nor Mary has a home of their/his or her *own*

If it is known that the individuals referred to are all of the
same sex, there is no difficulty; use *he* or *she* as appropriate:

Everyone in the women's movement has had her *own experience of sexual discrimination*

If, however, the sex of those referred to is unknown or
deliberately left indefinite, or if the reference is to a mixed
group, the difficulty arises that English has no singular pronoun to denote common gender.

The grammarians' recommendation, during the past two centuries, has been that *he* (*him*, *himself*, *his*) should be used.
Many good writers follow this:

Everyone talked at the top of his *voice* (W. Somerset
Maugham)

> *Everyone took his place in a half-circle about the fire* (Malcolm Bradbury)
> (The context of each shows that the company was mixed.)
> *The long street in which nobody knows* his *neighbour* (G. B. Shaw)
> *Each person should give as* he *has decided for* himself (*Revised English Bible*)

Popular usage, however, has for at least five centuries favoured the plural pronoun *they* (*them, themselves, their*).

This is entirely acceptable in informal speech:

> *Nobody would ever marry if* they *thought it over* (G. B. Shaw)
> *It's the sort of thing any of us would dislike, wouldn't* they? (C. P. Snow)

It is by no means uncommon in more formal contexts:

> *Nobody stopped to stare, everyone had* themselves *to think about* (Susan Hill)
> *His own family were occupied, each with* their *particular guests* (Evelyn Waugh)
> *Delavacquerie allowed everyone to examine the proofs as long as* they *wished* (Anthony Powell)

(The context of the second and third example shows that the company was mixed.)

Many people regard it as inequitable that the masculine pronoun *he* should be used to include both sexes, and therefore prefer to use *they*. This use of *they* as a singular pronoun is increasingly common but, it should be noted, is not yet universally acceptable as standard.

One can avoid the difficulty from time to time by writing *he or she*, as many writers do on awkward occasions:

> *Nobody has room in* his or her *life for more than one such relationship at a time* (G. B. Shaw)

But this grows unwieldy with repetition:

> *If I ever wished to disconcert anyone, all I had to do was to ask* him (or her) *how many friends* he/she *had* (Frederic Raphael)

There are some contexts in which neither *he* nor *they* will seem objectionable. In others, where *he* and *they* both seem inappropriate for the reasons given, it may be necessary simply to recast the sentence.

● The form *themself* is sometimes used as a singular pronoun in contexts where *themselves* is normally used: *I think somebody should immediately address themself to this problem* (Alice Thomas Ellis)

This use is not generally regarded as acceptable in Standard English.

group possessive

The group possessive is the construction by which the ending -'s of the possessive case can be added to the last word of a noun phrase, which is regarded as a single unit, e.g.

The king of Spain's daughter
John and Mary's baby
Somebody else's umbrella
A quarter of an hour's drive

Expressions like these are natural and acceptable.

Informal language, however, permits the extension of the construction to long and complicated phrases:

The people in the house opposite's geraniums
The woman I told you about on the phone yesterday's name is Thompson
The man who called last week's umbrella is still in the hall

In these, the connection between the words forming the group possessive is much looser and more complicated than in the earlier examples. The effect is often somewhat ludicrous.

● Expressions of this sort should not be used in serious prose. Substitute:

The geraniums of the people in the house opposite
The name of the woman I told you about on the phone yesterday is Thompson
The umbrella of the man who called last week is still in the hall

have

1. The verb *to have*, in some of its uses, can form its interrogative and negative either with or without the verb *to do*, e.g. *Do you have/have you?, You don't have/you haven't.*

In sentences like those below, *have* is a verb of event, meaning 'experience'. The interrogative (in the first example) and the negative (in the second example) are always formed in the regular way, using the verb *do*:

> Do you *ever* have *nightmares?*
> *We* did not have *an easy time getting here*

In the next pair of sentences, *have* is a verb of state, meaning 'possess'. When used in this sense, the interrogative (in the first example) and negative (in the second example) can be formed in the manner of an auxiliary verb, without the verb *do*:

> *What* have you *in common with the child of five whose photograph your mother keeps?* (George Orwell)
> *The truth was that he* hadn't *the answer* (Joyce Cary)

In more informal language, the verb *got* is added, e.g. *What have you got, He hadn't got the answer.* This is not usually suitable for formal usage and is not usual in American English.

It was formerly usual to distinguish the sense 'experience' from the sense 'possess' by using the *do*-formation for the first and the auxiliary formation for the second (but only in the present tense). Hence *I don't have indigestion* (as a rule) was kept distinct from *I haven't (got) indigestion* (at the moment). The use of the *do*-construction when the meaning was 'possess' was an Americanism, but it is now generally acceptable.

● However, the use of *do* as a substitute verb for *have*, common informally, is not acceptable in formal prose:

> *I had stronger feelings than she* did (substitute *than she had*)
> *Some have money, some* don't (substitute *some haven't*)

2. *Have* is often wrongly inserted after *I'd* in sentences like:

> *If I'd* have *known she'd be here I don't suppose I'd have come* (Character in play by John Osborne)

This is common, and hardly noticed, in speech, but should not occur in formal writing. The correct construction is:

If I'd known *she'd be here* . .

Without the contraction, the clause would read: *If I had known*, with the past perfect, which is the correct form in this kind of *if*-clause. The only expression that the mistaken *If I'd have known* could stand for is *If I would have known*, which is impossible in this context.

he who, she who

He who and *she who* are correctly used when *he* and *she* are the subject of the main clause, and *who* is the subject of the relative clause:

He who *hesitates is lost*
She who *was a star in the old play may find herself a super in the new* (C. S. Lewis)

In these examples *he* and *she* are the subjects of *is lost* and *may find* respectively; *who* is the subject of *hesitates* and *was*.

He who and *she who* should not be treated as invariable. They should change to *him who* and *her who* if the personal pronouns are not the subject of the main clause:

The distinction between the man who gives with conviction and him (not *he*) *who is simply buying a title*

Similarly *who* must become *whom* — if it is not the subject of the relative clause:

I sought him whom *my soul loveth* (Authorized Version)

See also **who and whom (interrogative and relative pronouns)**.

-ics, nouns in

Nouns ending in *-ics* denoting subjects or disciplines are sometimes treated as singular and sometimes as plural. Examples are:

apologetics	*dynamics*	*ethics*
classics (as a study)	*economics*	*genetics*
	electronics	*linguistics*

mathematics	optics	politics
mechanics	phonetics	statistics
metaphysics	physics	tactics
obstetrics		

When used strictly as the name of a discipline they are treated as singular:

> *Psychometrics* is *unable to investigate the nature of intel-ligence* (*Guardian*)
> *The quest for a hermeneutics* (TLS)

So also when the complement is singular:

> *Pure mathematics* is *a non-inductive .. science* (Gilbert Ryle).

When used more loosely, to denote a manifestation of qualities, often accompanied by a possessive, they are treated as plural:

> *His politics* were *a mixture of fear, greed and envy* (Joyce Cary)
> *I don't understand the mathematics of it, which* are *complicated*
> *The acoustics in this hall* are *dreadful*
> *Their tactics* were *cowardly*

So also when they denote a set of activities or pattern of behaviour, as commonly with words like

acrobatics	dramatics	heroics
athletics	gymnastics	hysterics
callisthenics		

e.g. *The mental gymnastics required to believe this* are *beyond me*

These words usually retain a plural verb even with a singular complement:

> *The acrobatics* are *just the social side* (Tom Stoppard)

infinitive, present or perfect

The perfect infinitive is correctly used when it refers to a state or action earlier in time than that referred to by the verb on which it depends, e.g.

> *If it were real life and not a play, that is the part it would be*
> *best* to have acted (C. S. Lewis)
> *Someone seems* to have been making *a beast of himself here*
> (Evelyn Waugh)

In the above examples, the infinitives *to have acted* and *to have been making* relate to actions earlier in time than the verbs *would be best* and *seems*.

Only if the first verb relates to the past and the infinitive relates to a state or action prior to that should a perfect infinitive follow a past or perfect verb, forming a sort of 'double past', e.g.

> *When discussing sales with him yesterday, I* should have
> liked to have seen *the figures beforehand*

In this example *I should have liked* denotes the speaker's feelings during the discussion and *to have seen* denotes an action imagined as occurring before the discussion.

If the state or action denoted by the infinitive is thought of as occurring at the same time as the verb on which it depends, then the present infinitive should be used:

> *She* would have liked to see *what was on the television*
> (Kingsley Amis)

The 'double past' is often accidentally used in this kind of sentence informally, e.g.

> *I* should have liked to have gone *to the party*

A literary example is:

> *Mr. McGregor threw down the sack on the stone floor in a*
> *way that would have been extremely painful to the Flopsy*
> *Bunnies, if they* had happened to have been *inside it*
> (Beatrix Potter)

This should be avoided.

-*ing* (gerund and participle)

1. The -*ing* form of a verb can in some contexts be used in either of two constructions:

(i) as a gerund (verbal noun) with a noun or pronoun in the possessive standing before it, e.g.

> *In the event of* Randall's not going (Iris Murdoch)
> *She did not like* his being *High Church* (L. P. Hartley)

(ii) as a participle with a noun in its ordinary form or a pronoun in the objective case standing before it, e.g.

> *What further need would there have been to speak of another* priest arising? (*New English Bible*)
> *Dixon did not like* him doing *that* (Kingsley Amis)

The option of using either arises only when the word before the -*ing* form is a proper or personal noun (e.g. *John, father, teacher*) or a personal pronoun.

It is sometimes said that the construction with the possessive (as in (i) above) is obligatory. This rule, in its strict form, should be disregarded. Instead one should, in formal usage, try to employ the possessive construction wherever it is possible and natural:

> *To whom, without* its being *ordered, the waiter immediately brought a plate of eggs and bacon* (Evelyn Waugh)
> *The danger of* Joyce's turning *them into epigrams* (Anthony Burgess)

But it is certainly not wrong to use the non-possessive construction if it sounds more natural, as in the *New English Bible* quotation above. Moreover, there is sometimes a nuance of meaning. *She did not like his being High Church* suggests that she did not like the fact that he was High Church, and need not imply personal antipathy, whereas *Dixon did not like him doing that* suggests an element of repugnance to the person as well as to his action.

When using most non-personal nouns (e.g. *luggage, meaning, permission*), groups of nouns (e.g. *father and mother, surface area*), non-personal pronouns (e.g. *anything, something*), and groups of pronouns (e.g. *some of them*), there is no choice of construction: the possessive would not sound idiomatic at all. Examples are:

> *Travellers in Italy could depend on their* luggage *not being stolen* (G. B. Shaw)

Altogether removing possibility of its meaning *being driven home* (Anthony Powell)

His lines were cited .. without his permission having *been asked* (*The Times*)

Due to her father and mother being *married* (Compton Mackenzie)

Owing to its surface area being *so large relative to its weight* (George Orwell)

The air of something *unusual* having *happened* (Arthur Conan Doyle)

He had no objection to some of them listening (Arnold Bennett)

When the word preceding the -*ing* form is a regular plural noun ending in -*s*, there is no spoken distinction between the possessive and the non-possessive form. It is unnecessary to write an apostrophe:

If she knew about her daughters *attending the party* (Anthony Powell)

2. There is also variation between the gerundial and the participial uses of the -*ing* form after nouns like *difficulty*, *point*, *trouble*, and *use*.

Formal English requires the gerundial use, the gerund being introduced by *in* (or *of* after *use*):

There was .. no difficulty in finding *parking space* (David Lodge)

There doesn't seem much point in trying *to explain everything* (John Osborne)

Informal usage permits the placing of the -*ing* form immediately after the noun, forming a participial construction, e.g.

He had some trouble convincing *Theo Craven* (Lynne Reid Banks)

The chairman had difficulty concealing *his irritation*

● This is not acceptable in formal usage.

I or *me*, *we* or *us*, etc.

There is often confusion about which case of a personal pronoun to use when the pronoun stands alone or follows the verb *to be*.

1. When the personal pronoun stands alone, as when it forms the answer to a question, formal usage requires it to have the case it would have if the verb were supplied:

Who killed Cock Robin?—I (in full, *I killed him*)
Which of you did he approach?—Me (in full, *he approached me*)

Informal usage permits the objective case in both kinds of sentence, but this is not acceptable in formal style. However, the subjective case often sounds stilted. It is then best to avoid the problem by providing the substitute verb *do*, or, if the preceding sentence contains an auxiliary, by repeating the auxiliary, e.g.

Who likes cooking?—I do
Who can cook?—I can

2. When a personal pronoun follows *it is, it was, it may be, it could have been*, etc., it should have the subjective case in formal usage:

Nobody could suspect that it was *she* (Agatha Christie)
We are given no clue as to what it must have felt like to be he (C. S. Lewis)

Informal usage favours the objective case:

I thought it might have been him *at the door*
Don't tell me it's them *again!*

● This is not acceptable in formal usage.

When *who* or *whom* follows, the subjective case is obligatory in formal usage and quite usual informally:

It was she *who winched up that infernal machine* (Joseph Conrad)
My task was stenographic—it was they *who spoke* (R. L. Stevenson)

The informal use of the objective case often sounds substandard:

It was her *who would get the blood off* (Character in work by Patrick White)

(For agreement between the personal pronoun antecedent and the verb in *It is I who* etc., see **I who, you who, etc.**)

In constructions which have the form *I am* + noun or noun phrase + *who,* the verb following *who* agrees with the noun (the antecedent of *who*) and is therefore always in the third person (singular or plural):

> *I am the sort of person who* likes *peace and quiet*
> *You are the fourth of my colleagues who's told me that* (Character in work by Angus Wilson) (*'s* = *has,* agreeing with *the fourth*)

I should or *I would*

There is often uncertainty whether to use *should* or *would* in the first person singular and plural before verbs such as *like* or *think* and before the adverbs *rather* and *sooner*.

1. *Should* is correct before verbs of liking, e.g. *be glad, be inclined, care, like,* and *prefer*:

> *Would you like a beer?*—I should prefer *a cup of coffee, if you don't mind*
> *The very occasions on which* we should *most like to write a slashing review* (C. S. Lewis)

2. *Should* is correct in tentative statements of opinion, with verbs such as *guess, imagine, say,* and *think*:

> I should imagine *that you are right*
> I should say *so*
> I shouldn't *have* thought *it was difficult*

3. *Would* is correct before the adverbs *rather* and *sooner*, e.g.

> I would *truly* rather *be in the middle of this than sitting in that church in a tight collar* (Susan Hill)

Would is always correct with persons other than the first person singular and plural.

See also *should* and *would*.

I who, you who, etc.

The verb following a personal pronoun (*I, you, he,* etc.) + *who* should agree with the pronoun and should not be in the third person singular unless the third person singular pronoun precedes *who*:

I, who have *no savings to speak of, had to pay for the work*

This remains so even if the personal pronoun is in the objective case:

They made me, who have *no savings at all, pay for the work* (not *who has*)

When *it is* (*it was*, etc.) precedes *I who*, etc., the same rule applies: the verb agrees with the personal pronoun:

It's I who have *done it*
It could have been we who were *mistaken*

Informal usage sometimes permits the third person to be used (especially when the verb *to be* follows *who*):

You who's *supposed to be so practical!*
Is it me who's *supposed to be keeping an eye on you?* (Character in work by David Lodge)

● This is not acceptable in formal usage.

like

The objective case of personal pronouns is always used after *like* and *unlike*:

Unlike my mother and me, *my sister is fair-haired* (not *Unlike my mother and I*)

-lily adverbs

When the adverbial suffix *-ly* is added to an adjective which already ends in *-ly*, the resulting adverb tends to have an unpleasant jingling sound, e.g. *friendlily*.

Adverbs of this kind are divided into three groups, here arranged in order of decreasing acceptability:

(i) Those formed from adjectives in which the final *-ly* is an integral part of the word, not a suffix, e.g. *holily, jollily, sillily*. These are the least objectionable and are quite often used.

(ii) Those of three syllables formed from adjectives in which the final -*ly* is itself a suffix, e.g. *friendlily, ghastlily, lovelily, statelily, uglily*. These are occasionally found.

(iii) Those of four (or more) syllables formed from adjectives in which the final -*ly* is itself a suffix, e.g. *heavenlily, scholarlily*. Such words have been recorded but are deservedly rare.

The adverbs of groups (ii) and (iii) should be avoided if possible, by using the adjective with a noun like *manner* or *way*, e.g. *In a scholarly manner*.

A few adjectives in -*ly* can be used adverbially to qualify other adjectives, e.g. *beastly cold, ghastly pale*.

may or *might*

There is sometimes confusion about whether to use *may* or *might* with the perfect infinitive referring to a past event, e.g. *He may have done* or *He might have done*.

1. If uncertainty about the action or state denoted by the perfect infinitive remains, i.e. at the time of speaking or writing the truth of the event is still unknown, then either *may* or *might* is acceptable:

> *As they all wore so many different clothes of identically the same kind . ., there* may *have been several more or several less* (Evelyn Waugh)
> *For all we knew we were both bastards, although of course there* might *have been a ceremony* (Graham Greene)

2. If there is no longer uncertainty about the event, or the matter was never put to the test, and therefore the event did not in fact occur, use *might*:

> *If that had come ten days ago my whole life* might *have been different* (Evelyn Waugh)
> *It* might *have been better if the Russian Revolution had never taken place* (*The Times*)

● It is a common error to use *may* instead of *might* in these circumstances:

> *If he* (President Galtieri) *had not invaded, then eventually the islands* may *have fallen into their lap*

I am grateful for his intervention without which they may
have remained in the refugee camp indefinitely
Schoenberg may *never have gone atonal but for the break-up
of his marriage*

(*Might* should be substituted for *may* in each of the above
sentences.)

measurement, nouns of

There is some uncertainty about when to use the singular
form, and when the plural, of nouns of measurement.

1. All nouns of measurement remain in the singular form
when compounded with a numeral and used attributively
before another noun:

    A six-foot *wall*   *A five*-pound *note*
    A three-mile *walk*   *A 1,000*-megaton *bomb*

This rule includes metric measurements:

    A ten-hectare *field*   *A three*-litre *bottle*

2. *Foot* remains in the singular form in expressions such as:

    I am six foot   *She is five foot two*

But *feet* is used where an adjective, or the word *inches*,
follows, e.g.

    I am six feet tall   *She is five feet three inches* .
    It is ten feet long

Stone and *hundredweight* remain in the singular form in plural
expressions, e.g.

    I weigh eleven stone   *Three hundredweight of coal*

Metric measurements always take the plural form when not
used attributively:

    This measures three metres by two metres
    Two kilos of sugar

Informally, some other nouns of measurement are used in the
singular form in plural expressions, e.g.

    That will be two pound fifty, please

● This is non-standard.

See also **quantity, nouns of**.

need

The verb *to need*, when followed by an infinitive, can be used either like an ordinary verb or like an auxiliary.

1. *Need* is used like an ordinary verb, and followed by the *to*-infinitive, in the present tense when the sentence is neither negative nor interrogative, in the past tense always, and in all compound tenses (e.g. the future and perfect):

> *One needs friends, one* needs to *be a friend* (Susan Hill)
> *One* did not need to *be a clairvoyant to see that war . . was coming* (George Orwell)

2. *Need* can be used like an auxiliary verb in the present tense in negative and interrogative sentences. This means that:

(*a*) The third person singular does not add -*s*:

> *I do not think one* need *look farther than this* (George Orwell)

(*b*) For the negative, *need not* replaces *does not need*:

> *One* need not *be an advocate of censorship to recommend the cautious use of poison* (Frederic Raphael)

(*c*) For the interrogative, *need I* (*you*, etc.) replaces *do I need*:

> Need I *add that she is my bitterest enemy?* (G. B. Shaw)

(*d*) The bare infinitive follows instead of the *to*-infinitive:

> *Company that keeps them smaller than they need* be (*Bookseller*) (This is negative in sense, for it implies *They need not be as small as this*)

This auxiliary verb use is optional, not obligatory. The regular constructions are equally correct:

> *I do not think one needs to look . .*
> *One does not need to be . .*
> *Do I need to add . .*
> *Smaller than they need to be . .*

One should choose whichever sounds more natural. It is important, however, to avoid mixing the two kinds of construction, as in the two following examples:

One needs not be *told that* (etc.)
What proved vexing, it needs be *said, was* (etc.)

neither . . nor

Two singular subjects linked by *neither . . nor* can be constructed with either a singular or a plural verb. Strictly and logically a singular verb is required (since both subjects are not thought of as governing the verb at the same time). When the two subjects are straightforward third person pronouns or nouns, it is best to follow this rule:

Neither he nor his wife has *arrived*
There is *neither a book nor a picture in the house*

Informal usage permits the plural and it has been common in the writings of good authors for a long time:

Neither painting nor fighting feed *men* (Ruskin)

When one of the two subjects is plural and the other singular, the verb should be made plural and the plural subject placed nearer to it:

Neither the teacher nor the pupils understand *the problem*

When one of the subjects is *I* or *you* and the other is a third person pronoun or a noun, or when one is *I* and the other *you*, the verb can be made to agree with the subject that is nearer to it. However, this does not always sound natural, e.g.

Neither my son nor I am *good at figures*

One can recast the sentence, but this can spoil the effect intended by using *neither . . nor*. It is often better to use the plural, as good writers do:

Neither Isabel nor I are *timid people* (H. G. Wells)
Neither Emily nor I were *quite prepared for the title* (Anthony Powell)

This is not illogical if *neither . . nor* is regarded as the negative of *both . . and*.

neither (pronoun)

Neither is a singular pronoun and strictly requires a singular verb:

> *Neither of us* likes *to be told what to do*

Informal usage permits not only a plural verb, but also a plural complement:

> *Neither of us* like *tennis*
> *Neither of us* are good players

Although this is widely regarded as incorrect, it has been an established construction for three or four centuries:

> *Thersites' body is as good as Ajax', When neither* are *alive* (Shakespeare)
> *Neither* were great inventors (Dryden)

It is recommended that one should follow the rule requiring the singular unless it leads to awkwardness, as when neither *he* nor *she* is appropriate:

> *John and Mary will have to walk. Neither of them* have *brought* their *cars*

none (pronoun)

The pronoun *none* can be followed either by singular verb and singular pronouns, or by plural ones. Either is acceptable, although the plural tends to be more common.

Singular: *None of them* was *allowed to forget for a moment* (Anthony Powell)

Plural: *None of the fountains ever* play (Evelyn Waugh)
None of the authors expected their *books to become best-sellers* (Cyril Connolly)

ought

Oughtn't or *didn't ought?*

The standard form of the negative of *ought* is *ought not* or *oughtn't*:

> *A look from Claudia showed me I* ought not *to have begun it* (V. S. Pritchett)

Being an auxiliary verb, *ought* can precede *not* and does not require the verb *do*. It is non-standard to form the negative with *do* (*didn't ought*):

> *I hope that none here will say I did anything I* didn't ought. *For I only done my duty* (Character in work by Michael Innes)

When the negative is used to reinforce a question in a short extra clause or 'question tag', the negative should be formed according to the rule above:

> *You ought to be pleased,* oughtn't you? (not *didn't you?*)

In the same way *do* should not be used as a substitute verb for *ought*, e.g.

> *Ought he to go?—Yes, he* ought (not *he did*)
> *You ought not to be pleased,* ought *you?* (not *did you?*)

participles

A participle used in place of a verb in a subordinate clause must have an explicit subject to qualify. If no subject precedes the participle within the clause, the participle is understood to qualify the subject of the main sentence. In the following sentences the participles *running* and *propped* qualify the subjects *she* and *we*:

> *Running to catch a bus, she just missed it* (Anthony Powell)
> *We both lay there,* propped *on our elbows* (Lynne Reid Banks)

It is a frequent error to begin a sentence with a participial clause, with no subject expressed, and to continue it with a main clause in which the subject is not the word which the participle qualifies:

> Driving *along the road,* the church *appeared on our left*
> (*We*, not *the church*, is the subject of *driving*)

> Having been relieved *of his portfolio in 1976,* the scheme *was left to his successor at the Ministry to complete*
> (*He*, or a proper name, is the subject of *having been relieved*)

Participles that appear to be attached to the wrong subject are sometimes known as dangling (or unattached or hanging) participles.

In sentences like these one must either recast the main clause so that its subject is the same as that of the subordinate clause, or recast the subordinate clause using a finite verb:

> *Driving along the road*, we saw *the church* appear *on our left*
> As we were *driving along the road, the church appeared on our left*

Sometimes a subject can be supplied in the participial clause, the clause remaining otherwise unchanged. This is usually only possible when the participle is *being* or *having*:

> Jones *having been relieved of his portfolio in 1976, the scheme was left to his successor at the Ministry to complete*

If the subject supplied in accordance with this rule is a personal pronoun it should be in the subjective case:

> He being *such a liar, no one will believe him when he tells the truth*
> *He rose bearing her,* she *still weeping, and the others formed a procession behind* (Iris Murdoch)

When the participial clause includes a subject it should not be separated by a comma from the participle:

> Bernadette being her niece, *she feels responsible for the girl's moral welfare* (David Lodge) (Not: *Bernadette, being her niece, she . .*)

This is in contrast with the punctuation of the other kind of participial clause, in which the participle qualifies the subject of the main sentence. If this type of participial clause follows the subject, it is either marked off by a pair of commas or not marked off at all:

> *The man*, hoping to escape, *jumped on to a bus*
> *A man* carrying a parcel *jumped on to the bus*

The rule that a participle must have an explicit subject does not apply to participial clauses whose subject is indefinite (= 'one' or 'people'). In these the clause is used adverbially, standing apart from and commenting on the content of the sentence:

> Judging *from his appearance, he has had a night out*

> Taking *everything into consideration, you were lucky to escape*
> Roughly speaking, *this is how it went*

The participial clauses here are equivalent to 'If one judges . .', 'If one takes . .', 'If one speaks . .' Expressions of this kind are entirely acceptable.

See also **unattached phrases**

preposition at end

It is a natural feature of the English language that many sentences and clauses end with a preposition, and has been since the earliest times. The alleged rule that forbids the placing of the preposition at the end of a clause or sentence should be disregarded.

The preposition *cannot* be moved to an earlier place in many sentences, e.g.

> *What did you do that* for?
> *What a mess this room is* in!
> *The bed had not been slept* in
> *She was good to look* at *and easy to talk* to (W. Somerset Maugham)

There are other kinds of construction which, generally speaking, allow a choice between placing the preposition at the end or placing it earlier—principally relative clauses, in which the preposition can stand before the relative pronoun if it is not placed finally. The choice is very often a matter of style. The preposition has been placed before the relative pronoun in:

> *The present is the only time* in which *any duty can be done* (C. S. Lewis)
> *The . . veteran* for whom *nothing has been real since the Big Push* (David Lodge)

But it stands at or near the end in:

> *Harold's Philistine outlook, which she had acquiesced* in *for ten years* (L. P. Hartley)
> *The sort of attentive memory . . that I should have become accustomed* to (C. P. Snow)

But notice that some prepositions cannot come at the end:

An annual sum, in return for *which she agreed to give me house room* (William Trevor)
During *which week will the festival be held?*

It would be unnatural to write *Which she agreed to give me house room in* return for, and *Which week will the festival be held* during?

Conversely, some relative clauses will not allow the preposition to stand before the relative pronoun:

The opposition (that) I ran up against was fierce
A sort of world apart which one can quite easily go through life without ever hearing about (George Orwell)

These cannot be changed to:

The opposition against which I ran up . .
A sort of world apart without ever hearing about *which . .*

One should be guided by what sounds natural. There is no need to alter the position of the preposition merely in deference to the alleged rule.

quantity, nouns of

The numerals *hundred, thousand, million, billion, trillion,* and the words *dozen* and *score* are sometimes used in the singular and sometimes in the plural.

1. They always have the singular form if they are qualified by a preceding word, whether it is singular (e.g. *a, one*) or plural (e.g. *many, several, two, three,* etc.), and whether or not they are used attributively before a noun or with nothing following:

A hundred days
Three hundred will be enough
I will take two dozen
Two dozen eggs

● The use of the plural form after a plural qualifier and when nothing follows is incorrect:

The population is now three millions (correctly *three million*)

Although they have the singular form, they always take plural verbs, even after the indefinite article:

> *There* were *about a dozen of them approaching* (Anthony Powell)
> *There* were *a score of them at a table apart* (J. I. M. Stewart)

2. They take the plural form when they denote indefinite quantities. Usually they are followed by *of* or stand alone:

> *Are there any errors?—Yes, hundreds*
> *He has dozens of friends*
> *Many thousands of people are homeless*

reflexive pronouns

The reflexive pronouns are normally used to refer back to the subject of the clause or sentence in which they occur, e.g.

> I *congratulated* myself *on outwitting everyone else*
> *Can't* you *do anything for* yourself?

Sometimes it is permissible to use a reflexive pronoun to refer to someone who is not the subject. Very often the person referred to may be the subject of a preceding or following clause, e.g.

> It *was their success, both with* myself *and others, that confirmed* me *in what has since been my career* (Evelyn Waugh)
> You *have the feeling that all their adventures have happened to* yourself (George Orwell)
> *He was furious with the woman, with a rancorous anger that surprised* himself (Joyce Cary)

In each of the above, there is a nearby *me, you,* or *he* to which the reflexive refers, but to have written *me, you,* and *him* respectively in these sentences would not have been grammatically incorrect.

A reflexive pronoun is often used after such words as

as	*but for*	*like*
as for	*except*	*than*
but	*except for*	

e.g. *For those who*, like himself, *felt it indelicate to raise an umbrella in the presence of death* (Iris Murdoch)

It can be a very useful way to avoid the difficult choice between *I, he, she*, etc. (which often sounds stilted) and *me, him, her*, etc. (which are grammatically incorrect) after the words *as, but*, and *than*, e.g.

Up to the nineteenth century Protestants were just as convinced as ourselves *of the importance of right beliefs if you were going to attain heaven* (Ronald Knox)
None of them was more surprised than myself *that I'd spoken* (Lynne Reid Banks)

Here *than I* would be strictly correct, while *than me* would be informal.

Naturally a reflexive pronoun cannot be used in the ways outlined above if confusion would result. One would not write:

John was as surprised as himself *that he had been appointed*

but would substitute the person's name, or *he himself was*, for *himself*, or recast the sentence.

relative clauses

A relative clause is a clause introduced by a relative pronoun and used to qualify a preceding noun or pronoun (called its antecedent), e.g. *The visitor* (antecedent) *whom* (relative pronoun) *you were expecting* (remainder of relative clause) *has arrived*; *He* who hesitates *is lost*.

Exceptionally, there are nominal relative clauses in which the antecedent and relative pronoun are combined in one *wh*-pronoun, e.g. What you need *is a drink*: see **what (relative pronoun)**.

Relative clauses can be either restrictive or non-restrictive. A restrictive relative clause serves to restrict the reference of the antecedent, e.g. *A suitcase* which has lost its handle *is useless*. Here the antecedent *suitcase* is defined or restricted by the clause.

A non-restrictive relative clause is used not to narrow the reference of the antecedent, but to add further information, e.g. *He carried the suitcase*, which had lost its handle, *on one shoulder*. Here the suitcase is already identified, and the relative clause adds explanatory information.

Notice that no commas are used to mark off a restrictive relative clause from the rest of the sentence, but when, as above, a non-restrictive relative clause comes in the middle of the sentence, it is marked off by a comma at each end.

There are two kinds of relative pronouns:

(i) The *wh*-type: *who, whom, whose, which*, and, in nominal relative clauses only, *what*.

(ii) The pronoun *that* (which can be omitted in some circumstances: see *that* **(relative pronoun), omission of**).

When one relative clause is followed by another, the second relative pronoun

    (*a*) may or may not be preceded by a conjunction; and
    (*b*) may or may not be omitted.

(*a*) A conjunction is not required if the second relative clause qualifies an antecedent which is a word inside the first relative clause:

> *I found a firm* which *had a large quantity of components* for
> which *they had no use*

Here *for which . . use* qualifies *components* which is part of the relative clause qualifying *firm*. *And* or *but* should not be inserted before *for which*.

But if the two clauses are parallel, both qualifying the same antecedent, a conjunction is required:

> *Help me with these shelves which I have to take home* but
> *which will not fit in my car*

(*b*) The second relative pronoun can be omitted if (i) it qualifies the same antecedent as the first, and (ii) it plays the same part in its clause as the first (i.e. subject or object):

> *George,* who *takes infinite pains and* (who) *never cuts cor-
> ners, is our most dependable worker*

Here the second *who* qualifies the same antecedent (*George*) as the first *who*, and, like it, is the subject of its clause. It can therefore be omitted.

But if the second relative pronoun plays a different part in its clause, it cannot be omitted:

> *George,* whom *everybody likes but* who *rarely goes to a party, is shy*

Here the first relative pronoun, *whom*, is the object, the second, *who*, is the subject, in their clauses. The second relative pronoun must be kept. This rule applies even if the two pronouns have the same form; it is the function that counts:

> *Like a child spelling out the letters of a word* which *he cannot read and* which *if he could would have no meaning* (Jean Rhys)

The second *which* cannot be omitted.

See also **preposition at end,** *that* **(relative pronoun), omission of,** *what* **(relative pronoun),** *which* **or** *that* **(relative pronouns),** *who* **and** *whom* **(interrogative and relative pronouns),** *who* **or** *which* **(relative pronouns),** *whose* **or** *of which* **in relative clauses,** *who/whom* **or** *that* **(relative pronouns).**

shall and *will*

> *'The horror of that moment', the King went on, 'I shall never, never forget!' 'You will, though,' the Queen said, 'if you don't make a memorandum of it.'* (Lewis Carroll)

There is considerable confusion about when to use *shall* and *will*. Put simply, the traditional rule in standard British English is:

1. In the first person, singular and plural.

(*a*) *I shall, we shall* express the simple future, e.g.
> *I am not a manual worker and please God I never* shall *be one* (George Orwell)
> *In the following pages we* shall *see good words . . losing their edge* (C. S. Lewis)

(*b*) *I will, we will* express intention or determination on the part of the speaker (especially a promise made by him or her), e.g.

> *I* will *take you to see her tomorrow morning* (P. G. Wodehouse)
>
> *I* will *no longer accept responsibility for the fruitless loss of life* (Susan Hill)
>
> *'I don't think we* will *ask Mr. Fraser's opinion', she said coldly* (V. S. Pritchett)

2. For the second and third persons, singular and plural, the rule is exactly the converse.

(*a*) *You, he, she, it*, or *they will* express the simple future, e.g.
> Will *it disturb you if I keep the lamp on for a bit?* (Susan Hill)
>
> *Seraphina* will *last much longer than a car. She'll probably last longer than you* will (Graham Greene)

(*b*) *You, he, she, it*, or *they shall* express intention or determination on the part of the speaker or someone other than the actual subject of the verb, especially a promise made by the speaker to or about the subject, e.g.
> *In future you* shall *have as many taxis as you want* (G. B. Shaw)
>
> *One day you* shall *know my full story* (Evelyn Waugh)
>
> Shall *the common man be pushed back into the mud, or* shall *he not?* (George Orwell)

The two uses of *will*, and one of those of *shall*, are well illustrated by:

> *'I* will *follow you to the ends of the earth,' replied Susan, passionately. 'It* will *not be necessary,' said George. 'I am only going down to the coal-cellar. I* shall *spend the next half-hour or so there.'* (P. G. Wodehouse)

In informal usage *I will* and *we will* are quite often used for the simple future, e.g.

> *I* will *be a different person when I live in England* (Character in work by Jean Rhys)

More often the distinction is covered up by the contracted form *'ll*, e.g.

> *I don't quite know when* I'll *get the time to write again* (Susan Hill)

● The use of *will* for *shall* in the first person, though common, is not regarded as fully acceptable in formal usage.

should and *would*

When used for (*a*) the future in the past or (*b*) the conditional,

> *should* goes with *I* and *we*
> *would* goes with *you, he, she, it,* and *they*

(*a*) The future in the past.

First person:

> *I had supposed these to be the last* . . I should *ever set eyes on* (Anthony Powell)
> *Julia and I, who had left* . . , *thinking* we should *not return* (Evelyn Waugh)

The person's imagined statement or thought at the time was:

> *These are the last* I shall *ever set eyes on*
> We shall *not return*

with *shall*, not *will* (see **shall** and **will**).

Second and third persons:

> *I told you that* you would *find Russian difficult to learn*
> *He was there. Later,* he would *not be there* (Susan Hill)

The person's statement or thought at the time was

> You will *find Russian difficult to learn*
> He will *not be there*

(*b*) The conditional.

First person:

> I should *view with the strongest disapproval any proposal to abolish manhood suffrage* (C. S. Lewis)
> *If I had* . . *had my way with you,* I should *never have known what you are* (Joseph Conrad)

Second and third persons:

> *If you took 3 ft off the average car,* you would *have another six million feet of road space* (*The Times*)
> *Isobel* would *almost certainly have gone in any case* (Anthony Powell)

In informal usage, *I would* and *we would* are very common in both kinds of sentence:

> *I wondered whether* I would *have to wear a black suit*
> I would *have been content, I would never have repeated it*
> (Both examples from Graham Greene)

The use of *would* with the first person is understandable, because *should* (in all persons) has a number of uses which can clash with the conditional and the future in the past; sometimes the context does not make it clear, for example, whether *I should do* means 'it would be the case that I did' or 'I ought to do', e.g.

> *I wondered whether, when I was cross-examined,* I should *admit that I knew the defendant*

● This use of *I would* and *we would* is not, however, regarded as fully acceptable in formal language.

See also **I should or I would**.

singular or plural

1. When subject and complement are different in number (i.e. one is singular, the other plural), the verb normally agrees with the subject, e.g.

(Plural subject)

> *Ships* are *his chief interest*
> *Their wages* were *a mere pittance*
> *Liqueur chocolates* are *our speciality*

The Biblical *The wages of sin* is *death* reflects an obsolete idiom by which *wages* took a singular verb.

(Singular subject)

> *The ruling passion of his life* was *social relationships*
> *What we need* is *customers*
> *Our speciality* is *liqueur chocolates*

2. A plural word or phrase used as a name, title, or quotation counts as singular, e.g.

> Sons and Lovers has *always been one of Lawrence's most popular novels*

Native Americans is *now the preferred term for the original inhabitants of America*

3. A singular phrase that happens to end with a plural word should nevertheless be followed by a singular verb, e.g.

Everyone except the French wants (not *want*) *Britain to join*
One in six has (not *have*) *this problem*

4. A problem often arises when such words as *average, maximum, minumum*, and *total* are used in constructions of the type shown below:

An average of 27,000 quotations has (or *have*) *been sent in each year*
A maximum of nine people is (or *are*) *allowed to travel in the lift*
A total of 335 British cases of AIDS has (or *have*) *been reported*

Strictly speaking the verb should, as with (3) above, agree with the singular noun, but in practice it is often made to agree with the nearest (and in the above examples, plural) noun. This does in fact often seem more natural.

5. If the subject of a relative clause is the same as the antecedent, the verb in the relative clause agrees in number with the antecedent, e.g.

I *thought it was just some* female *who* was *coming out to boss things* (Agatha Christie)
It is the children *who* are *the first consideration* (E. M. Forster)

If the relative clause follows *one of the* + a plural noun it may qualify either *one* or the noun, i.e. either *one* or the noun may be the antecedent. If *one* is the antecedent the verb should be singular, e.g.

One of the most dependable of the older girls, who was *made responsible* (Flora Thompson)

If the plural noun is the antecedent the verb should be plural, e.g.

He is one of the few businessmen who like *journalists* (i.e. 'one of the few journalist-liking businessmen')
Lord Reith—one of the few twentieth-century Britons who have *been willing to cast themselves as the community's superego* (*Listener*)

- The singular is often used by mistake, e.g. in

The theory of black holes . . may perhaps be considered as one of the aspects of general-relativistic physics which is *better understood* (*Nature*)

Where the sense must be 'one of the better-understood aspects'.

In the following

Lysine is one of the amino acids that is *an essential component of protein in human nutrition*

it is not clear whether lysine is one of several amino acids that are essential components, or (more probably) the only one of the amino acids that is an essential component.

See also **collective nouns, compound subject, -ics, nouns in, quantity, nouns of, -s plural or singular,** *what* **(relative pronoun).**

split infinitive

The split infinitive is the name given to the separation of *to* from the infinitive by means of an adverb (or sometimes an adverbial phrase), e.g. *He used* to continually refer *to the subject.* In this the adverb *continually* splits the infinitive *to refer* into two parts.

It is often said that an infinitive should never be split. This is an artificial rule that can produce unnecessarily contorted sentences. Rather, it is recommended that a split infinitive should be avoided by placing the adverb before or after the infinitive, unless this leads to clumsiness or ambiguity. If it does, one should either allow the split infinitive to stand, or recast the sentence.

1. Good writers usually avoid splitting the infinitive by placing the adverb before the infinitive:

I am not able, and I do not want, completely to abandon *the world-view that I acquired in childhood* (George Orwell)
One meets people who have learned actually to prefer *the tinned fruit to the fresh* (C. S. Lewis)
He did not want positively to suggest *that she was dominant* (Iris Murdoch)

On the other hand, it is quite natural in speech, and permissible in writing, to say:

> *What could it be like* to actually *live in France?*
> To really let *the fact that these mothers were mothers sink in*
>   (Both examples from Kingsley Amis)
> *Only one thing stops me from jumping up and screaming . . ,*
>   *it is* to deliberately think *myself back into that hot light*
>   (Doris Lessing)

2. Avoidance of ambiguity.

When an adverb closely qualifies the infinitive verb it may
often be better to split the infinitive than to move the adverb
to another position. The following example is ambiguous in
writing, though in speech stress on certain words would make
the meaning clear:

> *It fails completely to carry conviction*

Either it means 'It totally fails . .', in which case *completely*
should precede *fails*, or it means 'It fails to carry complete
conviction', in which case that should be written, or the
infinitive should be split.

3. Avoidance of clumsiness.

> *It took more than an excited elderly man . . socially to
>   discompose him . .* (Anthony Powell)

In this example *socially* belongs closely with *discompose*: it is
not 'to discompose in a social way' but 'to cause social
discomposure' or 'to destroy social composure'. There are
quite a number of adverb + verb collocations of this kind.
When they occur in the infinitive, it may be better either to
split the infinitive or to recast the sentence than to separate
the adverb from the verb.

4. Unavoidable split infinitive.

There are certain adverbial constructions which must immediately precede the verb and therefore split the infinitive, e.g.
more than:

> *Enough new ships are delivered* to more than make up *for the
>   old ones being retired*

And a writer may have sound stylistic reasons for allowing a
parenthetic expression to split an infinitive:

> *It would be an act of gratuitous folly* to, as he had put it to
> Mildred, make *trouble for himself at this stage* (Iris
> Murdoch)

-s plural or singular

Some nouns, though they appear to have the plural ending -*s*,
are treated as singulars, taking singular verbs and pronouns
referring back to them.

1.   *news*
2. Diseases:

diabetes	*rabies*
measles	*rickets*
mumps	*shingles*

Measles and *rickets* can also be treated as ordinary plural
nouns. *Diabetes* and *rabies* do not contain the plural ending
-*s* and are treated as ordinary singular nouns.

3. Games:

billiards	*dominoes*	*ninepins*
bowls	*draughts*	*skittles*
darts	*fives*	*tiddlywinks*

4. Countries:

the Bahamas	*the Philippines*
the Netherlands	*the United States*

These are treated as singular when considered as a unit, which
they commonly are in a political context, or when the complement is singular, e.g.

> *The Philippines* is *a predominantly agricultural country*
> *The United States* has *withdrawn its ambassador*

The Bahamas and *the Philippines* are also the geographical
names of the groups of islands which the two nations comprise, and in this use can be treated as plurals, e.g.

> *The Bahamas* were *settled by British subjects*

Flanders and *Wales* are always singular. So are the city names
Athens, Brussels, Naples, etc.

See also *-ics*, **nouns in.**

subjects joined by (*either* . .) *or*

When two singular subjects (either may be a noun, a pronoun,
or a noun phrase) are joined by *or* or *either* . . *or*, the strict
rule is that they require a singular verb and singular pronouns, since *or* (or *either* . . *or*) indicates that only one of them
is the logical subject:

> *Either Peter or John* has *had* his *breakfast already*
> *A traffic warden or a policeman* is *always on the watch in this
> street*

However, 'at all times there has been a tendency to use the
plural with two or more singular subjects when their mutual
exclusion is not emphasized' (*OED*), e.g.

> *On which rage or wantonness vented* themselves (George
> Eliot)

When one of the subjects joined by *or* is plural, it is best to
put the verb in the plural, and place the plural subject nearer
to the verb:

> *Either the child or the parents* are *to blame*

When one subject is *I, we,* or *you,* and the other is a noun or a
third person pronoun, or when the subjects are *you* and *I,* the
verb is usually made to agree with the nearer of the two subjects:

> *Either he or I* am *going to win*
> *Either he or you* have *got to give in*
> *Either you or your teacher* has *made a mistake*

This form of expression very often sounds awkward, especially when the sentence is a question:

> Am *I or he going to win?*
> Is *he or we wrong?*

It is usually best to recast the sentence by adding another verb:

> *Am I going to win, or is he?*

Is he wrong, or are we?
Either he has got to give in, or you have

subjunctive

The subjunctive mood is indicated by the basic form of the verb, a form that is identical with the bare infinitive and imperative. In most verbs, e.g. *do, give,* and *make,* this will be the same as all the persons of the present tense except the third, which ends in *-s.* In the verb *to be,* however, the subjunctive is *be,* whereas the present tense is *am, are,* or *is.* For the past subjunctive of *to be* (*were*) see **were or was.**

The subjunctive is normal, and quite familiar, in a number of fixed expressions which cause no problems:

Be *that as it may*	*Heaven* help *us*
Come *what may*	*Long* live *the Queen*
God bless *you*	*So* be *it*
God save *the Queen*	Suffice *it to say that*
Heaven forbid	

There are two other uses of the subjunctive that may cause difficulty, but they are entirely optional. This means that the ordinary user of English need not be troubled by the use of the subjunctive, apart from the past subjunctive *were.*

1. In *that*-clauses after words expressing command, hope, intention, wish, etc. Typical introducing words are

be adamant that	*propose that*
demand that	*proposal that*
insist that	*resolve that*
be insistent that	*suggest that*
insistence that	*suggestion that*

Typical examples are:

He had been insisting that they keep *the night of the twenty-second free* (C. P. Snow)
Joseph was insistent that his wishes be *carried out* (W. Somerset Maugham)
Chance . . dictated that I be *reading Sterne when . . Bellow's new novel arrived* (Frederic Raphael)

Your suggestion that I fly *out* (David Lodge)

Until recently this use of the subjunctive was restricted to very formal language, where it is still usual, e.g.

> *The Lord Chancellor put the motion that the House* go *into Committee*

It is, however, a usual American idiom, and is now quite acceptable in British English, but there is no necessity to use the subjunctive in such contexts. *Should* or *may* with the infinitive, or (especially in informal use) the ordinary indicative, depending on the context, will do equally well:

> *Your demand that he* should *pay the money back surprised him*
> *I insist that the boy* goes *to school this minute*

● Beware of constructions in which the sense hangs on a fine distinction between subjunctive and indicative, e.g.

> *The most important thing for Argentina is that Britain* recognize *her sovereignty over the Falklands*

The implication is that Britain does not recognize it. A small slip that changed *recognize* to *recognizes* would drastically reverse this implication. The use of *should recognize* would render the sense quite unmistakable.

2. In certain concessive and conditional clauses, i.e. clauses introduced by *though* and *if*, the subjunctive can be used to express reserve on the part of the speaker about an action or state which is contemplated or in prospect, e.g.

> *Though he* be *the devil himself he shall do as I say*
> *Though your sins* be *as scarlet, they shall be as white as snow* (Authorized Version)
> *The University is a place where a poor man, if he* be *virtuous, may live a life of dignity and simplicity* (A. C. Benson)
> *Things .. are also together in space, and together in time, even if they* be *not contemporaneous* (A. N. Whitehead)

This is now restricted to very formal literary language. It should not be used in ordinary prose, where sometimes the indicative and sometimes an auxiliary such as *may* are entirely acceptable, e.g.

Though he may be *an expert, he should listen to advice*
If this is the case, then I am in error

than, case following

A personal pronoun following *than* should have the case that it would have if a verb were supplied. In the following sentences, the subjective case is required because the personal pronoun would be the subject:

You are two stone heavier than I (G. B. Shaw) (in full, *than I am*)
We pay more rent than they (in full, *than they do*)

In the sentence below, the objective case is used, because the pronoun would be the object if there were a verb:

Jones treated his wife badly. I think that he liked his dog better than her (in full, *than he liked her*)

Informal English permits the objective case to be used, no matter what case the pronoun would have if a verb were supplied:

You do it very well. Much better than me

This is unacceptable in formal usage. The preferred alternative, with the subjective, often sounds stilted. When this is so, it can be avoided by supplying the verb:

We pay more rent than they do

The interrogative and relative pronoun *whom* is always used after *than*, rather than the subjective form *who*:

Professor Smith, than whom *there is scarcely anyone better qualified to judge, believes it to be pre-Roman*

that (conjunction), omission of

1. The conjunction *that* introducing a noun clause and used after verbs of saying, thinking, knowing, etc., can often be omitted in informal usage:

I told him (that) *he was wrong*
He knew (that) *I was right*
Are you sure (that) *this is the place?*

Generally speaking, the omission of *that* confers a familiar tone on the sentence, and is not usually appropriate in formal prose.

That should never be omitted if other parts of the sentence (apart from the indirect object) intervene:

I told him, as I have told everyone, that *he was wrong*
Are you sure in your own mind that *this is the place?*

The omission of *that* makes it difficult, in written prose, to follow the sense.

2. When the conjunction *that* is part of the correlative pairs of conjunctions *so .. that* and *such .. that*, or of the compound conjunctions *so that*, *now that*, it can be omitted in informal usage.

● It should not be omitted in formal style:

He walked so fast (or *at such a speed*) that *I could not keep up*
I'll move my car so that *you can park in the drive*
Are you lonely now that *your children have left home?*

that (relative pronoun), omission of

The relative pronoun *that* can often be omitted. Its omission is much more usual informally than formally.

In formal contexts the omission of *that* is best limited to relative clauses which are fairly short and which stand next to their antecedents:

The best thing (that) *you can do is make up for lost time*
None of the cars (that) *I saw had been damaged*
Nothing (that) *I could say made any difference*

That cannot be omitted when it is the subject of the relative clause, e.g.

Nothing that *occurred to me made any difference*
None of the cars that *were under cover had been damaged*

See also **adverbial relative clauses** and *way*, **relative clause following**.

there is or *there are*

In a sentence introduced by *there* + part of the verb *to be*, the latter agrees in number with the noun, noun phrase, or pronoun which follows:

> *There* was *a great deal to be said for this scheme*
> *There* are *many advantages in doing it this way*

In very informal language *there is* or *there was* is often heard before a plural:

> *There's two coloured-glass windows in the chapel* (Character in work by Evelyn Waugh)

● This is non-standard.

to

The preposition *to* can stand at the end of a clause or sentence as a substitute for an omitted *to*-infinitive, e.g.

> *He had tried not to think about Emma . . , but of course it was impossible not* to (Iris Murdoch)
> *I gave him her message, as I should have been obliged* to *if she had died* (C. P. Snow)

This is standard usage.

unattached participles: see **participles**.

unattached phrases

An adjectival or adverbial phrase, introducing a sentence, must qualify the subject of the sentence, e.g.

> While not entirely in agreement with the plan, *he had no serious objections to it*
> After two days on a life-raft, *the survivors were rescued by helicopter*

The introductory phrases *While . . plan* and *After . . life-raft* qualify the subjects *he* and *the survivors* respectively.

It is a common error to begin a sentence with a phrase of this kind, anticipating a suitable subject, and then to continue the sentence with a quite different subject, e.g.

After six hours without food in a plane on the perimeter at
Heathrow, *the flight was cancelled*

The phrase *After . . Heathrow* anticipates a subject like *the
passengers*: a flight cannot spend six hours without food in a
plane on an airport perimeter. Such a sentence should either
have a new beginning, e.g.

After the passengers had spent *six hours . .*

or a new main clause, e.g.

After six hours . . Heathrow, the passengers learnt that *the
flight had been cancelled*

unlike: see **like**.

used to

The negative and interrogative of *used to* can be formed in two
ways:

(i) Negative: *used not to*
    Interrogative: *used X to?*

This formation follows the pattern of the other auxiliary verbs.
Examples:

Used you to beat your mother? (G. B. Shaw)
You used not to have a moustache, used you? (Evelyn Waugh)

(ii) Negative: *did not use to, didn't use to*
    Interrogative: *did X use to?*

This formation is the same as that used with regular verbs.
Examples:

She didn't use to find sex revolting (John Braine)
Did you use to be a flirt? (Eleanor Farjeon)

□ Either form is acceptable. On the whole *used you to*, *used he
to*, etc. tend to sound rather stilted and over-formal.

● The correct spellings of the negative forms are:

usedn't to and *didn't use to*

not:

usen't to and *didn't used to*

way, relative clause following

(*The*) *way* can be followed by a relative clause with or without *that*. There is no need for the relative clause to contain the preposition *in*:

> *It may have been* the way he smiled (Jean Rhys)
> *Whatever* way they happened *would be an ugly way* (Iris Murdoch)
> *She couldn't give a dinner party* the way the young lad's mother could (William Trevor)

were or was

There is often confusion about whether to use the past subjunctive *were* or the past indicative *was* in the first or third person singular.

Formal usage requires *were*

1. In conditional sentences where the condition is 'unreal', e.g.

> *It would probably be more marked if the subject* were *more dangerous* (George Orwell)
> (The condition is unreal because 'the subject' is not very 'dangerous' in fact)
> *If anyone* were *to try to save me, I would refuse* (Jean Rhys)
> (The condition is regarded as unlikely)

2. Following *as if* and *as though*, e.g.

> *He wore it with an air of melancholy, as though it* were *court mourning* (Evelyn Waugh)
> (For a permissible exception see p. 120)

3. In *that*-clauses after *to wish*, e.g.

> *He wishes he* were *travelling with you* (Angus Wilson)

4. In the fixed expressions *As it were, If I were you*

Notice that in all these constructions the clause with *were* refers to something unreal, something that in fact is not or will not be the case.

Were may also be used in dependent questions, where there is doubt of the answer, e.g.

Hilliard wondered whether Barton were *not right after all*
(Susan Hill)
Her mother suddenly demanded to know if she were *pregnant*
(Joyce Cary)

☐ This is not obligatory even in very formal prose. *Was* is
acceptable instead.

we (with phrase following)

Expressions consisting of *we* or *us* followed by a qualifying
word or phrase, e.g. *we English, us English,* are often misused
with the wrong case of the first person plural pronoun. In fact
the rules are exactly the same as for *we* or *us* standing alone.

If the expression is the subject, *we* should be used:

(Correct)   *Not always laughing as heartily as* we
English *are supposed to do* (J. B.
Priestley)
(Incorrect) *We all make mistakes, even* us anarchists
(Character in work by Alison Lurie)
(Substitute *we anarchists*)

If the expression is the object or the complement of a preposition, *us* should be used:

(Correct)   *Had shut down all their Dutch ports
against* us English (Kipling)
(Incorrect) *The Manchester Guardian has said some
nice things about* we in the North-East

what (relative pronoun)

What can be used as a relative pronoun only when introducing
nominal relative clauses, e.g.

So much of what *you tell me is strange, different from* what
I was led to expect (Jean Rhys)

In this kind of relative clause, the antecedent and relative
pronoun are combined in the one word *what*, which can be
regarded as equivalent to *that which* or *the thing(s) which.*

- *What* cannot act as a relative pronoun qualifying an antecedent in standard English. This use is found only in non-standard speech, e.g.

> *The young gentleman* what's *arranged everything* (Character in work by Evelyn Waugh)

A *what*-clause used as the subject of a sentence almost always takes a singular verb, even if there is a plural complement, e.g.

> *What one first became aware of* was *the pictures* (J. I. M. Stewart)
> *What interests him* is *less events* . . *than the reverberations they set up* (Frederic Raphael)

Very occasionally the form of the sentence may render the plural more natural, e.g.

> *What once were great houses* are *now petty offices*
> *I have few books, and what there are* do *not help me*

which or *that* (relative pronouns)

There is a degree of uncertainty about whether to use *which* or *that* as the relative pronoun qualifying a non-personal antecedent (for personal antecedents see *who/whom* or *that*).

The general rule is that *which* is used in relative clauses to which the reader's attention is to be drawn, while *that* is used in clauses which mention what is already known or does not need special emphasis.

Which is almost always used in non-restrictive clauses, i.e. those that add further information about an antecedent already defined by other words or the context. Examples:

> *The men are getting rum issue*, which they deserve (Susan Hill)
> *Narrow iron beds with blue rugs on them*, which *Miss Fanshawe has to see are all kept tidy* (William Trevor)

- The use of *that* in non-restrictive clauses should be avoided. It is not uncommon in informal speech, and is sometimes employed by good writers to suggest a tone of familiarity, e.g.

Getting out of Alec's battered old car that *looked as if it had been in collision with many rocks, Harold had a feeling of relief* (L. P. Hartley)

It should not, however, be used in ordinary prose.

Both *which* and *that* can be used in restrictive relative clauses, i.e. clauses that limit or define the antecedent.

There is no infallible rule to determine which should be used. Some guidelines follow:

1. *Which* preferred.

(*a*) Clauses which add significant information often sound better with *which*, e.g.

> *Was I counting on Israel to work some miracle* which *would give me the strength?* (Lynne Reid Banks)
> *Not nearly enough for the social position* which *they had to keep up* (D. H. Lawrence)

(*b*) Clauses which are separated from their antecedent, especially when separated by another noun, sound better with *which*, e.g.

> *Larry told her the story of the young airman* which *I narrated at the beginning of this book* (W. Somerset Maugham)

(*c*) When a preposition governs the relative pronoun, *which* preceded by the preposition is often a better choice than *that* with the preposition at the end of the sentence (see also **preposition at end**), e.g.

> *I'm telling you about a dream* in which *ordinary things are marvellous* (William Trevor)
> (*A dream that ordinary things are marvellous in* would not sound natural)
> *Those secondary causes* to which *we attribute this or that effect in our daily experience* (Ronald Knox)
> (*Those secondary causes which we attribute this or that effect in our daily experience to* would sound very informal and awkward)

2. *That* preferred.

In clauses that do not fall into the above categories *that* can usually be used. There is no reason to reject *that* if

(*a*) the antecedent is impersonal,
(*b*) the clause is restrictive,
(*c*) no preposition precedes the relative pronoun, and
(*d*) the sentence does not sound strained or excessively colloquial.

Examples:

> *I read the letters, none of them very revealing,* that *littered his writing table* (Evelyn Waugh)
> *He fell back on the old English courtesy* that *he had consciously perfected to combat the increasing irritability* that *came with old age and arthritis* (Angus Wilson)

In these examples, *which* would be acceptable, but is not necessary.

When the antecedent is an indefinite pronoun (e.g. *anything, everything, nothing, something*) or contains a superlative adjective qualifying the impersonal antecedent (e.g. *the biggest car, the most expensive hat*) English idiom tends to prefer *that* to *which*:

> *Is there nothing small* that *the children could buy you for Christmas?*
> *This is the most expensive hat* that *you could have bought*

Note that *that* can sometimes be used when one is not sure whether to use *who* or *which*:

> *This was the creature, neither child nor woman,* that *drove me through the dusk that summer evening* (Evelyn Waugh)

who and *whom* (interrogative and relative pronouns)

1. Formal usage restricts the use of the interrogative and relative pronoun *who* to the subject of the clause only, e.g.

> *I* who'd *never read anything before but the newspaper* (W. Somerset Maugham)

When the pronoun is the object or the complement of a preposition, *whom* must be used:

> *Why are we being served by a man* whom *neither of us likes?* (William Trevor)

The real question is food (or freedom) for whom (C. S. Lewis)
A midget nobleman to whom *all doors were open* (Evelyn
  Waugh)

● The use of *who* as object or prepositional complement is
acceptable informally, but should not be carried over into
serious prose, e.g.

Who *are you looking for?*
The person who *I'm looking for is rather elusive*

See also **than, case following**.

2. *Whom* for *who.*

Whom is sometimes mistakenly used for *who* because the
writer believes it to be the object, or the complement of a
preposition.

(*a*) For the interrogative pronoun the rule is: the case of the
pronoun *who/whom* is determined by its role in the interrogative clause, not by any word in the main clause:

> *He never had any doubt about* who *was the real credit
> to the family* (J. I. M. Stewart)

Who here is the subject of *was*. One should not be confused
by *about*, which governs the whole clause, not *who* alone.

The error is seen in:

> Whom *among our poets .. could be called one of the
> interior decorators of the 1950s?*
> (Read *Who* .. because it is the subject of the passive
> verb *be called*)

Whom is correct in:

> *He knew* whom *it was from* (L. P. Hartley)
> (Here *whom* is governed by *from*)

> Whom *he was supposed to be fooling, he couldn't ima-
> gine* (David Lodge)
> (Here *whom* is the object of *fooling*)

(*b*) For the relative pronoun, when followed by a parenthetic
clause such as *they say, he thinks, I believe*, etc., the rule
is: the case of the pronoun *who/whom* is determined by the
part it plays in the relative clause if the parenthetic
statement is omitted:

Sheikh Yamani, who they say *is the richest man in the Middle East*

(Not *whom they say* since *who* is the subject of *is*, not the object of *say*)

But *whom* is correct in:

Sheikh Yamani, whom they believe to be *the richest man in the Middle East*

Here *they believe* is not parenthetic, since it could not be removed leaving the sentence intact. *Whom* is its object: the simple clause would be *They believe* him to be *the richest man.*

See also *I who, you who,* etc.

who or which (relative pronouns)

If a *wh*-pronoun is used to introduce a relative clause it must be *who* (*whom*) if the antecedent is personal, e.g.

Suzanne was a woman who *had no notion of reticence* (W. Somerset Maugham)

But it must be *which* if the antecedent is non-personal. e.g.

There was a suppressed tension about her which *made me nervous* (Lynne Reid Banks)

If the relative clause is non-restrictive, i.e. it adds significant new information about an antecedent already defined, the *wh*-type of pronoun *must* be used (as above).

If the relative clause is restrictive, i.e. it defines or limits the reference of the antecedent, one can use either the appropriate *wh*-pronoun (as indicated above), or the non-variable pronoun *that*. For guidance about this choice see **which or that (relative pronouns)** and **who/whom or that (relative pronouns)**.

whose or of which in relative clauses

The relative pronoun *whose* can be used as the possessive of *which*, i.e. with reference to a non-personal antecedent, just as much as it can as the possessive of *who*. The rule sometimes enunciated that *of which* must always be used after a non-personal antecedent should be ignored, as it is by good writers, e.g.

> *The little book* whose *yellowish pages she knew* (Virginia Woolf)
>
> *A robe* whose *weight and stiff folds expressed her repose* (Evelyn Waugh)
>
> *A narrow side street,* whose *windows had flower boxes and painted shutters* (Doris Lessing)

In some sentences, *of which* would be almost impossible, e.g.

> *The lawns about* whose *closeness of cut his father worried the gardener daily* (Susan Hill)

There is, of course, no rule prohibiting *of which* if it sounds natural, e.g.

> *A little town the name* of which *I have forgotten* (W. Somerset Maugham)

Whose can only be used as the non-personal possessive in *relative* clauses. Interrogative *whose* refers only to persons, as in *Whose book is this?*

who/whom or *that* (relative pronouns)

In formal usage, *who/whom* is always acceptable as the relative pronoun following an antecedent that denotes a person. (For the choice between *who* and *whom* see **who and whom (interrogative and relative pronouns)**.)

In non-restrictive relative clauses, i.e. those which add significant new information about an antecedent already defined, *who/whom* is obligatory, e.g.

> *It was not like Coulter,* who *was a cheerful man* (Susan Hill)

In restrictive relative clauses, i.e those which define or limit the reference of the antecedent, *who/whom* is usually quite acceptable:

> *The masters* who *taught me Divinity told me that biblical texts were highly untrustworthy* (Evelyn Waugh)

It is generally felt that the relative pronoun *that* is more impersonal than *who/whom*, and is therefore slightly depreciatory if applied to a person. Hence it tends to be avoided in formal usage.

However, if

 (i) the relative pronoun is the object, and
(ii) the personality of the antecedent is suppressed

that may well be appropriate, e.g.

> *Then the woman* that *they actually caught and pinned down*
>   *would not have been Margot* (Evelyn Waugh)
> *They looked now just like the GIs* that *one saw in Viet Nam*
>   (David Lodge)

Informally *that* is acceptable with any personal antecedent, e.g.

> *You got it from the man* that *stole the horse* (G. B. Shaw)
> *Honey, it's me* that *should apologize* (David Lodge)

● This should be avoided in formal style.

you and I or *you and me*

When a personal pronoun is linked by *and* or *or* to a noun or another pronoun there is often confusion about which case to put the pronoun in. In fact the rule is exactly as it would be for the pronoun standing alone.

1. If the two words linked by *and* or *or* constitute the subject, the pronoun should be in the subjective case, e.g.

> *Only* she *and her mother cared for the old house*
> *That's what we would do, that is, John and* I
> *Who could go?—Either you or* he

The use of the objective case is quite common in informal speech, but it is non-standard, e.g. (examples from the speech of characters in novels)

> *Perhaps only* her *and Mrs Natwick had stuck to the christ-*
>   *ened name* (Patrick White)
> *That's how we look at it,* me *and Martha* (Kingsley Amis)
> *Either Mary had to leave or* me (David Lodge)

2. If the two words linked by *and* or *or* constitute the object of the verb, or the complement of a preposition, the objective case must be used:

The afternoon would suit her *and John better*
It was time for Sebastian and me *to go down to the drawing-room* (Evelyn Waugh)

The use of the subjective case is very common informally. It probably arises from an exaggerated fear of the error indicated under 1 above.

● It remains, however, non-standard, e.g.

It was this that set Charles and I *talking of old times*
Why is it that people like you and I *are so unpopular?*
    (Character in work by William Trevor)
Between you and I

This last expression is very commonly heard. *Between you and me* should always be substituted.

PRINCIPLES OF PUNCTUATION

apostrophe

1. Used to indicate the possessive case: see pp. 44 f.

2. Used to mark an omission, e.g. *e'er, we'll, he's, '69.*

● Sometimes written, but unnecessary, in a number of curtailed words, e.g. *bus, cello, flu, phone, plane* (not *'bus*, etc.). See also p. 44.

brackets

See: 1. **parentheses.**
     2. **square brackets.**

colon

1. Links two grammatically complete clauses, but marks a step forward, from introduction to main theme, from cause to effect, or from premiss to conclusion, e.g. *To commit sin is to break God's law: sin, in fact, is lawlessness.*

2. Introduces a list of items (a dash should not be added), e.g. *The following were present: J. Smith, J. Brown, P. Thompson, M. Jones.*
   It is used after such expressions as *for example, namely, the following, to resume, to sum up.*

3. Introduces, in an especially formal and emphatic way, speech or a quotation, e.g. *I told them last week: 'Do not in any circumstances open this door.'*

comma

The least emphatic separating mark of punctuation, used:

1. Between adjectives which each qualify a noun in the same way, e.g. *A cautious, eloquent man.*

But when adjectives qualify the noun in different ways, or when one adjective qualifies another, no comma is used, e.g. *A distinguished foreign author, a bright red tie*.

2. To separate items (including the last) in a list of more than two items, e.g. *Potatoes, peas, and carrots*; *Potatoes, peas, or carrots*; *Potatoes, peas, etc.*; *Red, white, and blue*; *He has shares in Guinness, Tate and Lyle, and Marks and Spencer*.

● But *A black and white TV set*.

3. To separate coordinated main clauses, e.g. *Cars will turn here, and coaches will go straight on*. But not when they are closely linked, e.g. *Do as I tell you and you'll never regret it*.

4. To mark the beginning and end of a parenthetical word or phrase, e.g. *I am sure, however, that it will not happen*; *Fred, who is bald, complained of the cold*.

● Not with restrictive relative clauses, e.g. *Men who are bald should wear hats*.

5. After a participial or verbless clause, a salutation, or a vocative, e.g. *Having had breakfast, I went for a walk*; *The sermon over, the congregation filed out* or *The sermon being over, (etc.)*; *Ladies and gentlemen, I give you a toast*.

● Not *The sermon, being over, (etc.)*

● No comma in expressions like *My friend Lord X* or *My son John*.

6. To separate a phrase or subordinate clause from the main clause so as to avoid misunderstanding, e.g. *In the valley below, the villages looked very small*; *He did not go to church, because he was playing golf*; *In 1982, 1918 seemed a long time ago*.

● A comma should not be used to separate a phrasal subject from its predicate, or a verb from an object that is a clause: *A car with such a high-powered engine, should not let you down* and *They believed, that nothing could go wrong* are both incorrect.

7. Following words introducing direct speech, e.g. *They answered, 'Here we are.'*

8. Following *Dear Sir, Dear John*, etc., in letters, and after *Yours sincerely*, etc.

- No comma is needed between month and year in dates, e.g. *In December 1992* or between number and road in addresses, e.g. *12 Acacia Avenue.*

dash

1. The *en rule* is distinct (in print) from the **hyphen** (see pp. 27 ff.) and is used to join pairs or groups of words wherever movement or opposition, rather than cooperation or unity, is felt; it is often equivalent to *to* or *versus*, e.g. *The 1914–18 war; current-voltage characteristic; The London–Horsham–Brighton route; The Fischer–Spassky match; The Marxist–Trotskyite split.*

- Note *The Marxist-Leninist position; The Franco-Prussian war* with hyphens.

It is also used for joint authors, e.g. *The Lloyd–Jones hypothesis* (two men), distinct from *The Lloyd-Jones hypothesis* (one man with double-barrelled name).

2. The *em rule* (the familiar dash) is used to mark an interruption in the structure of a sentence. A pair of them can be used to enclose a parenthetic remark or to make the ending and resumption of a statement interrupted by an interlocutor; e.g. *He was not—you may disagree with me, Henry—much of an artist; 'I didn't—' 'Speak up, boy!' '—hear anything; I was just standing near by.'* It can be used informally to replace the **colon** (use 1).

exclamation mark

Used after an exclamatory word, phrase, or sentence. It usually counts as the concluding full stop, but need not, e.g. *Hail source of Being! universal Soul!* It may also be used within square brackets, after a quotation, to express the editor's amusement, dissent, or surprise.

full stop

1. Used at the end of all sentences which are not questions or exclamations. The next word should normally begin with a capital letter.

2. Used after **abbreviations**: see p. 12. If a point making an abbreviation comes at the end of a sentence, it also serves as the closing full stop, e.g. *She also kept dogs, cats, birds, etc.* but *She also kept pets (dogs, cats, birds, etc.).*

3. When a sentence concludes with a quotation which itself ends with a full stop, question mark, or exclamation mark, no further full stop is needed, e.g. He cried *'Be off!' But the child would not move.* But if the quotation is a short statement, and the introducing sentence has much greater weight, the full stop is put outside the quotation marks, e.g. *Over the entrance to the temple at Delphi were written the words 'Know thyself'.*

4. A sequence of three full stops marks an ellipsis or omission; a fourth is added if this comes at the end of a sentence, e.g. *One critic wrote 'A guidebook . . . that I would not want to be without. . . . It has been my constant companion.'*

hyphen: see pp. 27 ff.

parentheses
Enclose:

1. Interpolations and remarks made by the writer of the text himself, e.g. *Mr. X (as I shall call him) now spoke.*

2. An authority, definition, explanation, reference, or translation.

3. In the report of a speech, interruptions by the audience.

4. Reference letters or figures (which do not then need a full stop), e.g. (1), (*a*).

5. Optional words, e.g. *There are many (apparent) difficulties.*

period: see **full stop**.

question mark
1. Follows every question which expects a separate answer. The next word should begin with a capital letter.

● Not used after indirect questions, e.g. *He asked me why I was there.*

2. May be placed before a word, etc., whose accuracy is doubted, e.g. *T. Tallis ?1505–85.*

quotation marks

1. Single quotation marks are used for a first quotation; double for a quotation within this; single again for a further quotation inside that.

2. The closing quotation mark should come before all punctuation marks unless these form part of the quotation itself, e.g. *Did Nelson really say 'Kiss me, Hardy'?* but *Then she asked, 'What is your name?'* (see also **full stop,** 3).

The comma at the end of a quotation, when words such as *he said* follow, is regarded as equivalent to the final full stop of the speaker's utterance, and is kept inside the quotation, e.g. *'That is nonsense,' he said.* The commas on either side of *he said*, etc., when these words interrupt the quotation, should be outside the quotation marks, e.g. *'That', he said, 'is nonsense.'* But the first comma goes inside the quotation marks if it would be part of the utterance even if there were no interruption, e.g. *'That, my dear fellow,' he said, 'is nonsense'.*

3. Quotation marks (and roman type) are used when citing titles of articles in magazines, chapters of books, poems not published separately, and songs.

● Not for titles of books of the Bible; nor for any passage that represents only the substance of an extract, or has any grammatical alterations, and is not a verbatim quotation.

Titles of books and magazines are usually printed in italic.

semicolon

Separates those parts of a sentence between which there is a more distinct break than would call for a comma, but which are too closely connected to be made into separate sentences. Typically these will be clauses of similar importance and grammatical construction, e.g. *To err is human; to forgive, divine.* It is often used as a stronger division in a sentence that already includes divisions by means of commas, e.g. *He came out of the house, which lay back from the road, and saw her at the end of the path; but instead of continuing towards her, he hid until she had gone.*

square brackets

Enclose comments, corrections, explanations, interpolations, notes, or translations, which were not in the original text, but have been added by subsequent authors, editors, or others, e.g. *My right honourable friend [John Brown] is mistaken.*

CLICHÉS AND MODISH AND INFLATED DICTION

A CLICHÉ is a phrase that has become worn out and emptied of meaning by over-frequent and careless use. Never to use clichés at all would be impossible: they are too common, and too well embedded in the fabric of the language. On many occasions they can be useful in communicating simple ideas economically, and are often a means of conveying general sociability. When writing serious prose, however, in which clear and precise communication is intended, one should guard against allowing clichés to do the work which the words of one's own choosing could do better. 'Modish and inflated diction' is a rough and ready way of referring to a body of words and phrases that is familiar, but hard to delineate and delimit. In origin some of these expressions are scientific or technical and are, in their original context, assigned a real and useful meaning; others are the creation of popular writers and broadcasters. What they all have in common is their grip on the popular mind, so that they have come to be used in all kinds of general contexts where they are unnecessary, ousting ordinary words that are better but sound less impressive. As their popularity and frequency increase, so their real denotative value drains away, a process that closely resembles monetary inflation. As with clichés, it would be difficult, and not necessarily desirable, to ban these expressions from our usage completely, but, again, one should carefully guard against using them either because they sound more learned and up to date than the more commonplace words in one's vocabulary, or as a short cut in communicating ideas that would be better set out in simple, clear, basic vocabularly.

The list that follows does not claim to be an exhaustive collection of clichés or of modish diction, but presents some contemporary expressions which are most frequently censured and are avoided by good writers.

actual (tautologous or meaningless, e.g. *Is this an actual Roman coin?*)

actually (as a filler, e.g. *Actually it's time I was going*)

articulate (verb = express)

at the end of the day

at this moment (or *point*) *in time*

-awareness (e.g. *brand-awareness*)

back burner (*on the* ——)

ball game (*a different*, etc., ——)

basically (as a filler)

bottom line

by and large (sometimes used with no meaning)

-centred (e.g. *discovery-centred*)

conspicuous by one's absence

constructive (used tautologously, e.g. *A constructive suggestion*)

definitely

-deprivation (e.g. *status-deprivation*)

dialogue

dimension (= feature, factor)

-directed (e.g. *task-directed*)

dispense (= give)

-driven (e.g. *consumer-driven*)

environment

escalate (= increase, intensify)

eventuate (= result)

framework (in the framework of)

fresh (= new, renewed, etc.)

-friendly (e.g. *consumer-friendly*)

grind to a halt (= end, stop)

identify (= find, discover)

if you like (explanatory tag)

integrate, integrated

in terms of

in the order of (= about)

in this day and age

-ize (suffix, forming vogue words, e.g. *normalize, permanent-ize, prioritize, respectabilize*)

leave severely alone

life-style

look closely at

loved ones (= relatives)
low profile (*keep, or maintain, a* ——)
massive (= huge)
matrix
meaningful (can often be omitted without any change in meaning)
methodology (= method)
-minded (e.g. *company-minded*)
name of the game, the
-oriented (e.g. *marketing-oriented*)
overkill
participate in
persona (= character)
proliferation (= a number)
proposition
quantum jump/leap
real (especially in *very real*)
-related (e.g. *church-related*)
simplistic (= oversimplified)
sort of (as a filler)
spell (= mean, involve)
syndrome
take on board (= accept, grasp)
target (figuratively used)
terminate (= end)
totality of, the
track-record (= record)
until such time as
utilize (= use)
valid
viability
vibrant
you know (as a filler)
you name it

See also the entries in Section III for:

antithetical	*character*
author	*crucial*
aware	*decimate*

dichotomy
differential
dilemma
event (in the event that)
excess (in excess of)
exposure
feasible
following
hopefully
impact
interface
ironic
literally
locate
maximize
nature

neighbourhood (in the neighbourhood of)
no way
obligate
obscene
ongoing
overly
parameter
pivotal
predicate
pre-empt
pristine
proportion
region (in the region of)
scenario
situation
substantial

APPENDIX III

ENGLISH OVERSEAS

OUTSIDE the United Kingdom and the Republic of Ireland, English is an important language in many countries, and the major language of four—the United States, Canada, Australia, and New Zealand—and of a large minority in another, South Africa. Despite the great distances separating these five English-speaking communities from each other and from the British Isles, and the great social and cultural differences between them, the forms of English which they use remain mutually intelligible to a remarkable degree. Partly this is because all English-speaking communities have held to a standard spelling system. There are a number of points of difference in spelling between the English of the United States and that of Britain (the other communities follow the British mode, except that many US spellings are usual, or acceptable, in Canada); but these are all relatively minor. The major differences are in pronunciation, vocabulary, and, to a lesser degree, grammar.

1. *The United States*

The main differences between General American pronunciation and British Received Pronunciation are set out on pp. 68–9. The General American accent is a supra-regional way of speaking acceptable throughout the country, but there are very marked differences of accent between different regions of the United States. Two varieties familiar in Great Britain are 'Brooklynese' (the New York City accent), in which *earl* and *oil* sound alike (the sound is somewhere between the two), and the southern 'drawl' (the accent of the states from Virginia southward) in which *I* and *time* sound like *ah* and *tahm*.

The difference in vocabulary between American and British English is too well known to need extensive illustration. Most British people are familiar with many American equivalents for British terms, e.g. *checkers* (draughts), *cookie* (biscuit), *diaper* (nappy), *elevator* (lift), *faucet* (tap), *gas* (petrol), *rooster* (cock), *vest* (waistcoat). It is not so often realized that many words and phrases now normal in Britain originated in North America, e.g. *belittle, boost, coverage, fall for, fly off the handle, hitchhike, off-beat, punch line, quiz* (as a noun), *round trip, round-up, snoop.* Nor is it fully realized how many words and phrases used every day in the United States are unknown, or nearly so, in Britain, and show no sign of being adopted here. Many, but not all, are colloquial, e.g. *boondock* (rough country), *gouge* (swindle), *realtor* (estate agent), *rotunda* (concourse), *running gear* (vehicle's wheels and axles), *sassy* (cheeky), *scofflaw* (habitual law-breaker), *second-guess* (be wise after the event). Many words have slightly different meanings in the United States, e.g. *jelly* (jam), *mean* (nasty, *not* stingy), *nervy* (impudent, *not* nervous). Some familiar words have a slightly different form, e.g. *behoove, crawfish, dollhouse, math, normalcy, rowboat, sanitarium* (British *sanatorium*), *tidbit.* There are some notable differences between American and British grammar and construction, e.g. *aside from* (apart from), *back of* (behind), *different than, in school, meet with, most* (almost), *protest* (protest against), *some* (to some extent), *through* (up to and including); *he ordered them arrested, I just ate* (I have just eaten), *teach school, on the street, a quarter of ten.*

While, therefore, the formal and literary varieties of British and American English are mutually intelligible, the most colloquial spoken varieties of each are in some ways very different, and each can, in some contexts, be almost incomprehensible to a speaker of the other.

2. *Canada*

Canadian English is subject to the conflicting influences of British and American English. On the whole British English has a literary influence, while American has a spoken one. The Canadian accent is in most respects identical with General American. But where British English has four vowels in (i) *bat,* (ii) *dance, father,* (iii) *hot, long,* (iv) *law,* and General American three, Canadian has only two: *bat* and *dance* with a front *a,* and *father, hot, long,* and *law* with a back *ah*-sound. Peculiar to the Canadian accent is a distinction between two varieties of the *I*-sound and two of the *ow*-sound: *light* does not have the same vowel as *lied,* nor *lout* as *loud.* Canadians pronounce some words in the American way, e.g. *dance, half, clerk, tomato*, but others in the British way, e.g. *lever, ration, process, lieutenant*, and the name of the letter Z. Some American spellings have caught on, e.g. *honor, jail, plow, program, tire*, but many, such as *-er* in words like *center*, single *l* in *traveled, jeweler*, and the short *ax, catalog, check*, have not. In vocabulary there is much US influence: Canadians use *billboard, gas, truck, wrench* rather than *hoarding, petrol, lorry, spanner*; but on the other hand, they agree with the British in using *blinds, braces, porridge, tap*, rather than *shades, suspenders, oatmeal, faucet*. The Canadian vocabulary reflects to some extent the contact between English and Native American peoples and between English and the large French-speaking community of Canada, e.g. *muskeg* (type of swamp), *rouge* (member of Quebec liberal party), *sasquash* (mythical monster), *tuque* (knitted cap). And as there have been different degrees of settlement by the various non-English-speaking European nationalities in Canada than in the United States, so the range of European loan-words in Canadian English is markedly different, many American colloquialisms being unknown. On the other hand, there are several regional dialects that differ markedly from the standard language, notably that of Newfoundland. Canadian English naturally has a range of vocabulary reflecting its own political, social, and economic life, e.g. *hydro* (hydro-electric power or power company), *loonie* (one-dollar coin), *metro* (metropolitan area), *triactor* (form of betting).

3. *Australia and New Zealand*

There are no important differences in written form between the English of Great Britain and that of Australia, New Zealand, or indeed South Africa. The literary language of the four communities is virtually identical. Grammatically, too, the English of all four is uniform, except that each has developed its own colloquial idioms. Thus it is in the everyday spoken language that the main differences lie. The Australian accent is marked by a number of divergences from the British. (i) The vowels of *fleece, face, price, goose, goat*, and *mouth* all begin with rather open, slack sounds not unlike those used in

Cockney speech. (ii) The vowels of *dress, strut, start, dance, nurse* have a much closer, tighter, more fronted sound than in RP. (iii) In unstressed syllables, typically *-es* or *-ed* (*boxes, studded*), where RP would have a sound like *i* in *pin*, Australian English has a sound like *e* in *open* or *a* in *comma*. (iv) In unstressed syllables, typically *-y*, or *-ie* + consonant (*study, studied*), where RP has the sound of *i* in *pin*, Australian English has a close *-ee* sound, as in *tree*. The result of (iii) and (iv) is that in Australia *boxes* and *boxers* sound the same, but *studded* and *studied*, which are the same in RP, sound different. (v) *-t-* between vowels, and *l*, are often sounded rather as they are in American English. A number of individual words are differently pronounced, e.g. *aquatic* and *auction* with an *o* sound as in *hot* in the stressed syllable; *Melbourne* with a totally obscured second syllable, but *Queensland* with a fully pronounced one (the reverse of the RP). Australian vocabulary reflects, of course, the very different nature of the landscape, climate, natural history, and way of life. Familiar English words like *brook, dale, field*, and *forest* are unusual, whereas *bush, creek, paddock*, and *scrub* are normal. There are of course a large number of terms (often compounded from English elements) for the plants and animals peculiar to the country, e.g. *blue gum, stringybark* (plants), *flathead, popeye mullet* (fish). The borrowings from Aboriginal languages hardly need extensive illustration; many are familiar in Britain, e.g. *billabong, boomerang, budgerigar, didgeridoo, wallaby*. Many of them have taken on transferred meanings and have lost their Aboriginal associations, e.g. *bogey* (swim), *gibber* (boulder, stone), *mulga* (an inhospitable region), *warrigal* (wild, untamed person or animal). But above all it is in the colloquial language that Australian English differs from British. Not only are there terms relating to Australian life and society, e.g. *jackaroo, rouseabout, walkabout*, but ordinary terms, e.g. *chiack* (tease), *crook* (bad, irritable, ill), *dinkum, furphy* (rumour), *smoodge* (fawn, caress); formations and compounds like those ending in *-o* (e.g. *arvo* (afternoon), *Commo* (communist), *jollo* (party), *smoko* (teabreak)); *ratbag* (eccentric, troublemaker), *ropeable* (angry); and expressions like *come the raw prawn, down the gurgler, she'll be right, have a shingle short*. While it is true that many Australianisms are known in Britain, and form the basis of various kinds of humorous entertainment, and while British English has borrowed some Australian vocabulary (e.g. the verb *to barrack* or the noun *walkabout*), there is yet a wide gap between the popular spoken forms of the two kinds of English.

The gap is less wide in the case of New Zealand English, where British influence has on the whole remained stronger. To a British ear, the New Zealand accent is hardly distinguishable from the Australian. Its main peculiarities are: (i) *i* as in *kit* is a very slack sound almost like *a* in *cadet*; (ii) *a* as in *trap* and *e* as in *dress* are almost like British *e* in *pep* and *i* in *this*; (iii) the vowels of *square* and *near* are very tense and close, and may even be sounded alike; (iv) the vowels of *smooth* and *nurse* are sounded forward in the mouth, and rather close. The chief differences between New Zealand and Australian English are lexical. The words of Aboriginal origin are mostly unknown in New Zealand, while the New Zealand words drawn from Maori are unknown in Australia. Many of the latter, naturally, refer to natural history and landscape specific to the country, e.g. *biddy-bid* (kind of plant), *cockabully*, *tarakihi* (kinds of fish), *pohutukawa* (kind of tree). There is a large everyday vocabulary, much of it, but by no means all, colloquial or slang, used neither in Britain nor in Australia, e.g. *booay* (remote rural district), *greenstone* (stone used for ornaments), *return to the mat* (resume Maori way of life), *shake* (earthquake), *tar-sealed* (surfaced with tar macadam), *Taranaki gate* (gate made of wire strands attached to upright battens). While a fair amount of colloquial vocabulary is shared by Australia and New Zealand (e.g. *sheila*, *Pommy*, *paddock* (field), *shout* (to treat to drinks)), there are important nuances. In both *to bach* is to live as a bachelor, but in New Zealand only is there a noun *bach*, a small beach or holiday house. Similar organizations are the *RSA* (Returned Servicemen's Association) in New Zealand, but the *RSL* (Returned Servicemen's League) in Australia; the initials of the one would be meaningless to a member of the other. *Mopoke* or *morepork* is the name for a kind of owl in New Zealand, but for either a nightjar, or a different kind of owl, in Australia.

4. *South Africa*

English is one of the two official languages of the Republic of South Africa, the other being Afrikaans (derived from Dutch, but now an entirely independent language). Afrikaans has had a fairly strong influence on the English of the Republic: the South African accent is distinctly 'clipped'; *r* is often rolled, and the consonants *p*, *t*, and *k* have a sharper articulation, usually lacking the aspiration (a faint *h* sound) found in other varieties of English. *I* is sometimes very lax (like *a* in *along*), e.g. in *bit*, *lip*, at other times very tense (like *ee*), e.g. in *kiss*, *big*; the vowels of *dress*, *trap*, *square*, *nurse* are very tense and close, while that of *part* is very far back, almost like *port*. As in the other forms of English of the Southern Hemisphere, the different landscape, flora and fauna, and way of life are reflected in the South African vocabulary, e.g. *dorp* (village), *go-away bird*, *kopje*, *nartjie* (tangerine), *rand, rhenosterbos* (a kind of plant), *roman*, *snoek* (both fish), *springbok*, *stoep* (veranda), *veld*. There are many loan-words from Afrikaans and African languages, e.g. (besides most of those above) *braai* (barbecue), *donga* (eroded watercourse), *erf* (building plot), *gogga* (insect), *impala* (kind of antelope), *indaba* (meeting for discussion), *lekker* (nice), *rondavel* (hut). There are also many general colloquial words and phrases, e.g. *the farm* (the country), *homeboy* (African from one's own area), *location* (Black township), *robot* (traffic light), *tackies* (plimsolls). Some of these reflect the influence of Afrikaans idiom, e.g. *come there* (arrive), *just now* (in a little while), *land* (a field), *wait on* (wait for). Only a few words have entered the main stream of English, but they are important ones, including *apartheid, commandeer, commando, laager, trek*, and the slang *scoff* (to eat; food).

The spoken language of each of the main English-speaking communities, as well as of the smaller communities scattered around the world, manifests enormous differences in pronunciation, vocabulary, and idiom. The relative uniformity of the written, and especially the literary, language, stands in tension with this. The outcome is a world language of unparalleled richness and variety.

INDEX

Words and phrases are entered in strict alphabetical order, ignoring spaces between two or more words forming a compound or phrase (hence *as for* follows *ascendant* and *court martial* follows *courtesy*).

An asterisk is placed in front of forms or spellings that are not recommended; reference to the page(s) indicated will show the reason for this ruling in each case.

Individual words, parts of words, and phrases discussed in this book are given in *italics*, to distinguish them from subjects, which are in roman type.

165, 166, 168, 172, 190, 221, 247 f.
pronunciation 68 f., 70, 77, 92, 93, 247
spelling 13, 14, 18, 20, 22, 30, 32, 34, 36, 37, 47, 51, 52 ff., 249
amoeba 14
amok 53
among 121
amontillado 67
ampere 53
amphitheatre 46
amuck 53
amusedly 73
an 15 f., 175 f.
*analog 22
analogous 95, 117
analysable 21
analyse 51
analysis 42
ancillary 53
*ancilliary 53
and 41, 182 f., 234 f.
androgynous 75
anger 78
Anglicism 17
Anglicize 18
annex 53
annexe 53
annul 34
annulment 34
Antarctic 95
antecedent 1, 197, 209 f., 215, 223, 227 f.
  non-personal 228 ff., 232 f.
  personal 232, 233 f.
antechamber 15
anticipate 118
anti-Darwinian 30
anti-g 29
antiquary 95
antique 181
antithesis 42
antithetical 118, 245
antitype 15
anxiety 85
anxious 85
any 152, 187

anybody 152, 187
any one 53, 152
anyone 53, 152, 187
anything 78, 194, 230
any time 53
any way 53
anyway 53
apache 95
apartheid 95, 252
apologetics 191
apophthegm 53, 76, 80, 95
apophthegmatic 76
*apothegm 53
apostasy 53
apostrophe 40, 44, 44 ff., 195, 237
appal 34
apparatus 67, 95
appendix 42
appetite 33
appetize 33
applicable 89, 95
appliquéd 25
appliquéing 25
apposite 95
apposition 1, 175
appraise 118
appreciate 83
appreciation 83
apprise 33, 118
approve 118
apt 119
aquatic 250
Arab 119
arabic 18
Arabic 86
Araldite 18
arbitrage 68
arbitrarily 70, 90, 95
arced 17
archaeology 53
arcing 17
Arctic 95
are 220
area 81
areas 25
aren't 116
Argentine 95, 119
Argentinian 119

curriculum 43
curse 71
cursed 71
curtsy 54
cyclical 99
czar 54

D
daily 35, 51
dais 99
dale 250
dance 249
dandified 30
dangling participles 204 ff.
dare 177, 184 f.
dare say 54
*daresay 54
darts 218
dash 237, 239
data 44, 67, 99, 127
database 54
*datas 127
datum 43, 44, 67, 127
day 174
dearie 49
death 90
debatable 13
debater 35
debonair 54
decade 99
decaf 12
deceit 23
deceive 23
decided 72
decidedly 72, 127
decimate 128, 245
decisively 127
declaredly 73
decline 128
declining 128
decorous 88
deep 174
deeply 175
de-escalate 29
defaulter 36
defect 87, 99
defence 18
defensible 13
deficit 88, 99

definite 128
definite article, *see* article
definitely 22, 244
definitive 128
deflection 48
degree:
  comparative 2, 51, 145, 167, 180 ff., 182
  superlative 7, 51, 180 ff., 182, 230
dégringolade 67
deify 99
deism 74
deist 74
deity 74, 99
delirious 99
delude 128
deluge 92
delusion 128
demagogic 76
demagogy 76
demand that 220
demean 129
demesne 99
demise 33
demo 12
democratic 17
Democratic 17
demonstrable 13, 89, 99
demonstrate 90
deniable 51
denied 51
denies 52
denote 126
depend 129
dependant 15
dependence 15
dependent 15
depositary 54
depository 54
depravedly 73
deprecate 129
depreciate 129
depressedly 73
deprivation 99, 244
derby 69
derisive 99, 129
derisory 99, 129
descendant 15, 54

momentum 150
monarch 85
monarchic 85
moneyed 58
moneys 58
mongoose 58
mongooses 58
mongrel 78
monies 58
monophthong 80
monstrous 24
montage 68
mood 4, 177 f., 220 ff.
mopoke 251
more 145, 180 ff.
moreish 22
morepork 251
more than 136, 217
more than one 150
morish 22
morning 174
mortgager 36
*Moslem 58
mosquitoes 40
most 180 ff., 248
moth 90
motif 150
motivate 150
motive 150
motor cycle 27
motor-cyclist 27
motorway 27
mottoes 40
mould 36
moulder 36
moult 36
Mountie 49
moustache 58
mousy 22
mouth 58, 91
*mouthe 58
movie 49
mow 38
mown 38
MPs 44
Mr 12
Mrs 12
Ms 12
MS 16

much 145, 174
mucous 58
mucus 58
Muhammad 58
mulga 250
mullah 105
mumps 218
municipal 105
Munros 40
murderous 24
murky 58
muskeg 249
Muslim 58
must 177, 178
*mustache 58
mustachioed 25
mutual 150
mynah 58
mysterious 85
mystery 85

N
Naafi 12
nadir 105
naive 59, 105
naivety 59, 105
naked 70
nameable 13
namely 114, 237
name of the game, the 245
names 214 f.
  Greek and Latin 45
  of business 46
  of cities 219
  of countries 17, 84, 218 f.
  of denominations 17
  of diseases 218
  of games 218
  of organizations 17
  of political parties 17
  proper 18, 40
  proprietary 18
naphtha 80
Naples 219
nappy 48
narcissus 44
narrow 180
narrower 180
narrowest 180

pasta 81
pastel 59
pasteurize 18
pastille 59
pastoralia 67
pasty 107
patent 107
path 91
pathos 107
patina 88, 107
patois 43
patriarch 107
patricide 155
patriot 107
patriotic 107
patron 107
patronage 107
patroness 107
patronize 107
pavior 59
pawpaw 59
pay 37
pay-bed 27
pay phone 27
peaceable 21
peccadilloes 40
*pedagog 22
pedagogic 76
pedagogy 76
pedal 59
peddle 59
*peddler 59
pederast 59
pedigreed 59
pedlar 59
peer 155
peewit 59
pejorative 89, 107
Pekinese 59
Pekingese 59
pence 106, 155
pendant 15
pendent 15
penetralia 67
peninsula 59, 92
peninsular 59
pennant 59
pennon 60
penny 106, 155

peony 60
perceive 23
perceptible 14
peremptory 89, 107
perfecter 36
perfectible 14
perhaps 107
perimeter 155
peripeteia 23
peristalsis 67
peristaltic 67
periwig 20
perk 155
permanentize 244
permissible 14
perquisite 155
Persian 84
persiflage 68
persistence 155
persistency 155
person 187
person:
    first 197, 211, 213 f., 227
    second 212, 213
    third 197 f., 212, 213
    singular 47 f., 182, 201, 220
persona 245
perspicacious 156
perspicacity 156
perspicuity 156
perspicuous 156
persuasible 14
petit bourgeois 156
petite bourgeoisie 156
petrol 249
petty bourgeois 156
pewit 59
pharmacopoeia 107
phenomena 44, 156
*phenomenas 156
phenomenon 43, 156
philharmonic 107
Philippines, the 218
philtre 47
phlegm 76
phlegmatic 76
phone 60, 237
'phone 60
phonetics 192

politics 86, 192
polity 156
poll 79
pollen 79
pomade 67
pomegranate 78, 107
pommel 60, 78
Pommy 251
popeye mullet 250
poppadam 60
pore 60
porpoise 108
porridge 249
*portentious 157
portentous 156
porticoes 40
porticos 40
poseur 75
possessive case:
    formation of 44 ff., 237
    group 189
    of measure 46
    of nouns ending in -s 45
    of plural nouns 44 ff.
    of pronouns 45 f.
    use of 192, 194 f.
possible 14
post 157
posthumous 108
postilion 60
potatoes 40
pot-pourri 108
potty 48
pound 200
powwow 60
practicable 157
practical 157
practicality 85
practically 85
practice 18, 60
practise 18, 60
*praps 83
pre 157
precede 18, 60
precedence 88, 108
precedent 88, 108
precedented 108
precipitate 157
precipitous 157

precise 32
précised 20, 60
preclude 157
*predaceous 60
predacious 60
predicate 157, 246
predilection 108
predominant 60
predominantly 60
*predominately 60
pre-empt 29, 157, 246
prefer 158, 197
preferable 13, 89, 108
preferable to 158
preference 158
preference to, in 158
prefixes:
    ad- 31
    ante- 15
    anti- 15, 95
    bi- 121
    by- 16
    co- 19, 31, 120
    col-, com-, con-, cor- 31
    de- 31
    di(s)- 31
    em- 31
    en- 23 f., 31
    ex- 29, 31
    for-, fore- 25
    gyn(o)- 75
    haema-, haemo- 56
    homo- 102
    im- 31
    in- 13, 23 f., 30 ff.
    inte(r)- 31
    Mac, Mc, M^c, M' 58
    milli- 58
    neo- 29
    non- 29, 137
    palaeo- 59
    per- 31
    pre- 157, 159
    pro- 29, 159
    pseudo- 92
    re- 47
    requiring a hyphen 29 f.
    schizo- 111
    self- 29

villa 81
villagey 49
villain 63
villein 63
vincible 14
viola 114
virile 77
virtuoso 43
virtuosos 43
*vise 63
visible 14
visor 63
visual 84
vitamin 114
viz. 114
vizor 63
vocal cord 63
volcanoes 40
volume 92
voluminous 91
voluntarily 70, 114
voluntary 89
vortex 42
voyeur 75
vying 32

W
waggery 19
waggon 63
wagon 63
wainscoted 20
waistcoat 114
wait on, to 252
waive 170
waiver 63
Wales 219
walkabout 250, 251
walkie-talkie 49
wallaby 250
walnut 114
walrus 114
waltz 67
waltzes 39
*wanna 83
*wannit 83
want 171
warrigal 250
warrior 63
was 226

wastable 63
water-colourist 37
wave 171
waver 63
way 63, 174, 199, 226
we 176, 195 ff., 213, 219, 227
weather-wise 30
weir 23
weird 23, 63
well 171
were 220, 226
werewolf 114
we shall 211
Western Australia 17
we will 211
wharf 26
wharfs 26
wharves 26
what 210, 227 f.
what ever 135
whatever 135
whence 171
when ever 135
whenever 135
where ever 135
wherever 135
wheyey 50
wheyiness 50
which 173, 180, 210, 227, 228 ff.,
    232, 232 f.
whippers-in 41
whiskey 63
whisky 63
whiteness 22
whitish 22
Whit Monday 63
Whit Sunday 63
Whitsunday 63
whiz 63
whizz 63
whizzes 48
who 180, 191, 196 f., 197 f., 210,
    222, 230 ff., 232, 233 f.
who ever 135
whoever 135, 171
wholly 22, 35, 79
whom 191, 196, 210, 222, 230 ff., 233 f.
whomever 171
whoop 114